cirencester
college
a beacon college

Question& Answer
TORT LAW

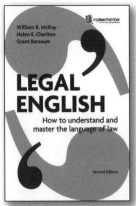

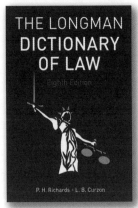
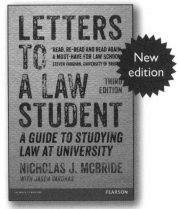

Question&Answer

TORT LAW

3rd edition

Neal Geach
University of Hertfordshire

Harlow, England • London • New York • Boston • San Francisco • Toronto • Sydney • Auckland • Singapore • Hong Kong
Tokyo • Seoul • Taipei • New Delhi • Cape Town • São Paulo • Mexico City • Madrid • Amsterdam • Munich • Paris • Milan

Pearson Education Limited
Edinburgh Gate
Harlow CM20 2JE
United Kingdom
Tel: +44 (0)1279 623623
Web: www.pearson.com/uk

First published 2012 (print and electronic)
Second edition published 2014 (print and electronic)
Third edition published 2016 (print and electronic)

ISBN: 978-1-292-06678-3 (print)
       978-1-292-06680-6 (PDF)
       978-1-292-06681-3 (ePub)
       978-1-292-06682-0 (eText)

British Library Cataloguing-in-Publication Data
A catalogue record for the print edition is available from the British Library

10 9 8 7 6 5 4 3 2 1
19 18 17 16 15

Front cover bestseller data from Nielsen BookScan (2009–2013, Law Revision Series).

Print edition typeset in 10/13 Helvetica Neue LT W1G by 35
Print edition printed and bound in Malaysia (CTP-PJB)

NOTE THAT ANY PAGE CROSS REFERENCES REFER TO THE PRINT EDITION

Contents

Supporting resources

Visit the **Law Express Question&Answer** series companion website at
www.pearsoned.co.uk/lawexpressqa to find valuable learning material
including:

- **Additional essay and problem questions** arranged by topic for each chapter
  give you more opportunity to practise and hone your exam skills.
- **Diagram plans** for all additional questions assist you in structuring and writing
  your answers.
- **You be the marker** questions allow you to see through the eyes of the examiner
  by marking essay and problem questions on every topic covered in the book.
- Download and print all **Before you begin** diagrams and **Diagram plans** from
  the book.

Also: The companion website provides the following features:

- Search tool to help locate specific items of content.
- Online help and support to assist with website usage and troubleshooting.

For more information please contact your local Pearson sales representative or
visit **www.pearsoned.co.uk/lawexpressqa**

Acknowledgements

I would like to thank all of the academics and students who have reviewed and recommended, and helped develop, this work; and especially the team at Pearson for providing me with the opportunity to produce it. Primarily though I would like to thank the person who makes all of this possible through her never-ending support and encouragement: my wife, Sarah. Thank you for everything.

Neal Geach

Publisher's acknowledgements

Our thanks go to all reviewers who contributed to the development of this text, including students who participated in research and focus groups which helped to shape the series format.

What you need to do for every question in Tort Law

It is also important not to worry about trying to learn all of the case citations. These are listed in the answers for information purposes only. You are unlikely to be expected to include these in an exam. Tort is predominantly a case-based subject and so you would be using a lot of your time if you listed the citations every time. However, you should obviously just confirm this with your tutors. Citations for journal articles are slightly different. While, again, it is very unlikely that you will be expected to write the full details of articles, you should give some indication as to where they are from, such as the journal abbreviation and year.

All torts have an inherent structure because of the elements which make up each tort. Use these elements to form the basis of your structure, particularly for problem questions. Deal with the first element and then move on to the next. The key is to spot how much weight you need to give each element, as questions are likely to focus on particular elements of the tort.

Tort also has a large amount of theory underpinning it and is influenced by certain principles. Make sure you learn these and try to incorporate these into your answer. This is particularly beneficial when the question is an essay assessing the merits of an overall tort, or the component elements required by the courts for a particular tort.

Guided tour

What you need to do for every question in Tort Law

What to do for every question – Identify the key things you should look for and do in any question and answer on the subject, ensuring you give every one of your answers a great chance from the start.

Negligence: Duty of care for economic loss

2

How this topic may come up in exams

The law restricts when a duty of care arises in negligence for purely economic losses. This area can come up as a distinct question, independent from a more general negligence one, or within the sole examination of negligence. In this chapter we look at common essay questions only for which you will need to know about the policy factors behind the law's restrictive approach. The topic is equally liable, though, to appear as a problem question dealing with either form of economic loss (i.e. resulting from negligent misstatements or negligent acts) or both (see Chapter 5). As such, you will need to learn the whole area, alongside the other components of negligence.

How this topic may come up in exams – Understand how to tackle any question on this topic by using the handy tips and advice relevant to both essay and problem questions. In-text symbols clearly identify each question type as they occur.

 Essay question

 Problem question

Before you begin – Use these diagrams as a step-by-step guide to help you confidently identify the main points covered in any question asked. Download these from the companion website to add to your revision notes.

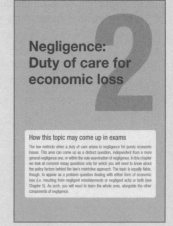

Answer plans and Diagram plans – A clear and concise plan is the key to a good answer and these answer and diagram plans support the structuring of your answers, whatever your preferred learning style.

Answer plan

→ Take Noel first, and establish whether he is a visitor under the 1957 Act.

→ Explain the extent of the duty under the Act.

→ Assess Paul's liability and the applicability of any defences.

→ Highlight how Liam is a non-visitor under the 1984 Act.

→ Consider the scope of the Act and whether Paul will owe Liam a duty under it.

Diagram plan

Answer with accompanying guidance – Make the most out of every question by using the guidance to recognise what makes a good answer and why. Answers are the length you could realistically hope to produce in an exam to show you how to gain marks quickly when under pressure.

Case names clearly highlighted – Easy-to-spot bold text makes those all important case names stand out from the rest of the answer, ensuring they are much easier to remember in revision and an exam.

Make your answer stand out – Really impress your examiners by going the extra mile and including these additional points and further reading to illustrate your deeper knowledge of the subject, fully maximising your marks.

Don't be tempted to – Points out common mistakes ensuring you avoid losing easy marks by understanding where students most often trip up in exams.

Bibliography – Use this list of further reading to really delve into the subject and explore areas in more depth, enabling you to excel in exams.

Answer

The issue to determine here is the extent to which Kyle may have redress in tort for the publication of his hosting of poker nights and his subsequent rehabilitation. This will involve assessing the extent to which the law recognises rights to privacy and protects them under the tort of misuse of private information.[1] It will be argued that Kyle may be entitled to damages because of the parallels with *Campbell v MGN Ltd* [2004] UKHL 22,[2] depending on the level of detail published in relation to his treatment.

Notwithstanding that privacy is a fundamental human right under Article 8 of the ECHR, which has been incorporated into English law by the Human Rights Act 1998, the absence of any horizontal effect between private citizens[3] means there is no general tort protecting invasions of privacy as has happened here. This was clearly stated in *Wainwright v Home Office* [2003] UKHL 53 which saw no need for its creation, particularly by the judiciary. However, Kyle should be advised that this does not mean he automatically has no redress. As Hunt (1998) has argued, while the courts do not have the power to

[1] Indicate your awareness of the extent of privacy protection in tort and what Kyle's action could be.

[2] By mentioning *Campbell*, you show the parallels between Kyle's situation and *Campbell*, and how that authority will form the basis of your answer.

[3] Use this wording to show your awareness of the context of the debate on privacy and the workings of the Act. This allows you to develop this point later to show how Kyle's action may be about.

by the employer to the children, which clearly failed to do. Further, as Lord Steyn stated, the tort was 'inextricably interwoven' with his duties. This link warranted liability and not simply the fact that the employment created an opportunity for committing the tort; which is why it was stated that liability would not have arisen if the tortfeasor had been the gardener.

The test offers no exact guidance on what is a sufficient connection (*Dubai Aluminium Co. Ltd v Salaam & Others* [2003] 1 AC 366) and so can lead to seemingly inconsistent results, as seen in the factually similar cases of *Weddall v Barchester Healthcare Ltd; Wallbank v Wallbank Fox Designs Ltd* [2012] EWCA Civ 25. Arbitrary operation raises questions as to the doctrine's rationale,

✓ **Make your answer stand out**

- Although the question is specifically on psychiatric injury, contrast the position of a rescuer in a claim for psychiatric injury with that of a rescuer suffering physical injury. In doing this, consider the point raised by Lord Hoffmann in *White*; that rescuers do not even receive special treatment in cases of physical injury.
- Tailor your answer to suit your view. Therefore, if you actually disagree with the minority in *White*, end your answer with the views of the majority and why they are more justified. This will ensure that your answer finishes strongly.
- Offer your own view as to what the law should be in order to be in a better state if you feel that to be the case. If you have identified a problem, try to solve it. Do make sure that you substantiate any opinion by expressing the basis for that opinion.
- Draw on the wealth of academic literature on the topic in order to support the different positions that you are considering, and then to lend support for your ultimate view on the question.

! **Don't be tempted to . . .**

- Stray into examining in depth the merits of recoverability for economic losses; remember the question is about whether the Council can establish a duty owed to them by either party.
- Focus heavily on the history of recovery in this area and the merits of *Anns*, as it has been overruled, and as this is a problem question you need to focus on what the law is and how it might be applied.
- Miss out reference to the other aspects of negligence. They are needed briefly for completeness.

Bibliography

Arden, M. (2010) Human rights and civil wrongs: tort law under the spotlight. *Public Law*, January: 140–59.

Bailey, S. (2010) What is a Material Contribution? *Legal Studies* 30: 167.
Barker, K. (1993) Unreliable Assumptions in the Modern Law of Negligence. *Law Quarterly*

Guided tour of the companion website

Book resources are available to download. Print your own **Before you begin** and **Diagram plans** to pin to your wall or add to your own revision notes.

Additional Essay and Problem questions with **Diagram plans** arranged by topic for each chapter give you more opportunity to practise and hone your exam skills. Print and email your answers.

You be the marker gives you a chance to evaluate sample exam answers for different question types for each topic and understand how and why an examiner awards marks. Use the accompanying guidance to get the most out of every question and recognise what makes a good answer.

All of this and more can be found when you visit
www.pearsoned.co.uk/lawexpressqa

Table of cases and statutes

■ Cases

TABLE OF CASES AND STATUTES

TABLE OF CASES AND STATUTES

Table of Statutes

■ European and International Legislation

Negligence: Duty of care

1

How this topic may come up in exams

While negligence is examinable as a whole (see Chapter 5), the various individual components can be, and often are, examined separately as essays. Duty of care is particularly ripe for essay questions because of its complexity and differing components. There is also a large amount of policy considerations in the decisions, and within the law's development which you should also be aware of. The more restrictive duty situations of psychiatric injury and economic loss may form part of an overall examination of the duty concept, or they may be treated distinctly, so do check your particular module guides for that.

■ Before you begin

It's a good idea to consider the following key themes of negligence: duty of care before tackling a question on this topic.

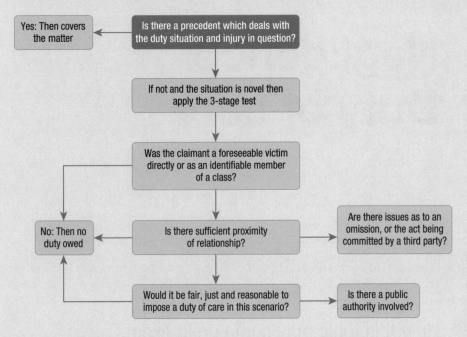

A printable version of this diagram plan is available from **www.pearsoned.co.uk/lawexpressqa**

 Question 1

'The concept of duty of care in negligence emerged towards the end of the eighteenth century, and is now so firmly rooted that there can be no doubt that actions in negligence must fail where a duty is not established.' (Murphy, J. and Witting, C. (2012) *Street on Torts.* Oxford: Oxford University Press, pp. 26–27)

In light of this statement critically evaluate the role of the duty concept and the need for it to be so firmly rooted in the tort.

Diagram plan

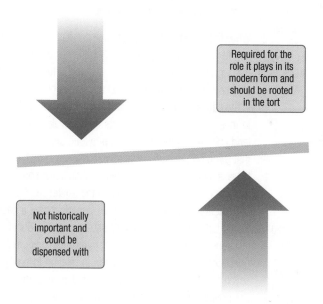

Required for the role it plays in its modern form and should be rooted in the tort

Not historically important and could be dispensed with

A printable version of this diagram plan is available from **www.pearsoned.co.uk/lawexpressqa**

Answer plan

➜ Provide the historical context and background to the role of the duty concept, discussing whether it needs to be firmly rooted in the tort.

➜ Evaluate the role played by the duty concept, including how and why it was developed in the way it has been.

➜ Assess the impact of the concept in the modern law and the extent to which it meets the needs of the tort.

➜ Conclude whether the concept is needed or could have a less prominent application.

Answer

The issue to be determined is whether it is right that the duty concept is so firmly rooted in negligence or could it operate without reliance on the concept, relying instead on the other aspects of negligence to perform the current duty function. This is important, as establishing a duty is the first hurdle which a claimant must overcome; a failure to do so means that, notwithstanding their injury and principles of corrective justice,[1] they will have no redress. It will be argued that while not always valued, the duty concept plays a useful function in seeking to achieve justice for those injured, while preventing punitive liability for those who are negligent.

While firmly rooted in the tort today, this has not always been the case and its importance has previously been questioned.[2] Winfield (1934) has argued that historically no case was in fact ever lost through the absence of a duty. He noted that the concept of duty was never raised in the cases from which the independent tort of negligence grew, and in those cases arising during its early development. Similarly Buckland (1935) saw the duty concept as merely a fifth wheel: he argued that the more rational explanation for cases is that, as in Roman law, there is a duty to everyone, which is then limited on the basis of other aspects of the tort. By insisting on the existence of a duty to succeed in an action, claimants today now lose claims on a basis which they would not have lost on historically. As such, in Buckland's view the insistence on the need for a duty in all situations creates injustice. A good example of this can be seen in relation to negligently inflicted psychiatric injury where, even if all of the other elements of negligence are present, the duty concept has long been used as the basis for denying liability. However, if liability can be justifiably limited by other factors and the duty's presence would not have mattered, then it is perhaps questionable how much injustice is caused. Arguably, using, say, remoteness to limit liability rather than duty was not any fairer.[3]

The debate around shifting the focus away from duty received fresh impetus in *D v East Berkshire Community Health NHS Trust* [2005] 2 AC 373 with Lord Bingham stating that he would 'welcome' such a shift in focus so that breach of duty becomes the dividing line between success and failure.[4] Lord Nicholls in the same case noted the argument is 'not without attraction'. However, he noted that while

[1] By including reference to this here you are showing your marker early on that you have an understanding of the underlying fundamental principles of tort and how they relate to the question.

[2] Due to the view I have of this issue, I am starting by dealing with the idea it should not be so rooted and we could do without the concept.

[3] While you have advanced Buckland's view, you still need to subject it to some critical evaluation – is there a link between the concept and injustice or would it exist anyway?

[4] The point here is for you to say that, notwithstanding the time lapse and the changes to the law since the above views were first aired, there is prominent, recent support. This will then strengthen any argument you may want to advance that the concept need not be so rooted in the law.

such a move would work in the field of human rights, in other cases it would cause lengthy uncertainty until a new control mechanism is devised which recognises that liability is not dependent on foreseeability. Therefore if remoteness would also potentially cause unfairness and breach is not yet set up to act as an adequate control mechanism to contain claims, the duty concept needs to remain rooted in the law.

Therefore, need to firmly root the duty concept in the law as a control mechanism grew in importance following **Anns v Merton LBC** [1978] AC 728. The test proposed there for establishing a duty was seen as expanding negligence into areas where the law had been reluctant for it to explore, particularly economic loss. Generally, claims have to fit within an existing precedent which has recognised a duty in that situation. This rejects arguments of corrective justice whereby a person should have redress for any injury suffered through a want of care. Although, it could be argued that by performing this role it reflects the fact that the law should also be just towards defendants.

[5] This part of your answer is quite important. Naturally, if you are discussing duty of care, you need to discuss how it arises. You need to link, though, how it arises to the wider discussion about what the role is and how well the test for establishment performs the role given to the concept.

However, negligence cannot be completely rigid and it needs to expand into new situations, but the duty concept firmly dictates when, so as to keep the law within acceptable bounds.[5] This role is reflected in the test for establishing a new duty situation. In **Caparo v Dickman** [1990] 2 AC 605 it was determined that the following factors would need to be present on the facts. Firstly, it must be reasonably foreseeable that the particular claimant would suffer the particular type of loss which did in fact occur. The issue of the foreseeable claimant leads to the second factor which is proximity. There must be a sufficient closeness between the parties in view of the type of loss which justifies imposing a duty. This, in turn, leads to the third element which is that it is 'fair, just and reasonable' to impose the duty. The presence of the first two factors means it generally will be, but this element is also where public policy comes in. Even today this still leads to injustice being caused, as with psychiatric injury; although the judges, rather than talking specifically about policy, can use the policy to find that there was insufficient proximity or foreseeability.

The converse can also be said to be true though. The third element and the presence of policy can lead to justice for the defendants and thus it reinforces the modern role of the concept. A good example of this would be **Caparo**, where the auditor's negligence was argued to have caused the claimant to buy, first, a significant shareholding,

[6] As the reasoning is from a specific judge, name him/her as this shows a greater level of knowledge and understanding of the case, and that you have read, learnt and understood the judge's views.

[7] Whereas normally you would not need the journal's full name, where it is one from another jurisdiction it is worth stating it in full, because the marker may not be familiar with the abbreviated initials, unlike, say, LQR.

[8] This is where you could still expand on a comparative evaluation if you have not chosen to include a paragraph in the main body on other jurisdictions. The benefit of doing this is that the quote suggests the concept is indispensable. Show how other jurisdictions get by without it. This will then tie in to your discussion of the history of English law from Buckland (1935) and Winfield (1934).

and then the entire third-party company. The claim was rejected by Lord Bridge[6] because to hold otherwise would result in an indeterminate amount of liability, owed to an indeterminate class of people for an indeterminate length of time. If a duty was owed to potential shareholders, or even shareholders in relation to publicly released information, there was nothing to stop banks and merchants supplying credit to the company in reliance on the accounts having a claim. Therefore, for these reasons it was determined that it would not be fair, just and reasonable to impose what would have been a potentially crushing duty of care on the auditors.

In conclusion, notwithstanding the arguments that the duty concept serves no function, or simply duplicates a role which could be performed by another aspect of negligence, as Winfield (1934) noted,[7] it is so deeply entrenched in the law now that only legislation can eradicate it. This is even more the case today, and therefore the debate now really is purely academic in nature even though different jurisdictions also provide a model as to how the law could operate without it.[8] The modern approach utilises the concept as a way of balancing when liability can justifiably be imposed on the one hand with the need to ensure the potential liability is not too excessive on the other. Although, as the cases show, this may not always be satisfactorily achieved, depending on how strictly one adheres to corrective justice.

✓ Make your answer stand out

- Read in full the following articles: Buckland, W.W. (1935) The duty to take care. *Law Quarterly Review,* 51: 637; Winfield, P.M. (1934) Duty in tortious negligence. *Columbia Law Review,* 34(1): 41–66; and Howarth, D. (2006) Many duties of care: or a duty of care? Notes from the underground. *Oxford Journal of Legal Studies,* 26: 449.

- Read the debate on the role of the duty concept in *D* v *East Berkshire Community Health NHS Trust* [2005] 2 AC 373.

- Draw on human rights arguments and the application of Article 6 as to whether there are further arguments against placing such importance on the duty concept.

- Consider how other jurisdictions deal with the issue and undertake a comparative evaluation to see if they have a better system.

- Get bogged down describing the historical development of the duty concept.
- Discuss in great detail the different specialist duty situations and their merits; just draw on specific examples where relevant to your argument.
- Discuss all the different components of the whole tort of negligence as the question is specifically on duty.

Question 2

'It is one matter to require a person to take care if he embarks on a course of conduct which may harm others. . . . It is another matter to require a person, who is doing nothing to take positive action to protect others from harm for which he is not responsible, and to hold him liable in damages if he fails to do so.' *Per* Lord Nicholls in *Stovin* v *Wise* [1996] AC 923 at 930.

Evaluate why this distinction does matter and the justification of the rationale of the courts for restricting the imposition of a duty of care for an omission.

Diagram plan

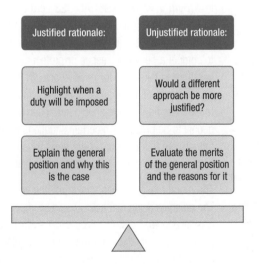

Answer plan

→ Evaluate why the law does make a distinction between these situations and the rationale behind this general position regarding omissions.

→ Discuss the alternative view of Lord Mackay in *Smith* v *Littlewoods Organisation Ltd* [1987] 1 AC 241.

→ Analyse the limited scenarios when a duty will exist and whether these offer, in light of the policy reasons, a justifiable departure from the general position.

→ Conclude by determining whether the general position is justified or whether adopting the approach of Lord Mackay is better.

Answer

English law makes an important distinction when it comes to the duty of care concept between positive acts and pure omissions, viewing them as very different situations which warrant different treatment. As Lord Keith observed in **Yeun Kun Yeu v A.G. of Hong Kong** [1988] AC 175, one would otherwise be liable for not warning another that they were walking off a cliff edge. The justifications for this distinction will be evaluated, and it is argued that the position is justified, partly due to the existence of limited exceptions which ensure a fair balance between parties.

In **Stovin v Wise** [1996] AC 923 Lord Hoffmann categorised the reasons for the distinction in political, moral and economic terms. The political reason is that it is a greater invasion of a person's freedom to compel a person to rescue or protect another than simply requiring them to take care for positive acts. This is indeed hard to argue against from a libertarian perspective. The alternative is for the state to mandate how people should act. It can be argued that compelling people to be proactive in certain situations is necessary and justified though, but this is arguably the basis for some of the limited exceptions to the rule which will be discussed below.[1]

The moral reason is also known as 'the why pick on me argument'. The rationale being that a duty could be imposed on an indeterminate class of people, therefore the question is why that one individual should be held liable for the omission, and not another. It is hard to justify, in the absence of other factors, why that person is picked. It is easy, however, to justify why a duty should be owed for positive conduct.

[1] You have a bit of a balance to strike. There is an argument for saying that, if you mention the point here, you should explain it more, but you need to bear in mind what part of your answer you are dealing with – the reasons for the general rule. If you go off into the exceptions you will lose the structure of your argument, so the safest thing to do is to raise the point and show that you will be discussing it in depth at some stage. You could give an example of such a situation here though.

This explains the repeated insistence that mere foreseeability of harm is insufficient (see Lord Hope in **Mitchell v Glasgow CC** [2009] UKHL 11). In **Stovin** Lord Hoffmann highlighted that a duty will be imposed where a person has undertaken to do something, or induced another to rely on them doing something. This illustrates the prominence of proximity when justifying the imposition of a duty in such cases,[2] which is why one exists, for example, between employers and employees; the class of potential claimant is clearly identifiable and limited in scope. This proximity makes the duty fair and just, while foreseeability of harm is generally quite obvious in such situations.

[2] Use this as an opportunity to highlight your broader knowledge of the duty concept and how it relates to this specific discussion.

The economic reason is based on the theory of efficient allocation of resources. Economic theory dictates that markets are distorted if the cost of performing an activity is passed on to others; as the activity becomes cheaper to perform. The activity should, therefore, bear its own costs. As a benefit is being gained from the activity, there is a justification for making people factor in the potential liability costs of this activity into its price. Compensation payments or increased insurance premiums for negligent performance mean that the activity will be performed more safely, so as to limit the activity's cost – it is economically inefficient to pay out higher costs. However, Lord Hoffmann noted that there was no equivalent justification for imposing a cost on someone who is not performing an activity for the benefit of another. As the reasoning is based on the benefit gained from performing the activity, it is clear why this position is correct in relation to omissions.[3]

[3] This is obviously the justification for not having a duty for omissions. Naturally, if you disagree with the reasoning, explain that here.

[4] The point that you should be seeking to make here is to show that Lord Hoffman was wrong, as the earlier case of Smith appears to have accepted a duty in relation to omissions.

The orthodox position, that there is no duty for omissions as set out by Lord Goff in **Smith v Littlewoods Organisation Ltd** [1987] 1 AC 241, was challenged in **Mitchell**, where it was argued that this was not the majority opinion. A submission was made to endorse the opinion of Lord Mackay in **Smith** who appeared contrastingly to recognise a notional duty of care for omissions.[4] His Lordship expressly rejected counsel's argument that there were policy grounds against recognising a duty. As Markesinis (1989), argued in the LQR[5] while Lord Mackay referred to foreseeability, he also stressed that it fell to be decided on the facts of each specific case. This view can be equated with the idea of likelihood of harm when determining the standard of care to be exercised. The case being decided on this basis meant that there was no breach on the particular facts as opposed to any general principle. It could be that Lord Mackay felt, again in contrast

[5] You would not need to give the full citation and title but you should give the marker some reference point as this enables him/her to check it and adds to the validity of the reference.

[6] After raising the issue and the argument for it, you should then make a decision as to which view is better and why.

[7] This firmly sets out when this situation would arise.

[8] This is just to give a firmer example of the situation and so the facts are not necessary; your marker should know the facts of the examples that you give in this section of your answer, so you do not have to use time explaining them. If you are doing fine for time, you could give some brief words, such as 'where a contracted decorator left the house unlocked'.

to Lord Goff, that the situation was within the scope of the limited exceptions. However, as Lord Mackay gave no detailed explanation as to why there were no policy reasons against imposing a duty, their Lordships in **Mitchell** were correct to follow Lord Goff's view that the general position is one of no duty.[6]

Notwithstanding the general position, as indicated, the law will recognise a duty in relation to omissions in certain limited situations. While Lord Nicholls in **Stovin** felt that the established situations for imposing a duty are not closed, it is clear that, for a new category to be recognised, it must be fit within the circumstances outlined by Lord Goff in **Smith**. The first is where 'special circumstances' exist warranting the duty's imposition. This includes where there is an assumption of responsibility, arising through contract or a fiduciary position,[7] between the maker of the omission and the claimant such as in **Stansbie v Troman** [8] [1948] 2 KB 48. Where the harm is caused through the acts of a third party, a duty may also be imposed if there is a special relationship between the maker of the omission and that third party, as was the case in **Dorset Yacht Club v Home Office** [1970] AC 1004. Crucially, there is a clear element of proximity in both situations which indicate why the individual is being chosen to owe the duty, overcoming any moral objection. Proximity also explains why it is fair for that individual to be required to act which overcomes the political reason.

Lord Goff also highlighted two general circumstances when a duty may be imposed. First, when someone causes, or allows to be created, a source of danger and it is reasonably foreseeable that a third party will interfere, sparking off the danger. Second, where an occupier has knowledge that a third party has created a fire, or the risk of one, on their premises and fails to prevent the fire spreading to neighbouring land. As Lord Hoffmann explained in **Stovin**, a mutuality of benefit exists in these two situations which creates enough proximity to overcome the main objections and justify the duty.

In conclusion, omissions need to be treated differently when it comes to the imposition of a duty of care, as otherwise individuals suffer unjustifiable burdens and personal intrusions. When factually warranted, the law has created limited exceptions to the general position which maintain fairness between the parties and achieve justice; thus ensuring flexibility in the law whilst maintaining the overall justified position.

Make your answer stand out

■ Read Markesinis, B. S. (1989) Negligence, nuisance and affirmative duties of action. *Law Quarterly Review,* 105: 104, and refer to this in support of your arguments. Offer a comparative evaluation from the jurisdictions which are covered in the article.

■ Give a bit of factual detail of *Stansbie* v *Troman* and *Dorset Yacht Club* v *Home Office* to illustrate more fully the application of the exceptions to the general position which you are setting out.

■ Explore in more depth whether the approach which Lord Mackay appeared to adopt has more merit than the general position.

■ Make sure you do offer an opinion as to the soundness of the reasons for the law's position. Do not just describe what that position is.

! Don't be tempted to . . .

■ Produce a list of situations when a duty for an omission does exist; make sure the answer flows from one to another.

■ Provide every specific example of a situation when a duty will arise. In the interests of the clarity of your structure and time, discuss the overall categories and then draw on specific examples.

■ Get tied down in specific situations, such as employer/employee relationships.

www.pearsoned.co.uk/lawexpressqa

 Go online to access more revision support including additional essay and problem questions with diagram plans, You be the marker questions, and download all diagrams from the book.

Negligence: Duty of care for economic loss

2

How this topic may come up in exams

The law restricts when a duty of care arises in negligence for purely economic losses. This area can come up as a distinct question, independent from a more general negligence one, or within the sole examination of negligence. In this chapter we look at common essay questions only for which you will need to know about the policy factors behind the law's restrictive approach. The topic is equally liable, though, to appear as a problem question dealing with either form of economic loss (i.e. resulting from negligent misstatements or negligent acts) or both (see Chapter 5). As such, you will need to learn the whole area, alongside the other components of negligence.

▌ Before you begin

It's a good idea to consider the following key themes of negligence: duty of care for economic loss before tackling a question on this topic.

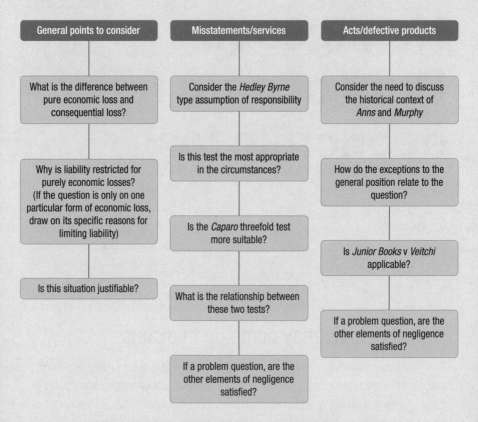

General points to consider	Misstatements/services	Acts/defective products
What is the difference between pure economic loss and consequential loss?	Consider the *Hedley Byrne* type assumption of responsibility	Consider the need to discuss the historical context of *Anns* and *Murphy*
Why is liability restricted for purely economic losses? (If the question is only on one particular form of economic loss, draw on its specific reasons for limiting liability)	Is this test the most appropriate in the circumstances?	How do the exceptions to the general position relate to the question?
	Is the *Caparo* threefold test more suitable?	
Is this situation justifiable?		Is *Junior Books* v *Veitchi* applicable?
	What is the relationship between these two tests?	
		If a problem question, are the other elements of negligence satisfied?
	If a problem question, are the other elements of negligence satisfied?	

A printable version of this diagram plan is available from **www.pearsoned.co.uk/lawexpressqa**

Question 1

'The language of "voluntary assumption" is particularly slippery . . . and judicial interpretations of what it is for a defendant to "voluntarily assume" a responsibility vary in strength.' (Barker, K. (1993) Unreliable Assumptions in the Modern Law of Negligence. *Law Quarterly Review,* 109: 461–484)

In light of this statement, critically analyse the application and development of the assumption of responsibility test and whether its ongoing use for negligently caused economic losses is warranted.

Diagram plan

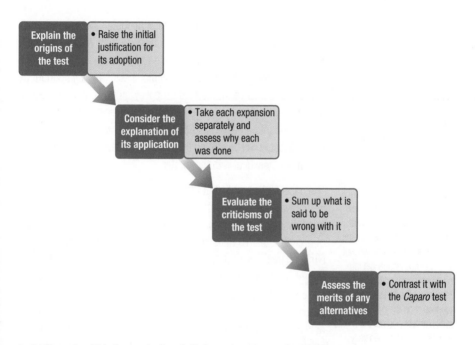

A printable version of this diagram plan is available from **www.pearsoned.co.uk/lawexpressqa**

Answer plan

→ Explain the background to the test and why it was developed.

→ Discuss the operation of the test including what is required to establish a duty.

→ Evaluate the criticisms to which the test is subjected to.

→ Consider the main alternative to the test; namely that in *Caparo* v *Dickman* [1990] 2 AC 605 and assess what limitations, if any, that may have.

→ Explore whether the two tests are, in fact, mutually exclusive or whether they could be used in conjunction with each other.

Answer

The proposition within the quote which needs analysing is whether the assumption of responsibility test, deriving from **Hedley Byrne v Heller** [1964] AC 465, is appropriate to use when determining if a duty of care for negligent misstatements arises. This is important as the law is restrictive in this field on policy grounds and any vagueness in the requirements could have severe implications for claimants and defendants. In assessing this test and the main alternative, the **Caparo** test, it will be argued that both can in fact work well together to appropriately deal with the matter.

The basis of the test is that the statement maker assumes responsibility towards the claimant, who then reasonably relies on the statement resulting in their loss. It applies regardless of the presence of a contractual or fiduciary relationship between the parties. The circumstances are said to be equivalent to a contractual situation, though lacking consideration.[1] As such, the relationship between the parties is viewed as 'special', which creates enough proximity to overcome the policy objections to such actions and thus justifies a duty being imposed.[2] As the claimants in **Hedley Byrne** had directly asked (albeit through their own bank) for the credit reference from the defendants, imposing the duty was easy to justify. While there was no contract for its provision, it was reasonable for the defendants to have anticipated reliance on the reference as the reason for the request was made clear. Therefore, by supplying it, the defendants had assumed responsibility towards the claimant in light of this reasonable reliance.[3] The idea that responsibility had been assumed is

[1] To fully explain the point you need to offer a little explanation here as to why it occurs outside of these situations.

[2] By including this line by way of explanation, you indicate that you are aware that there are policy reasons behind the law and that it is only because of special circumstances that the law recognises a duty, without having to necessarily get into too much depth as to why. Remember the thrust of the question is on the merits of the particular test and not the merits of imposing a duty generally.

[3] Adding any further facts from the case is not really going to add anything to your answer. What effectively you need to demonstrate through the facts is how the test operates and why it can be justified.

[4] By rounding off the paragraph with this line you further acknowledge the key policy concern which Lord Devlin discussed in *Hedley Byrne*.

[5] It is important to move your answer on into a discussion on this issue as it is the expansion of the test to new scenarios which are arguably the cause of the problems which the test faces and why it is criticised. Therefore, you can really start to engage with the question.

[6] It is important to consider the development of the test in distinct stages because this will allow you to consider the merits of the test through each development and discuss whether it has merit in all of the new situations, none or just particular ones.

supported by the directness of the request and so the merit of the test can be seen. The notion neatly fits the factual situation without leading to indeterminate liability which was part of the reluctance to find such a duty previously.[4]

Subsequently the test has developed to cover negligently provided services[5] (***Spring v Guardian Assurance plc*** [1995] 2 AC 296). Lord Goff felt that the test's correct basis is that the defendant has been trusted by the claimant to conduct their affairs. In ***Spring*** the issue concerned a job reference which was provided negligently. The direct relationship between both parties meant extending the test had merit. However, its continued development has caused doubts and criticism. In ***Henderson v Merrett Syndicates*** [1995] 2 AC 145 there was less reliance and what there was, was more indirect: A had contracted with B to perform a service for the benefit of C knowing that it was for C's benefit. Arguably the application still had merit as A knew that C was benefiting from the service and this justified the idea that A had assumed responsibility towards C. Again, Lord Goff argued that any criticisms of the test arose in order to prevent the scope of liability extending to an indeterminate class, but this was not an issue in ***Henderson*** as the knowledge and reliance created an identifiable and determinate class.

Therefore, the test seems to clearly require a directness between the parties or at least sufficient knowledge that the statement/service is being relied on by an identifiable class. The resultant proximity which this causes warrants the duty of care. However, the application of the test has not stuck to these situations and has developed to be used when a contract between A and B exists for the benefit of C, which C does not know about.[6] This situation occurred in ***White v Jones*** [1995] 2 AC 207, where the intended beneficiaries of a will received nothing following the negligent failure to redraft it as instructed. Lord Browne-Wilkinson suggested that the phrase referred to the task to be performed, not the legal obligation. As the defendant had involved himself in the claimant's affairs the case was aligned with previous ones justifying a duty. Lord Mustill, dissenting, argued though that for an assumption of responsibility to exist mutuality was needed between the parties so that both played an active role in the transaction in question. Such mutuality was present in all of the cases following

[7] By having a distinct paragraph on the criticisms of the assumption of responsibility test you reach the culmination of your discussion on it and provide a platform to then go on and cleanly assess the test's alternative, the *Caparo* test, which is the logical next step in the answer.

[8] Clearly, you will need to outline what the test involves but the actual issue of the question does not make it essential to break down these in depth. You could perhaps do this to make your answer stand out more.

[9] By highlighting a specific quote here you add substance to the general assertion that you are making.

[10] Whereas Lord Bridge's opinion is the most well-known from the case, by including reference to Lord Roskill you show a wider and deeper level of knowledge of the case; and secondly strengthen the assertion that you are making about the limits of the test by showing it was more of a widely held view.

[11] Although you have just highlighted some problems with the *Caparo* test, remember the point of the question and see if this test has any merit which might make it better than the assumption of responsibility test.

Hedley Byrne, including *Henderson* as, effectively, C had engaged B to contract with A; however, it was clearly lacking in *White*.

Lord Mustill's view built on that of Lord Griffiths' opinion in *Smith* v *Eric S. Bush* [1990] 1 AC 831 who felt the phrase only has any real meaning if assumption of responsibility refers to assuming responsibility towards the person who acts upon the advice. This was because, if asked, the maker of the statement would only consider himself to be assuming legal responsibility for the person they contracted with. This view has force due to its logic; and if correct, applying the test to situations such as *Smith* and *White* cannot be right. In any event, the lack of clear consensus as to the phrase's meaning and how the test operates raises a question mark over its suitability to determine liability.[7]

In *Smith*, applying what has become known as the *Caparo* test was preferred. This test requires the claimant and the injury suffered to be foreseeable, proximity between the parties and imposing a duty to be fair, just and reasonable.[8] Applying the *Caparo* test in certain situations may have more logic, and thus more merit. However, the judiciary have acknowledged that this test too does not always provide the answer. In *Customs and Excise Commissioners* v *Barclays Bank plc* [2007] 1 AC 181 Lord Walker commented that it merely provides 'a set of fairly blunt tools',[9] with the other judges expressing similar sentiments. Indeed, even in *Caparo*, both Lords Bridge and Roskill[10] highlighted how the three requirements lacked enough precision to be an effective practical test and were, at most, labels describing situations where a duty has been held to exist. This vagueness though does have some merit in that it allows judges scope to look at the entire circumstances in light of any prevailing policy and determine the matter.[11] Ultimately though, criticisms can be levelled at, and questions raised over, both tests equally.

¹² This allows you to conclude your answer by pulling the arguments for and against each test together. Your aim should be to consider the extent that the two tests can work together in a sensible and coherent manner. If you feel they cannot, you should advance this and suggest what you feel needs to be done to improve the state of the law. If you feel they can, you need to show how this is so.

¹³ When you abbreviate a case make sure you have written the name in full first and then use an appropriate name which still identifies the case in question. Avoid shortening the case name to that of the bank due to the number of cases involving each bank. The marker may not necessarily know what case you mean otherwise.

In conclusion, this leaves two tests which can be used, and questions regarding which should be used and when.[12] The test has merit as a mechanism for establishing the sufficient proximity between the parties, which makes it in turn just to impose a duty and, as such, it is simply a means of satisfying the **Caparo** requirements. As Lord Bingham noted in **Customs and Excise Commissioners**,[13] the outcomes in past cases were likely to have been the same whichever test was used. Consequently the tests are compatible with equal merit and effectiveness; although, each has a more appropriate realm of application. Therefore, the approach advocated by Lord Bingham is the best one; namely the whole circumstances of the case are viewed in light of policy considerations, and then the assumption of responsibility test is used as the starting point. If needed, **Caparo** is then applied.

 Make your answer stand out

- Explain briefly what the policy reasons are which make the law seek to limit when a duty arises for these types of losses.
- Read the article in the question along with: Murphy, J. (1996) Expectation losses, negligent omissions and the tortious duty of care. *Cambridge Law Journal*, 55(1): 43–55; Hedley, S. (1995) Negligence – pure economic loss – goodbye privity, hello contorts. *Cambridge Law Journal*, 54(1): 27–30; and Stanton, K. (2006) Professional negligence; duty of care methodology in the twenty first century. *Professional Negligence*, 22: 134, in order to gain some substance for your argument.
- Highlight specific strengths and weakness with the individual elements of the *Caparo* test.
- Consider whether, in fact, there needs to be a clearer distinction between the two tests, and their precise scope of application determined rather than merged.

Don't be tempted to . . .

- Labour the facts of the case. You need enough to show how the application of the test did, or did not, have merit to that particular situation but that is all.
- Stray into examining in depth the merits of recoverability for economic losses; remember the question is about the specific test used to find a duty.
- Chart the history of the development of the duty of care concept, especially in a narrative form.

Question 2

'The law regarding duties of care for a negligently caused economic loss is based on suspect policy considerations, and judicial approaches are inconsistent and rest on unsound principles.'

Evaluate when a duty will be owed in relation to negligent misstatements and assess the overall merit of this statement.

Diagram plan

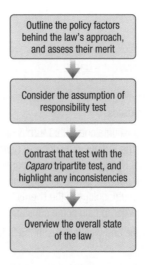

Outline the policy factors behind the law's approach, and assess their merit

↓

Consider the assumption of responsibility test

↓

Contrast that test with the *Caparo* tripartite test, and highlight any inconsistencies

↓

Overview the overall state of the law

A printable version of this diagram plan is available from **www.pearsoned.co.uk/lawexpressqa**

Answer plan

→ Explain and evaluate what policy factors influence this area of law.

→ Outline the initial approach of the courts to establishing the duty from *Hedley Byrne* v *Heller* [1964] AC 465.

→ Assess the creation of the test from *Caparo* v *Dickman* [1990] 2 AC 605 and whether its development is based on sounder principles.

→ Draw on *Customs and Excise Commissioners* v *Barclays Bank plc* [2007] 1 AC 181, evaluate the law and whether any inconsistencies from having two approaches can be reconciled.

Answer

A duty of care can be owed for negligent misstatements, but only in more tightly controlled situations for personal or property injury. Previously such a duty was denied on policy grounds which, despite the possibility of a duty now being owed, still exist. This is controversial as it means that a person who suffers an injury to their financial interests may be left without redress even though all other aspects of negligence are satisfied.[1] The issue is how the law ensures fairness to both parties in a dispute whilst also developing in a manner which is just and based on sound principle. Arguably, in aiming for this goal, the courts have approached the task in an inconsistent manner, but it is submitted that the statement in the question is without merit and the law is not in the problematic state that it suggests.

[1] Show from the start that you understand the area fully, know what the debate is getting at and what you are required to consider.

The duty was first recognised in **Hedley Byrne & Co. Ltd v Heller & Partners Ltd** [1964] AC 465. However, in doing so the House of Lords made clear that it would be on a restrictive basis as there were significant policy reasons for doing so. These reasons focus on ensuring that the statement maker is not disproportionately, and unfairly, burdened with liability. The reason why this was a concern and deemed important was because, first, people express definitive opinions in certain situations without considering the influence, due to the situation, that those words will have. Second, those words can spread rapidly as one person tells another, so that people who ultimately suffer the loss were not the persons to whom the statement was made and are people of whom the maker has no knowledge. This reasoning makes sense, and explains clearly why the person may not have taken so much care in the first place when making the statement.[2]

[2] Make sure that you offer a view as to the policy factors as the statement in the question suggests they are suspect. Don't just say what they are, consider *why* they are those as well.

In light of this policy reasoning, for a duty to be imposed, their Lordships held that what must be established is an assumption of responsibility by the defendant towards the claimant, which was reasonably relied on by the claimant, and the defendant knew that they were so relying on their skill and judgement (the assumption of responsibility test). This worked in **Hedley Byrne** because the defendant bank knew that the credit worthiness rating was for the purpose of enabling the claimant to make a business decision, albeit liability was ultimately excluded.[3]

[3] Don't forget this significant fact from the case. While the court recognised the duty, it did not find one on the facts. It is a good sign as to whether you have read and understood the case.

The test has been developed to cover the negligent provision of services, on the basis that the test is that the claimant has entrusted the defendant with the conduct of his or her affairs. The extension has merit as there is still a direct relationship between both parties; however, doubts arise from its application to more indirect service relationships. In **Henderson v Merrett Syndicates** [1995] 2 AC 145, A had contracted with B to perform a service for the benefit of C in the knowledge that it was for C's benefit. However, the test's application had merit because A's knowledge that C was benefiting from the service forged enough proximity between the parties to justify the idea that A had assumed responsibility towards C. However, this can be contrasted with **White v Jones** [1995] 2 AC 207 where a negligent failure to redraft a will meant that the intended beneficiaries, the claimants, received nothing. It was hard to see an assumption of responsibility for the claimants when the contract was between the defendant and the deceased, and the claimant would have had no knowledge of it. Lord Browne-Wilkinson suggested that the phrase 'assumption of responsibility' meant for the task performed, and not in relation to any legal obligation. As the solicitor had involved himself in the claimant's affairs by contracting to draft the will, there was a justifiable duty as in previous cases. There was a strong dissent by Lord Mustill[4] who argued that there must be mutuality between the parties which involves both playing an active role in the transaction for an assumption of responsibility to exist. In the previous cases, His Lordship argued, this was the case as, at the very least, B had contracted with A at the instigation of C. This builds on earlier criticisms of the test, in **Smith v Eric Bush** [1990] 1 AC 831, by Lord Griffiths,[5] who felt that the phrase only has any real meaning if it refers to when the law deems the maker of a statement to have assumed responsibility towards the person who acted upon the advice, i.e. they had assumed a legal obligation to them.

[4] Your aim in this section is to not only show the development of the assumption of responsibility test, but also to set a platform for the rest of your answer and link back to the question. The statement suggests judicial inconsistency and disagreement, which is what you are highlighting. You can then use this to suggest that is why a second test was needed, and then discuss that in that context.

[5] While what you are writing here naturally fits with your argument at this stage, placing this particular point at the end of the paragraph allows you to then go seamlessly into the *Caparo* test and the next part of your answer.

[6] As you are discussing a different test and explaining that it came about in light of criticism of the previous test, you need to assess the merit of this test. Link it back to your earlier discussion by considering whether it deals with any of the problems you discussed in relation to the assumption of responsibility test.

[7] Do not just assume that the test was designed to perform that role. Highlight how the judges have acknowledged it is not perfect. This allows you to address the sentiment in the question again.

[8] Even if you feel that the statement is without merit overall, do not be afraid of acknowledging where it may have a point on a certain issue. The key is to clearly explain your thinking throughout and maintain a coherent structure.

Lord Griffiths preferred to apply what became known as the *Caparo* test and was a response to the perceived weakness of the assumption of responsibility test. This test involves the claimant demonstrating that their injury was foreseeable to the defendant, there was sufficient proximity between them and, overall, it is fair, just and reasonable to impose a duty. This leaves a large degree of discretion in the courts' hands. This inherent flexibility has merit, but obviously it puts claimants firmly at risk of policy decisions. It is clear what needs to be satisfied though, which may not always be the case with the other test, as discussed above.[6] The test is only meant to be a practical test too, and no more than a blunt tool to help with the matter (*Caparo* itself and *Customs and Excise Commissioners* v *Barclays Bank plc* [2007] 1 AC 181).[7] As such we have two different tests, one which leads to questionable results in certain instances, and another which lacks sufficient precision to say with certainty when the duty will be imposed. As such the statement could be said to have some merit in relation to the law being inconsistent.[8]

However, in conclusion, while it may be said that having the two tests is inconsistent, arguably this is partially countered by saying that the *Caparo* test was intended to overcome the perceived problem of applying the initial assumption of responsibility test too broadly. Further, following *Customs and Excise Commissioners* v *Barclays Bank plc*, any inconsistency is more apparent than real with an assumption of responsibility establishing the sufficient proximity between the parties which makes it in turn just to impose a duty and, as such, it is simply a means of satisfying the *Caparo* requirements with the same outcomes largely being reached regardless of what test would have been used. Effectively, as Lord Bingham noted, both tests are compatible, although each has a more appropriate realm of application. Therefore, the approach of looking at the whole circumstances of the case in light of policy considerations and then using the assumption of responsibility test as a start before applying *Caparo*, if needed, arguably resolves any difficulties. The policy considerations do need to be justified though, and thus the concern in the statement is reasonable. However, the underlying policy rationale is justified; therefore, the statement, ultimately, has little merit.

Make your answer stand out

- Read Murphy, J. (1996) Expectation losses, negligent omissions and the tortious duty of care. *Cambridge Law Journal,* 55(1): 43–55; and Hedley, S. (1995) Negligence – pure economic loss – goodbye privity, hello contorts. *Cambridge Law Journal,* 54(1): 27–30, in order to gain some substance for your argument.

- Draw more on specific individual judicial comments on the issue and use these to highlight any inconsistencies in judicial attitudes. Also use them to fully explain how the different tests work, and why they are needed.

- Expand on the policy arguments in favour of a restrictive approach and assess whether any arguments can be made against them.

- Consider economic loss from negligent acts briefly in order to make a wider statement as to the coherence of the overall law, and the judicial approaches taken to economic losses.

! Don't be tempted to . . .

- Labour the facts of the cases. You need enough to show how the development of the test in that case was, or was not, justified, but that is all.

- Provide a full history of the duty concept even in relation to economic loss. Stick to a tight structure or you will risk running out of time.

- Ignore any merit that the statement may have, because overall you disagree with it. You need to have a balanced approach to the sentiment it is expressing throughout until your conclusion.

- Give unequal weight to the various issues which the statement throws up. You need to address adequately both the policy facts which the law is based on, and whether the law lacks consistency and principle.

- Go on to discuss the other elements of negligence, as the question is specifically on the duty aspect.

www.pearsoned.co.uk/lawexpressqa

 Go online to access more revision support including additional essay and problem questions with diagram plans, You be the marker questions, and download all diagrams from the book.

Negligence: Duty of care for psychiatric injury

How this topic may come up in exams

Psychiatric injury is an aspect of negligence concerned with mental harm which has been caused through the negligent act of another. However, it has its own specific criteria for establishing whether a duty of care is owed. For these reasons it is a common exam question in its own right, separate and distinct from the more normal questions on negligence and physical injury. You must ensure that you are familiar with the different rules for establishing liability and the distinctions that the law makes between the different categories of individuals within a problem question (see Chapter 5). The law has also been heavily criticised, with various proposals offered regarding reform. This also makes this topic equally favourable with examiners as an essay question.

■ Before you begin

It's a good idea to consider the following key themes of negligence: duty of care for psychiatric injury before tackling a question on this topic.

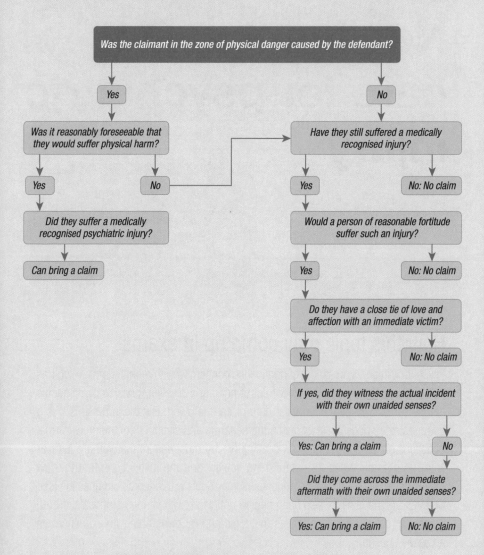

A printable version of this diagram plan is available from **www.pearsoned.co.uk/lawexpressqa**

Question 1

'I cannot, for my part, regard the present state of the law as either entirely satisfactory or as logically defensible.' (*Per* Lord Oliver in *Alcock* v *Chief Constable of South Yorkshire Police* [1992] 1 AC 310, 418)

Critically evaluate the reasoning and merits of the approach taken by the courts in relation to recognising a duty of care for negligently inflicted psychiatric injury.

Answer plan

→ Define psychiatric injury.

→ Explain the distinction between primary and secondary victims.

→ Explain the different control mechanisms for secondary victims, assessing their justification and, therefore, whether the law is 'satisfactory' and can be defended logically.

→ Explain some of the reform proposals and discuss whether they are better.

→ Conclude by summarising what state the current law is in and whether any reform proposals will help.

Diagram plan

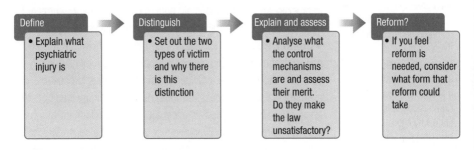

Define	Distinguish	Explain and assess	Reform?
• Explain what psychiatric injury is	• Set out the two types of victim and why there is this distinction	• Analyse what the control mechanisms are and assess their merit. Do they make the law unsatisfactory?	• If you feel reform is needed, consider what form that reform could take

A printable version of this diagram plan is available from **www.pearsoned.co.uk/lawexpressqa**

¹ Try to show off your wider, non-legal knowledge as it is important. You can use the fact of medical advances in relation to such injuries later in your answer to raise questions as to whether the concerns that the law has historically expressed are in fact warranted today.

Answer

Whether the law is 'satisfactory or logically defensible' matters as psychiatric injuries arguably are more devastating than physical ones and advancements in medical understanding requires the law to keep up.¹ Historically the law has taken a highly restrictive approach, based on issues of public policy, and put control mechanisms in place which claimants must satisfy to succeed. A large numbers of claimants

[2] This indicates straight away that you are aware of the wider issues relating to this area and that something needs to replace the current law.

[3] By referring to judicial comment you will demonstrate your authority for the statement and by referring to the actual judge add more authority to your answer by demonstrating more knowledge of the point you are making.

[4] You should include this in order to weigh up the merits of the requirement in order to avoid being too descriptive. By referring to medical advancement you also tie your comment back to your introduction. It also allows you to develop the argument, if you agree, that the rationale of the law is based on an outdated understanding of these injuries.

[5] State the justification for the distinction, although it is criticised by the Law Commission, it is important to state why it exists.

[6] You will find a lot of criticism of this case in the text books. However, rather than simply adopt it, look at the judicial reasoning carefully and see what arguments you can advance in its favour. You will impress your marker with the originality of your thinking.

[7] By setting out the policy justifications here you provide the context from which to assess the mechanisms.

have failed to do so leading to the area becoming very emotive. The different judicial approaches to different categories of victim will be assessed with the various control mechanisms evaluated in order to assess their merit. It is argued that the sentiment expressed by Lord Oliver is justified and that reform is needed.[2]

It must first be considered what amounts to an actionable psychiatric injury. As Lord Denning noted in *Hinz v Berry* [1970] 1 All ER 1084 English law does not compensate for mere grief or sorrow, what is needed is a medically recognised psychiatric injury.[3] Therefore, unlike physical injuries, a threshold of psychiatric harm is required. The rationale was highlighted by Lord Steyn in *White v Chief Constable of South Yorkshire* [1999] 2 AC 455: expensive expert witnesses are required to establish the exact nature of the psychiatric injury. This has time and cost implications for the administration of justice. Although simple grief should not warrant liability, it is questionable whether this reasoning is applicable today as science is more able to quickly and definitively diagnose genuine conditions due to a better understanding of them.[4]

In determining whether a duty is owed, the law categorises people as either primary or secondary victims. While the Law Commission has called the distinction 'more of a hindrance than a help', it exists in order to limit those who could bring a claim.[5] Primary victims must be exposed to a reasonably foreseeable risk of physical injury (*Page v Smith* [1996] 1 AC 155). Lord Lloyd in *Page* held that there was no justification in treating physical and psychiatric injury differently for such victims. Therefore, provided physical injury was foreseeable, the claimant would be successful even if psychiatric injury was not. This approach, while criticised, is acceptable[6] as the claimant has been placed in direct danger. Everyone else is deemed a secondary victim and must be of 'customary phlegm' to succeed (*Bourhill v Young* [1943] AC 92). They then must satisfy the control mechanisms from *Alcock v Chief Constable of South Yorkshire* [1992] 1 AC 310 to succeed, which puts such victims in a far less favourable position than primary victims.

The control mechanisms are heavily influenced, and underpinned, by policy considerations which were explained by Lord Steyn in *White*.[7] Principally, the judiciary have applied the 'floodgates' argument and sought to avoid a wide class of individuals being able to claim. This is then combined with the need to avoid imposing disproportionate

[8] In exams include citations of academic opinion as it strengthens the suggestion that you have read the texts and also helps the marker double check what you are saying as they have an idea where the opinion is from. That said, save time by abbreviating the citation; if it is a book or article, as here, then just put the year.

[9] The existence of the control mechanisms are really the key part of your answer and where you should focus your time. Ensure that what you write deals with the issue of whether they make the law satisfactory or not.

[10] Try and relate your criticism of the mechanism back to the policy justifications for imposing mechanisms as this will give more force to the point you are making.

[11] Try to vary your sources of academic opinion to illustrate your wider reading, rather than relying on the same academic.

[12] By highlighting a different result in another case you reinforce the idea that the law is inconsistent and unsatisfactory.

liability, as the negligence may only have been a momentary lack of concentration. These factors can be justified on the basis of fairness to the defendant as psychiatric injury could be caused to a wider range of people from a single incident than those physically injured. The final consideration is that the prospect of compensation may act as a disincentive to recovery. Stapleton (1994a) explains this is a well-intentioned desire to protect the claimant's condition deteriorating through the stress of a trial; however, as Teff (1998) highlights,[8] there is little evidence to support the assertion. As such, it is hard to sustain an approach based on this consideration.

The first control mechanism[9] is a close tie of love and affection with an immediate victim of the incident. In *Alcock* it was held that there is a rebuttable presumption of such a tie between a parent and child, and spouses. The defendant should reasonably foresee injury to these groups, but not necessarily others such as siblings who must prove their closeness with evidence. This creates uncertainty and is more likely to cause deterioration in a claimant's condition.[10] Weir (1992)[11] argues this risks causing 'embarrassment' to claimants who face cross-examination on their closeness, and contradiction by investigators.

The second mechanism requires the claimant to be present at the incident. *McLoughlin v O'Brien* [1983] 1 AC 410 extended this temporally forwards and spatially away from the scene to include the immediate aftermath, thus covering seeing the immediate victim in hospital. While *McLoughlin* eases some of the mechanism's strictness, it remains an arbitrary line drawn by the courts. In *McLoughlin* the claimant succeeded in arriving two hours later and seeing the unclean bodies, yet in *Alcock* relatives who arrived later, having travelled further, were unsuccessful.[12] It is also questionable whether the result would have been the same if the bodies had been cleaned in *McLoughlin*. The issue is far from clear and, again, reinforces the proposition that the law is unsatisfactory.

The final mechanism is that the psychiatric injury was a result of directly perceiving the incident or aftermath with one's own senses. While similar to the second mechanism, it requires the injury to arise from the sudden impact of witnessing the event rather than through gradual exposure. This can produce inconsistent results. No claim will stand if the injury is caused immediately upon being informed, by a

[13] Again, as with the other paragraphs, it is important to balance the discussion by stating what the reason for the mechanism is first before you provide any criticism of it. If you personally feel that the mechanism is justified, write the reason after the criticism so that the answer reads more strongly.

[14] By using a second judicial quote from another leading case, you build up the picture that the judiciary are not happy with the law even though they are applying it. Your argument, therefore, carries more weight and will lead in to a discussion as to reform.

[15] Depending on the number of proposals that you discuss, ensure that you state which one you prefer to round off your discussion.

third party of, say, the death of a child. Lord Keith in **Alcock** explained the reason as being a lack of proximity and because English law has never allowed for recovery in this way.[13] However, if the onset of injury is delayed until arrival at the mortuary in sufficient time, the claimants could succeed. This is hard to justify; if it is reasonably foreseeable that a parent would suffer injury as a result of witnessing an incident, surely it is a foreseeable occurrence from being informed of the incident.

There does seem to be judicial consensus around Lord Oliver's view of the law with Lord Steyn in **White** opining that the law is a 'patchwork quilt of distinctions'.[14] This has led to widespread calls for reform, notably from the Law Commission. A significant aspect of the Commission's proposals was to remove the second and third mechanisms owing to the unjust results they can bring; the first mechanism would be retained in amended form. A conclusive, automatic statutory presumption of closeness was proposed for the existing groups, but widened to include siblings and cohabitants. Those not within the list could still have to prove their closeness as now. If adopted, the floodgates could still be avoided as there would still be a restrictive control, but it would operate in a more logically defensible way.

To conclude, it is submitted that the statement describes the law correctly. Reform is not only desirable, but a necessity in order to ensure justice to victims of negligence. The Commission's proposals would vastly improve the situation while still maintaining the control required by policy.[15]

 Make your answer stand out

■ Contrast the approach taken in respect of physical injuries and discuss whether such a distinction between types of injury is warranted in more depth.

■ Explore in more detail whether the law for primary victims is as equally unsatisfactory as that for secondary victims.

■ Expand on the options for reform. Although the question does not expressly ask for a discussion regarding reforming the law, the quote does imply that reform is needed. By not discussing reform you would still pass the question, but by discussing the issue you will demonstrate that you understand the wider issues surrounding the area and achieving a higher mark.

■ Consider why the law has remained in its current state for so long in light of the consensus that it is not satisfactory.

! Don't be tempted to . . .

■ Just focus on the requirements for establishing a duty, you need to evaluate why the law requires those points for this type of duty.

■ Simply describe what criticisms and reforms exist. While you will pick up marks for this knowledge, to get the really high marks you need to consider whether the criticisms have merit and whether a certain reform will make things better. Give an opinion as to what you think.

■ Focus exclusively on case law. There are a number of academics who have questioned the merit of the law and/or offered reform proposals. Draw on these to build up just how large the consensus is on the proposition within the question.

Question 2

'What rescuer ever thinks of his own safety? It seems to me that it would be very artificial and unnecessary control to say a rescuer can only recover if he was in fact in physical danger. A danger to which he probably never gave thought, and which in any event might not cause physical injury . . . I do not share the view that the public would find it in some way offensive that those who suffered disabling psychiatric illness as a result of their efforts to rescue the victims should receive compensation.' (Lord Griffiths, *White* v *Chief Constable of South Yorkshire* [1999] 2 AC 455 at 465)

In view of this statement, evaluate the position of a rescuer in a claim for psychiatric injury and whether the law is at a justifiable position.

Answer plan

→ Briefly outline the background to *White* and highlight the decision of the case.

→ Highlight that while rescuers claiming for physical injury are treated favourably this is not the case when the claims are for psychiatric injury.

→ Outline the position of rescuers drawing on the opinions of the majority and evaluate the merits of their reasoning.

→ Contrast the reasoning of the majority with that of the minority.

→ Conclude as to which reasoning is the better view and why.

Diagram plan

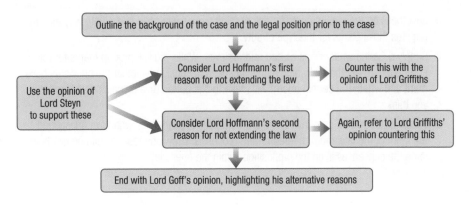

A printable version of this diagram plan is available from **www.pearsoned.co.uk/lawexpressqa**

Answer

The issue to address is the merit in the law's current approach to rescuers who, in undertaking the rescue, suffer psychiatric injury. This issue arose in ***White*** v ***Chief Constable of South Yorkshire Police*** [1999] 2 AC 455, where the House of Lords reinterpreted existing authority on the matter and created a new control mechanism for claimants to overcome. The rationale behind the majority's decision is evaluated before assessing the merits of the dissenting opinions. It is argued that while within the context of the factual background to the case the position is understandable, overall, the position in terms of legal principle cannot be justified.

In order to make a full assessment of the legal position, it is necessary to briefly outline the factual background from which it has originated.[1] The case originated out of the same incident as ***Alcock*** **v *Chief Constable of South Yorkshire Police*** [1992] 1 AC 310. However, whereas ***Alcock*** concerned the relatives of those that died, the claimants in ***White*** were the policemen who assisted in the aftermath of the incident and subsequently suffered psychiatric injury. The legal position, following ***Chadwick* v *BRB*** [1967] 1 WLR 912, was considered to be that, as with physical injury, rescuers would be in a special position and have a successful claim. The Court of Appeal

[1] By setting this out you have a yardstick from which to determine whether the decision of the case was correct. The history of the case illustrates why the judges formed the opinions that they did.

[2] Obviously, there were two grounds to the appeal, one regarding the duty owed as employee and one on the basis of their rescuer status. As the question is focused on rescuers, you need to focus on just that aspect of the appeal.

[3] It is important to state this, as the absence of authority allowed the majority to come at the matter as they did on policy grounds. It also sets up a contrast to Lord Goff, which can be evaluated later.

[4] As Lord Griffiths' reasons for dissenting on this point are at complete odds with Lord Hoffmann's, raise them as argument against the merit of the majority's view.

[5] If you include some of Lord Steyn's opinion in your answer, although essentially the same, it demonstrates your knowledge of the whole case and supports your argument.

had allowed the policemen's claims whereas the relatives in *Alcock* were unsuccessful. The defendant appealed, with one ground being[2] that, as the officers were not in any reasonably foreseeable physical danger, they would have to satisfy the *Alcock* control mechanisms to be successful. The majority, allowing the appeal, held that a rescuer who was not at any risk of physical danger could not be classified as a primary victim and, therefore, must satisfy the control mechanisms.

The majority decided that *Chadwick* was not authority for the proposition that a rescuer was in any sort of special position regarding psychiatric injury.[3] Mr Chadwick was what would now be considered a primary victim as he was at risk of physical injury. As for whether the law should be extended incrementally to impose liability where a rescuer, in no physical danger, suffers psychiatric injury, Lord Hoffman felt that there were two reasons for saying no. Firstly, it is clearly understood that a rescuer is someone who puts themselves in physical danger. If the term was extended, as proposed, to cover those who, such as the claimants, provide assistance in the aftermath, then difficulties would arise in distinguishing such a person from a mere bystander. Lord Griffiths disagreed with this analysis,[4] believing that, while a distinction is needed between providing immediate help at the scene and treatment once the victim is safe, this could easily be established on the facts of each case. Therefore, Lord Griffiths would have dismissed the appeals and allowed the law to be extended, provided it was still reasonably foreseeable that the rescuer in question would suffer psychiatric injury. This is arguably the better view; while some distinction is required in order to prevent too wide-ranging liability, taking matters on a case-by-case basis allows control to be maintained but also allows flexibility where warranted.

The second reason in Lord Hoffman's opinion was firmly one of public policy. He felt that allowing the claims would offend ordinary people in view of the fact that the claimants would become better off than the relatives in *Alcock*. Lord Steyn called such a situation, whereby the relatives lose out while spectators giving peripheral assistance could recover, an 'unedifying spectacle'.[5] In countering this point, Lord Griffiths felt that the public would not find it offensive that people who had actually been involved in the aftermath and, significantly, suffered a disabling psychiatric illness could receive compensation. The important difference was the suffering of such illness as opposed

[6] As the majority were so clearly swayed by the factual background to the case and the decision in *Alcock,* it is important to have raised this beforehand. By doing so you give yourself a platform from which to fully evaluate the reasoning given in the case.

[7] Therefore, your answer will benefit from Lord Goff's reasoning being looked at separately from Lord Griffiths'.

[8] It is quite central to explaining Lord Goff's opinion that you highlight the different way that he saw the question to be asked in the case. Therefore, you need to state what the question was in his view in order to fully demonstrate your understanding of his reasoning.

[9] As Lord Goff was basing his opinion firmly on tort principles, you need to provide some explanation as to the underlying principle and function of tort law. This will strengthen your discussion of Lord Goff's opinion and show the depth of your understanding of tort law generally.

to mere grief and bereavement. In view of the factual context of the decision, it is hard to argue with the concerns of the majority.[6] However, approaching the matter ignorant of the **Alcock** decision and looking simply at the principle to be determined, and the direct facts, it seems hard to disagree with the counter opinion of Lord Griffiths that a case-by-case look at the facts could adequately deal with the matter.

Lord Goff would also have dismissed the appeals; however, his reasoning was different and more forceful.[7] He noted first that Mr Chadwick did not actually rescue anyone but simply brought aid and comfort. Additionally, he noted that in **Chadwick** there had been some physical danger but this was treated as irrelevant as it was the whole horror of the event which caused his injuries. Each of these factors was important; the first meant that we should not be restricted as to what is meant by a rescuer. The second factor showed that there was no reason to single out for compensation only those who had done rescue acts where those acts were only incidental to the wider incident which, as a whole, caused the psychiatric injury. Lord Goff suggested that insisting that a rescuer be objectively exposed to the risk of physical injury was, in fact, contrary to authority. This meant that the majority were wrong in viewing the question as to whether the law should be extended, rather than whether the law should be restricted.[8] In his view, the majority were imposing an undesirable artificial barrier against recovery for foreseeable psychiatric injury. Furthermore, Lord Goff felt that the majority's concern in relation to public offence at certain claimants being seen to be better off, which underpinned their opinions, was misconceived. The role of tort is to compensate, at the expense of those whom the law deems responsible, those that have been injured.[9] Some claimants will always be more able to prove the defendants' responsibility than others. This did not warrant restricting their claims; all that should be done is that each claim be measured against the same legal principles. The control mechanism proposed by the majority would equally deny a relative who had attempted a rescue, while the existing mechanisms would defeat a claim by the policemen where they had no more than witnessed the event. It is hard to argue with this reasoning, particularly as it is firmly grounded in principle.

To conclude, it is now settled that a rescuer who is at no risk of physical injury must satisfy the **Alcock** control mechanism to be successful.

In reaching this position it could be said that the majority in **White** were unduly influenced in attempting to give solace to the relatives in **Alcock**. From an emotional perspective, the decision is understandable. However, in terms of legal principle, the current position is hard to justify, a point in fact conceded by the majority, and the view of the minority in relation to rescuers is preferable.

 Make your answer stand out

- Although the question is specifically on psychiatric injury, contrast the position of a rescuer in a claim for psychiatric injury with that of a rescuer suffering physical injury. In doing this, consider the point raised by Lord Hoffmann in *White;* that rescuers do not even receive special treatment in cases of physical injury.

- Tailor your answer to suit your view. Therefore, if you actually disagree with the minority in *White,* end your answer with the views of the majority and why they are more justified. This will ensure that your answer finishes strongly.

- Offer your own view as to what the law should be in order to be in a better state if you feel that to be the case. If you have identified a problem, try to solve it. Do make sure that you substantiate any opinion by expressing the basis for that opinion.

- Draw on the wealth of academic literature on the topic in order to support the different positions that you are considering, and then to lend support for your ultimate view on the question.

! Don't be tempted to . . .

- Dwell too long on setting out the factual backdrop to the case and provide too much detail. This is needed simply to illustrate why the majority reached the decision that they did and no more.

- Ignore the opinions of the dissenting Law Lords on the basis that their view is not the law. The question asks you whether the current position is justified and, therefore, in order to do this adequately, you have to evaluate the opposing views provided from the case.

- In particular, do not simply focus on Lord Griffiths from the minority just because the question quotes his opinion. Lord Goff gave a longer opinion based on different reasoning which should be referred to.

www.pearsoned.co.uk/lawexpressqa

Go online to access more revision support including additional essay and problem questions with diagram plans, You be the marker questions, and download all diagrams from the book.

Negligence: Breach, causation, remoteness and defences

4

How this topic may come up in exams

While these all naturally come together in a problem question, as shown in Chapter 5, as with the duty concept each is examinable as an individual essay. For breach questions you will need to ensure that you know what the factors are which the courts consider, and be able to evaluate how and why they are used; as well as when they will be adapted. Causation is very popular for essay questions as it has many different complex subsections. Therefore, you will need a firm understanding of the judicial reasoning in causation cases, and be able to evaluate whether those opinions have merit. Ensure you have also read sufficient academic opinion to support your argument. Remoteness and defences are less likely as individual essays.

◼ Before you begin

It's a good idea to consider the following key themes of negligence: breach, causation, remoteness and defences before tackling a question on this topic.

Non-Duty Elements of Negligence			
Breach: consider	**Causation: consider**	**Remoteness: consider**	**Defences: consider**
Factors extraneous to the defendant • The likelihood of harm • The likely magnitude of harm • The social utility of the defendant's conduct? • The cost of avoiding the harm? • Was the act in accordance with a trade or community practice? • Was it an emergency? • How much was the situation part of the demands of everyday life? **Factors related to the defendant** • Their age? • Do they possess any disability? • Were they able to foresee the acts of third parties? • Did they possess special knowledge of the claimant? • Their level of intelligence or knowledge • Were they a skilled professional?	• Is the situation one of distinct, alternate causes or cumulative causes? • Has the breach of duty caused or materially contributed to the injury? • Is the injury which has been caused one which is actionable? • Is there any medical uncertainty which permits the normal rules to be relaxed? • Did the breach materially increase the risk of injury? • Are there consecutive causes of the injury? • Can any of these be classed as an intervening act?	• What was the original test under *Re Polemis*? • Is the injury one which is of a type, kind or class which was reasonably foreseeable as required by the modern approach under *The Wagon Mound No. 1*?	• Has the claimant voluntarily assumed the risk of injury? • Is the injury one for which liability can be excluded or limited? • Is the claim substantially based on an illegal act by the claimant? • Has the claimant contributed to his injury through his own negligence?

A printable version of this diagram plan is available from **www.pearsoned.co.uk/lawexpressqa**

Question 1

'The standard of foresight of the reasonable man is, in one sense, an impersonal test. It eliminates the personal equation and is independent of the idiosyncrasies of the particular person whose conduct is in question.' (*Per* Lord MacMillan in *Glasgow Corporation* v *Muir* [1943] AC 448, at 457)

Evaluate the statement's validity in light of the factors pertaining to the defendant which the courts consider in assessing breach of duty.

Answer plan

→ Establish the role played by breach within negligence.

→ Explain what the standard of care of is.

→ Outline the factors considered which are impersonal to the defendant.

→ Contrast those with an evaluation of the factors which do relate to the defendant.

→ Conclude by assessing the overall validity of the statement.

Diagram plan

A printable version of this diagram plan is available from **www.pearsoned.co.uk/lawexpressqa**

Answer

When determining whether a person has reached an acceptable standard in their conduct, various factors are considered. The issue is the extent to which personal characteristics should be included. This is important as liability will vary according to how their conduct is assessed, while certain characteristics may prevent someone reaching a standard attainable by others. It is argued that while certain factors pertaining to the defendant are considered, Lord MacMillan's statement is correct owing to the objective nature of assessing those factors.

Breach is a crucial element of negligence as determining the standard expected to be shown impacts on whether the duty of care is discharged and thus potential liability. Breach is a mixture of law and fact. Firstly, the standard required by law needs establishing; then it becomes a question of fact whether the standard was reached or not. The legal standard to reach, as seen in **Paris v Stepney BC** [1951] AC 367, is reasonable care in the circumstances of the case. The scope of looking at the circumstances of the case allows the court to assess a range of factors in determining how the reasonable man would have acted.

Clearly, the emphasis on the reasonable man demonstrates that the factors are assessed objectively and therefore, are impersonal. There are several but the main ones[1] are the likelihood and magnitude of harm, plus the preventability of that harm. The greater the likelihood of the harm occurring, the more care should be taken, particularly where the harm can easily be prevented. A prime example is the case of **Paris** where supplying goggles would have prevented the harm occurring; it was more likely in view of the work and would be greater owing to his already limited eyesight.[2] A further external factor is the nature of the situation. Where there is an emergency, it is reasonable to act less cautiously than where there is more time to consider what one is doing.

However, notwithstanding these impersonal factors, it is not entirely accurate to say that the standard of care is completely without reference to the defendant.[3] As *Street* (Murphy and Witting, 2012)[4] states, to finalise the definition of the reasonable man the phrase 'in the circumstances' from **Paris** needs to be considered; and these words require the particular defendant to be taken into account. Although, as *Street* also highlights, the courts still eliminate considerations related to the defendant's idiosyncrasies and instead consider their attributes which are characteristic of a class of which they are a member. Objectively considering characteristics attributable to the defendant's class is necessary for justice, as clearly a child cannot be expected to reach the same standard as expected of an adult. Yet, focusing on the class rather than the actual individual prevents the key principle of negligence, namely that a required standard of behaviour must be reached,

[1] Use this to show that you know that there are more but also to indicate that you are consciously looking at a limited few. Looking only at the main factors will also allow you time to explore the factors which relate to the defendant in more depth.

[2] It is beneficial to show some of your knowledge of case law but remember that the question asks for a consideration of the factors more attributable to the defendant, so do not dwell too long on these points.

[3] This is your most important paragraph: you need to show that, while there are some factors which pertain to the defendant which are considered, these are still viewed objectively. This allows the latter part of your answer to explore these factors for their justifications and explains why your answer has gone in this direction.

[4] You ought to give an indication of what you have read and state this as your authority for the proposition. However, in the exam do not worry about trying to get the full citation down; simply give sufficient indication as to what you have read.

5 It is around this point that
you can, and should, include
some evaluation as to why
these factors are needed
and why a full subjective
account of the defendant's
characteristics is not
undertaken. This will prevent
your answer coming across
as just a list of factors.

6 Explain why this is the case
by relating your discussion
to the primary principles and
theories of tort. This will show
your deeper understanding of
the subject as a whole.

7 As such factors are not
considered, use them as
a contrast to how youth
is considered within this
paragraph rather than as a
separate paragraph.

being distorted.[5] Clearly, a subjective approach would negate tort's purpose in regulating social conduct by stressing how one should act.[6]

As indicated, one characteristic assessed is whether the tortfeasor is a child. If so, the question asks what degree of care and foresight is reasonable to expect of a child of that age (*Mullin v Richards* [1998] WLR 1304). This is necessary to allow children to indulge in natural horseplay and enjoy their youth without unduly stifling them with thoughts of potential injury while playing games like tag, as in *Orchard v Lee* [2009] EWCA Civ 295. By contrast, any disability or infirmity of the defendant[7] will not be considered, as it will be deemed that by doing the act in question with knowledge of their disability they have been negligent (*Roberts v Ramsbottom* [1980] 1 WLR 823).

Whether the defendant has, or ought to have, special knowledge of the claimant is another assessed factor attributable to the defendant (*Paris*). If the defendant knows of a condition which makes the claimant more susceptible to injury, or injury of a greater extent, then clearly it is right to expect a greater degree of care. As such, this can be seen as overlapping with the external factors considered earlier as it means they should be more aware of the likelihood and magnitude of harm.

Arguably, the most significant factors relating to defendants are their skill and knowledge. Negligence is not excused simply because someone is of lower intellect (*Vaughan v Menlove* (1837) 132 ER 490) nor does failing to use one's higher intellect necessarily attract liability (*Wooldridge v Sumner* [1963] 2 QB 43). The reasonable man simply has normal intelligence; however, where the defendant has a status which is relevant to the conduct in question, this is considered. For example, where a reasonable chief engineer would have known of the risk of discharging the oil in *The Wagon Mound (No. 2)* [1967] AC 88, liability resulted. Such circumstances warrant altering the reasonable man's knowledge to that of someone of the defendant's status so as to fully and fairly assess their conduct.

This leads into consideration of the defendant's skills and whether someone, possessing certain skills, who then injures another when exercising that skill should be judged by reference to the reasonable man who does not have that skill or to someone who does. The law takes a tough stance answering this question. For example, learner drivers are judged to the standard of reasonable, qualified drivers (*Nettleship v Weston* [1971] 2 QB 691). This scenario is based on

[8] This section is needed in order to illustrate why there is a tough stance taken. Use this to try and either justify or argue against the approach the law takes with regard to these factors.

policy as otherwise there would be problems in determining insurance and assessing liability based on experience. However, unlike scenarios such as ***Chaudhry* v *Prabhakar*** [1989] 1 WLR 29, it cannot be said that the learner holds themselves out as having more skill, hence their learner plates.[8] Similarly, professionals are judged to the standard of the reasonable person of their profession, regardless of their experience (***Bolam* v *Friern Hospital Management Committee*** [1957] 1 WLR 582). Patient confidence dictates doctors cannot plead inexperience for poor operations, thus also enhancing tort's deterrence and economic efficiency principles. However, under ***Bolam*** professionals do have leeway if they can show that a respected body of opinion from that profession would have acted in the same way, even if others would not have so acted. Provided the opinion supporting the conduct withstands scrutiny (***Bolitho* v *City and Hackney HA*** [1998] AC 232), this is permissible to reflect legitimate variations in professional opinions as to such conduct which makes it harder to say what is unreasonable.

In conclusion, it is clear the statement is largely correct, as breach is firmly determined on an objective basis. That reasonableness is determined objectively in view of the circumstances means some considerations of factors pertaining to the defendant are needed. However, these are still viewed objectively by looking at how a reasonable person of that class would have acted, thus reinforcing the statement.

✓ Make your answer stand out

- Ensure that you offer some evaluation of each factor. It is quite easy to have your answer simply slide into a descriptive narrative; that will only get so many marks.
- Similarly, add to the level of academic analysis of your work by drawing on academic journals and other texts around the approach of the courts to the various factors. This will allow you to then substantiate some of your views with academic authority.
- Show your awareness of section1 of the Compensation Act 2006, but more importantly your understanding of it by highlighting how it has not affected how the courts approach the issue of breach of duty.
- Explore whether the approach of the courts in dismissing subjective personal factors, specific to the particular defendant, could be said to be introducing a touch of strict liability to the issue. On this look at cases such as ***Nettleship* v *Weston*, *Roberts* v *Ramsbottom*** and ***Mansfield* v *Weetabix Ltd***.
- Ensure that you do reach a decision as to the issue in the question; do not just sit on the fence.

Don't be tempted to . . .

- Just list the different factors, make sure you evaluate each one. As noted above, it is easy to do this but you will lose out on marks.

- Turn your answer into a list of cases and facts if giving an example for each factor.

- Go through all the factors which are considered. You will struggle to get through them all in any significant depth and will end up with a series of brief points. Focus on the main ones and use your time and space to add depth to them.

- Cover all aspects of negligence; the question is very specifically concerned with breach of duty.

Question 2

'In a case where medical science cannot establish the probability that "but for" an act of negligence the injury would not have happened but can establish that the contribution of the negligent cause was more than negligible, the "but for" test is modified, and the claimant will succeed.' (*Per* Waller LJ in *Bailey* v *Ministry of Defence* [2009] 1 WLR 1052 at [46])

Evaluate the instances when a court will depart from the 'but for' test in favour of an alternative test and consider whether the law is satisfactory.

Diagram plan

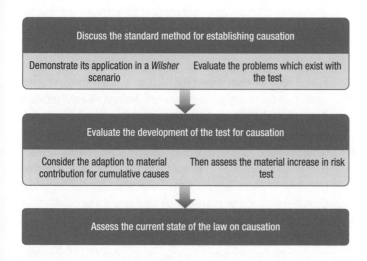

Discuss the standard method for establishing causation

Demonstrate its application in a *Wilsher* scenario

Evaluate the problems which exist with the test

Evaluate the development of the test for causation

Consider the adaption to material contribution for cumulative causes

Then assess the material increase in risk test

Assess the current state of the law on causation

A printable version of this diagram plan is available from **www.pearsoned.co.uk/lawexpressqa**

Answer plan

→ Outline the standard 'but for' test.

→ Demonstrate its standard application in scenarios consisting of distinct, alternative possible causes of injury.

→ Highlight what problems there can be with the application of the 'but for' test.

→ Chart the development of the 'material contribution' test through to the 'material increase in risk' test and evaluate their use in situations where the 'but for' test is deemed inappropriate.

→ Conclude by assessing the current state of the law.

Answer

The issue to address is the test used for determining causation in negligence and how it is modified depending on the circumstances. Strict adherence to the traditional approach has led to many claimants going uncompensated, whereas in certain circumstances claimants benefit from a relaxation of the rules. It will be argued that this discrepancy in the law can be justified and so the law is satisfactory.

The standard approach for determining causation was devised in **Cork v Kirby Maclean** [1952] 2 All ER 402, and is to apply a simple test to the facts. One asks whether, 'but for' the negligent act, the claimant would have suffered their injury. This requires looking at whether, on the balance of probabilities, the negligent act was the most likely cause of the claimant's injury. Where there is an over 50 per cent chance that the negligent act was the cause, it is treated as the 100 per cent cause. Where it is shown that the injury was likely to have occurred even without the negligence, the defendant cannot be deemed the factual cause of the injury. **Hotson v East Berkshire AHA** [1987] AC 750 illustrates this, with the judge holding that as there was only a 25 per cent chance that without the negligence the condition would have been avoided, the injury was already in place prior to the negligence.[1] In **Bonnington Castings Ltd v Wardlaw** [1956] AC 613 Lord Reid noted the authorities supported the proposition that the question is whether on the balance of probabilities the defendant caused or materially contributed to the injury. Although **Wardlaw** concerned cumulative causes, the issue of material contribution to the injury applies where the cause is one of several distinct factors as seen in **Wilsher v Essex AHA** [1988] AC 1074. Here a

[1] It is the decision of the case and its reasoning here which you need to illustrate your point, so there is no need to give a fuller factual account.

prematurely born baby was given excessive oxygen by the hospital and later suffered blindness, but there were four other completely separate risks which the baby was exposed to which could have caused the blindness. Lord Bridge framed the question throughout as one of showing that the excess oxygen administered to the baby was the cause or material contribution of the blindness. However, the problem was the presence of the other factors, which meant that it could not be shown that 'but for' the contribution of the negligent cause, the injury would not have occurred. The application of the 'but for' test for the material contribution of injury in such a case was affirmed in **Bailey v Ministry of Defence** [2009] 1 WLR 1052.

[2] The fact that these cases are set in a different context is important as to why the same policy factors as *Wilsher* have not been applied. Therefore, you need to flag up this difference in setting.

As **Wilsher** shows, the test has been rigorously applied in medical negligence cases: however, in cases of negligent exposure to industrial illnesses[2] the courts have been willing to relax the 'but for' test to overcome causal uncertainties. In **Wardlaw**, while the fact that a material contribution would suffice as opposed to actually causing the injury, the issue was complicated by the fact that the case concerned a cumulative cause scenario. Wardlaw contracted pneumoconiosis from inhaling silicon dust while at work. There were two sources of inhalation, an innocent cause from using a pneumatic hammer which could not be avoided, and a negligent cause by his employer who had failed to maintain the extraction plant. Wardlaw succeeded as, while it could not be said that 'but for' the negligence the injury would not have occurred – indeed the evidence showed it was insufficient to have caused it – the evidence showed that his employer's contribution to him contracting the illness was more than negligible.[3] In **Fairchild v Glenhaven Funeral Services Ltd** [2002] UKHL 22 Lord Rodger expressly stated[4] that the 'but for' test is departed from in such situations.

[3] Do not forget this qualification to the decision as this forms part of the justification to the decision.

[4] By referring to Lord Rodger in *Fairchild,* you have high level authority for the statement which you are making.

The approach was developed further by **McGhee v National Coal Board** [1973] 1 WLR 1. McGhee, through his job, was non-negligently exposed to brick-dust and then negligently not provided with washing facilities, which prolonged the exposure while he travelled home. Subsequently, he developed dermatitis which medical evidence showed was from the exposure. However, the evidence only showed that the prolonged exposure increased the risk of dermatitis but not that this negligent exposure had caused it. Lord Reid felt that there was no distinction between a material contribution and a material increase in risk, although this was rejected in **Fairchild**. Lord Wilberforce justified liability on the basis that where a person creates a risk by breaching a duty, and injury ensues from within the area of risk, he should bear the loss unless he can show there was another cause. This was a matter of justice as the employer should be taken to foresee the possible injury and thus bear the consequences.[5] At first glance this might seem unfair on the defendant who becomes liable for injury which it is unclear that he caused. However, it certainly achieves justice for the claimant and would seem to be grounded in tort principles such as ideas of corrective justice and loss distribution. A wrong has been done with a foreseeable outcome; the employer is in a better position to bear such a loss through insurance and could prevent liability through better working practices, another aim of tort.

Therefore, a shift in approach has been undertaken by the courts in relation to causation and the application of the 'but for' test, with departure permitted where, as Lord Rodger states in **Fairchild**, 'it is inherently impossible for the claimant to prove exactly how his injury was caused'. The principle, started in **Wardlaw** and developed in **McGhee**, can be applied where the claimant has proved all they can, with the causal link of the injury needing scientific investigation which cannot be concluded because science itself is uncertain as to the cause.[6] **Wilsher** appeared to make a distinction between industrial cases and medical cases. While justified on the grounds of protecting NHS funds, this has now rightly been removed by **Bailey** which stated there is no policy reason for not applying **McGhee** in cumulative-cause medical cases, which does provide some consistency.[7]

However, **Bailey** did retain a distinction between cases where the cause is cumulative but flowing from essentially the same substance or where there are distinct, alternative causes as in **Wilsher**. In the former, to alleviate the evidential uncertainty the 'but for' test is departed from, and possibilities are considered rather than probabilities. As noted above,[8] this is justifiable under tort principles but it raises questions as to why the same tort principles are not applied to a **Wilsher**-style case. However, the key distinguishing factor is that in **Wilsher** there were several independent causes.[9] No commonality existed and so it is hard to say that the hospital's negligence even contributed to the injury; the uncertainty is too great. Imposing liability would be too unfair and thus ensures justice between the parties in question; no wrong needs correcting.

[5] This is still part of Lord Wilberforce's reasoning which you need to set out before considering whether *McGhee* was an acceptable departure from the traditional position.

[6] Although a judicial quote has just been stated as to how/when the principle operates, you ought to demonstrate that you understand it by explaining it and developing the point.

[7] It is important to explore why the distinction existed and the nature of that distinction, i.e. you comment on whether it is right or wrong that *Bailey* has exposed the medical profession to potentially more litigation.

[8] Refer to your previous comment to justify your point without repeating in full what you have already said.

[9] If you are arguing that there is a distinction, you need to highlight why this is the case and then argue whether there is a good reason for it or not.

Make your answer stand out

- Evaluate the merits of the single agent theory as the basis for continuing to distinguish *Wilsher* from *McGhee*. Look at the opinion of Lord Hoffman in *Fairchild*, who did not think it was satisfactory although he did change his mind in *Barker* v *Corus UK Ltd* [2006] 2 AC 572.
- Offer a view as to whether material contribution is different to material increase in risk; if you think it is, are both equally justifiable?
- Include academic opinion throughout to support your discussion. Consider: Lee, J. (2008) Causation in Negligence: Another Fine Mess. *Professional Negligence*, 24: 194 and Bailey, S. (2010) What is a Material Contribution? *Legal Studies*, 30: 167.
- Analyse the specific approach taken in mesothelioma cases drawing on *Fairchild, Barker* and *Sienkiewicz* [2011] UKSC 10 and the Compensation Act 2006, section 3.
- Consider the potential overlap with issues for loss of a chance.

! **Don't be tempted to . . .**

- Focus your answer solely on mesothelioma and the discussion of such principles in cases such as *Fairchild, Barker* and *Sienkiewicz*. The question is framed more generally than that.
- Leave out a discussion of the policy factors which underpin why each case was decided in the way it was. These are needed to more fully assess whether the decisions reached in the cases as to test of causation to apply are justifiable for those situations.

 Question 3

'The common law imposes duties and seeks to provide appropriate remedies in the event of a breach of duty. If negligent diagnosis or treatment diminishes a patient's prospects of recovery, a law which does not recognise this as a wrong calling for redress would be seriously deficient today.' (*Per* Lord Nicholls in *Gregg* v *Scott* [2005] 2 AC 176 at 185E)

Critically evaluate whether the law on causation is 'deficient' and loss of a chance should be an actionable head of damage.

Answer plan

→ Outline the factual background of *Gregg*.

→ Set out the majority's view, evaluating the compatibility of each judge's reasoning.

→ Discuss whether the decision leaves the law 'deficient'.

→ Evaluate whether the opinion of Lord Nicholls satisfactorily counters the majority's concerns.

→ Conclude which view is more justifiable.

Diagram plan

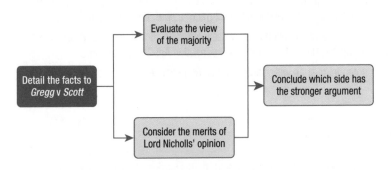

A printable version of this diagram plan is available from **www.pearsoned.co.uk/lawexpressqa**

Answer

[1] By stating these points here, you are showing that you are aware of the context in which the debate is taking place and providing the marker with insight into the reasoning that will form the basis of your argument.

Whether loss of a chance is an injury which warrants being an actionable head of damage in negligence is an important issue, as recognising such harm would give effect to a fundamental principle of tort, namely corrective justice. However, it would potentially increase litigation against the NHS and lead to defensive medical practices.[1] It will be argued that theoretically the stronger argument is that it should be adopted while equally any practical complaints can be overcome.[2]

[2] This is just my opinion and not necessarily what you should write. As with other areas, this question lends itself to having your own opinion which you should express and then seek to substantiate in your answer.

In **Gregg v Scott** [2005] 2 AC 176 the defendant misdiagnosed a lump under the claimant's arm as harmless when in fact it was cancerous. The misdiagnosis was revealed nine months later when Gregg visited another GP after the lump had grown.[3] Resultantly, the cancer spread, reducing Gregg's chances of recovery from 42 per cent to 25 per cent, therefore no injury had occurred which was caused by Scott. On the balance of probabilities, there was no chance of recovery to lose.

[3] Save yourself time by being brief with the factual background to the case. This is needed just to provide the context to the debate on the issue in the House of Lords.

Gregg unsuccessfully appealed on two grounds, the second being that loss of a chance should be an actionable injury itself.

Lord Hoffman dismissed this ground[4] for lacking a principled basis. He regarded the law as deeming everything to have a determinate cause even if that cause is not known. A lack of knowledge and evidential difficulty do not make the cause indeterminate. He considered economic loss cases could be explained owing to an act of an independent third party which was not the case here; it was simply whether the defendant caused the injury.

Responding to counsel's argument that a wrong required remedying,[5] he argued any remedy required widening the limited exception for departing from the normal rules of causation from **Fairchild v Glenhaven Funeral Services Ltd** [2003] 1 AC 32 and departing from **Wilshire v Essex AHA** [1988] AC 1074 and **Hotson v East Berkshire AHA** [1987] AC 750; yet the arguments had not changed since those cases. Gregg argued that the **Fairchild** principle could be narrowly extended by confining it to cases in which the claimant had already suffered an injury. Lord Hoffman felt this was artificial and akin to limitations which had 'disfigured' the law on psychiatric injury. Such a restriction had no underlying principle to it nor did the alternative restriction of limiting the principle to cases where medical knowledge as to the cause was lacking. While Lord Hoffman was adamant that the claim should not succeed, no reason was advanced against the latter restriction and it was the complete opposite of how Lord Nicholls saw that issue.[6]

Lord Nicholls, allowing the appeal,[7] felt the matter was, in principle, 'clear and compelling';[8] actionable loss should cover the loss of a favourable outcome rather than just the lost outcome itself. He argued this would 'match medical reality' and recognise what, in practice, the patient had before the negligent act and thus what has been lost. He further argued that the extent of the duty owed by doctors is to exercise care and skill when diagnosing and treating patients. This is hollowed by stating that just because a favourable outcome was originally less than 50 per cent it can be negligently reduced; there would be no need to exercise the requisite care on a patient in such a position.

[4] You need to state what position each of their Lordships was coming from as this was a majority decision.

[5] This indicates that you have read the case in full and know the full range of arguments advanced before their Lordships.

[6] This sentence allows your answer to flow naturally into how Lord Nicholls saw the matter.

[7] Make sure you show that you are aware that he was not in the majority, to give the context of why he took the opposite view.

[8] Starting with this part of his opinion straightaway gives weight to the comparative evaluation which you should be seeking to provide in your answer, as it is in direct contrast to the argument which you have advanced.

Underlying this reasoning was the recognition that tort's principal objective is to provide redress where a duty has been breached. The principle of corrective justice centres on injuries being corrected by the payment of compensation; it is hard to see even on grounds of distributive justice why the former should be departed from. Lord Nicholls argued that leaving a claimant without redress in this situation would leave the law deficient and, notwithstanding Lord Hoffman's view, 'open to reproach' in light of the differing approach taken to loss of financial opportunities.

He furthered countered Lord Hoffman's argument by considering that it is not always true that the patient's actual condition at the time of the negligence will determine the answer to the hypothetical question which must be asked as to what would have happened 'but for' the negligent act. As such, **Gregg** was not covered by authority as Lord Hoffman suggested. In **Gregg**, the answer to the latter question was laced with uncertainty and could only be answered by recourse to statistics expressed in percentage terms. Reflecting this, there were no theoretical grounds for holding that compensation could not be awarded for the diminution of recovery. By restricting the development to where the claimant already has the illness complained of, he felt it also left the **Fairchild** principle unaffected.[9]

[9] As you are seeking to rebut the arguments of the majority and show why it should be actionable, you must show how Lord Nicholls countered the arguments of the majority and tie it back to the points you advanced earlier.

It does appear that tort is placing financial interests above the chance of achieving personal well-being, which is strange considering that claims for pure economic loss are tightly restricted. The justification could lie in the practical difficulties in adopting this change. Lord Nicholls addressed some of these implications, although not in as much depth as the theoretical arguments. He simply stated that the fear of floodgates was not a convincing enough reason for departing from the principal objective of tort. In terms of increased costs to the NHS, he felt, while a formidable argument, it was 'unacceptable' and by keeping the development to the tightly defined circumstances which he did and insisting on a significant reduction in the chance of recovery this would combat the issue. Finally, regarding claims that defensive medical practices would result, he noted that doctors are already aware that they face being sued if they are negligent and thus this argument was unimpressive.

It could be said that his failure to go into more depth weakened his opinion and he certainly does not counter the argument of Lady Hale that nearly all claims based on loss of an outcome could be changed to a loss of a chance of that outcome. This would result, if both were retained, in the defendant always being liable, as the claimant would always have the fallback position of a proportionate claim. This could be unfair, but it misses the fact that they have been at fault and, therefore, based on corrective justice principles, it is not necessarily an unfair situation. A stronger argument was that for some claimants this could be a negative development. If both types of claims could not be retained and the latter were adopted, then claimants who currently get 100 per cent compensation would suddenly get less. This is detrimental to claimants but arguably fairer for defendants and would further best recognise the medical reality of the situation.

[10] Throughout your answer you will have been looking at the merits of both sides of the argument. However, in your conclusion it is essential, in order to fully answer the question, to come down on one side.

In conclusion, in principle a lost favourable outcome should be actionable.[10] **Gregg** differed from **Hotson**, the eventual outcome 'but for' the negligent act was not determined at the time of that act. Even Lady Hale's concerns could be argued as having some positive consequences, with any issues as to quantifying damages being resolved in practice. Potential implementation difficulties should not prevent the law's development in a fair manner consistent with fundamental principles. The potential impact on the NHS needs to be monitored, with Parliament stepping in if it proves detrimental.

✓ Make your answer stand out

- Look at the basic objective of tort in order to determine which view in *Gregg* was right.
- Explain the extent of the principle in *Fairchild*.
- Draw on the arguments of academics such as Reece, H. (1996) Losses of chances in the law. *Modern Law Review,* 59: 188.
- Consider whether loss of a chance needed to be actionable if the majority had been persuaded by the quantification argument within the first ground of appeal. On this point read Gore, R. (2012) Loss of chance, Lord Hope's dissent in *Gregg* v *Scott* [2005] UKHL 2, in Geach and Monaghan (eds), *Dissenting Judgments in the Law.* London: Wildy, Simmonds & Hill Publishing.

> **!** **Don't be tempted to . . .**
>
> ■ Put too much factual background surrounding the illness and misdiagnosis and get too technical in terms of medical terminology.
>
> ■ Cover all the points raised by their Lordships in *Gregg* as you will simply run out of time for your answer.
>
> ■ Dwell on the first ground of appeal, the quantification argument, as the question centres on the second ground. Therefore, in light of the point above you do not need to worry about Lord Hope so much in this question.

✒ Question 4

'The *Polemis* rule works in a very strange way. After the event a fool is wise. But it is not the hindsight of a fool; it is the foresight of the reasonable man which alone can determine responsibility.' (*Per* Viscount Simonds in *Overseas Tankship (UK) Ltd* v *Morts Dock & Engineering Co. Ltd (The Wagon Mound (No. 1))* [1961] AC 388 at 424)

In light of this statement evaluate the judicial approach to the issue of remoteness of damage.

Answer plan

→ Outline the requirements and operation of the test in *Re Polemis*.

→ Discuss what problems arose through the test's use.

→ Highlight the approach adopted in the *Wagon Mound (No. 1)*.

→ Evaluate the requirement for change and whether it has solved the highlighted problems.

→ Have there been adverse consequences because of the change?

Diagram plan

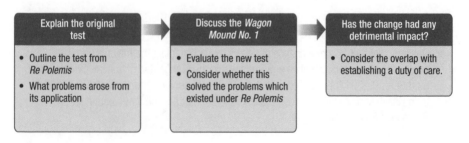

Explain the original test	Discuss the *Wagon Mound No. 1*	Has the change had any detrimental impact?
• Outline the test from *Re Polemis* • What problems arose from its application	• Evaluate the new test • Consider whether this solved the problems which existed under *Re Polemis*	• Consider the overlap with establishing a duty of care.

A printable version of this diagram plan is available from **www.pearsoned.co.uk/lawexpressqa**

Answer

For any claim to be successful in tort, the injury suffered must not be too remote from the act of the defendant. Therefore, the issue is how the courts should best go about determining whether negligent acts will be deemed to be the legal cause of injury. This has implications for claimants as, even if the defendant factually caused the injury, they may still not receive compensation. The current approach will be evaluated to explain why it is better than the original approach from ***Re Polemis*** [1921] 3 KB 560.

Remoteness is the law's attempt to limit liability on policy grounds even where the defendant has factually caused the injury.[1] This restriction is justified[2] as liability is based on the risk that the negligent creates. If the injury is outside of this risk, it is unfair to impose liability. The issue, therefore, is how the law determines whether the injury was within the scope of risk for which liability should result.

Originally, following ***Re Polemis***, remoteness was determined by looking at whether the injury was a direct consequence of the negligent act regardless of its foreseeability. In the case, a ship was destroyed when, through the negligence of the stevedores, a rope from a sling led to a wooden plank dropping into the ship's hold which in turn caused a spark because the hold contained benzine vapour.[3] The court acknowledged that this outcome was not a foreseeable consequence of the negligent act. However, it held that provided the outcome was a direct cause of the negligence, it was irrelevant whether the defendant could anticipate that outcome. Foreseeability of the consequences went towards negligence not compensation. What would amount to 'direct' was not explained, and questions could be asked about how someone is meant to guard against such an outcome if they do not know what they may be liable for. However, the decision itself can be said to be fair; a negligent act was performed which caused damage. As such, liability should ensue as that damage was caused by the negligence, thereby sanctioning negligent behaviour and awarding compensation for loss suffered, which are two functions of tort.[4] The decision could also be justified owing to the circumstances of the time. As Davies (1982) notes, the case was tried during a slump in the shipping industry[5] and so the decision would have been a further blow to a struggling shipping industry if liability was not found. While not stated as a reason within the case, Davies

---

[1] Before you can discuss whether the approach to remoteness is appropriate, you need to explain what this aspect of negligence is about and what it attempts to do.

[2] By then discussing whether the actual purpose of remoteness is justified, you have more scope to argue that perhaps the law should be different; would a change in approach allow the law to be more justifiable, or strengthen its overall purpose?

[3] You need the key facts in order to highlight how the test operates, and then you can decide whether the approach is fair or not by using these as an illustration.

[4] Give your own view on whether the test has merit. Your purpose here is to help set up the debate later in your answer as to whether a change was needed.

[5] The point of highlighting this is so you can give some context to the decision and then also argue whether, even if the principle behind the case is flawed, there is still some justification to the decision. You are looking to provide an explanation for the case.

argues it must surely have played a part; owing to the importance of shipping at the time this seems a fair assessment.

Although no criticism regarding excessive liability was made following the decision, negative comment did emerge after **Donoghue v Stevenson** [1932] AC 562 established a general principle for imposing a duty of care in novel situations. Academic criticisms over excessive liability were also combined with judicial comments, subsequent to **Donoghue**, which were at odds with **Re Polemis** and which never wholeheartedly endorsed the principle.

[6] By including reference to this you could explore how binding this decision should be.

This culminated in the Privy Council[6] decision of the **Wagon Mound (No. 1)**. Viscount Simonds felt that the **Polemis** approach overcomplicated matters with a prime example being a defence based around intervening acts. Furthermore, he felt that the basis of **Re Polemis**, whereby the issue of foreseeability related to liability rather than whether compensation was payable, was false. He noted that liability is founded upon the consequences of the act, not the act itself. Therefore a new approach was adopted whereby the question to ask is simply: was the injury of a type which was reasonably foreseeable to occur from the negligence? His Lordship felt that it was unjust to impose liability simply because an injury is a natural consequence, especially if completely unforeseeable.[7] Although he noted the opposite was true, where injury is reasonably foreseeable, even if an indirect consequence of the act, liability is fair and just. To hold otherwise would be at odds with principles of civil liability that a man is only liable for the probable causes of his acts, while still leaving minimum standards to be observed by society.

[7] As you are stating that the law was changed, you need to explain what his reasoning was. This then allows you to evaluate whether the reasoning, and by extension the change, was justifiable.

Interestingly, he did not feel that many cases would be decided any differently, and that in fact where damage was a direct or natural consequence of the act they would be reasonably foreseeable. However, by insisting on reasonable foreseeability as the limitation of liability, it meant that liability was kept within the bounds of common conscience. It is significant that the problems with **Re Polemis** began to emerge following the change to imposing duties in **Donoghue**; indeed Viscount Simonds states that to base remoteness on **Re Polemis** would be a departure from the sovereign principle of **Donoghue**. This ignores that **Re Polemis** was pre-**Donoghue** and decided at a time when the duty concept was narrowly applied to particular relationships. A wider test of remoteness only became an issue when the application of the duty concept was widened in **Donoghue**.

However, this development means it is more logical to treat compensation the same as culpability with both based on foreseeability. The injury suffered must be within the scope of any duty owed, otherwise the act cannot be said to be negligent. If duty is restricted on this basis, it is indeed unjust to still award compensation for injury which, while a cause of the act, was not something which the defendant could have foreseen and so taken steps to prevent.

[8] Even if you feel that the change was justified, you ought to explore what the consequences have been. Just because something has merit in theory you still need to look at how it works in practice.

However, the equating of remoteness with reasonable foreseeability has created an overlap with the imposition of the duty of care.[8] This was seemingly accepted by Viscount Simonds, as he states that culpability dependent on reasonable foreseeability is determined by reference to the foreseeability of what actually happened. This raises the question as to why this separate element of the tort is needed.[9] Arguably, for remoteness to have any independent purpose, notwithstanding the opinion of Viscount Simonds, hindsight must play a part.[10] If the aim of remoteness is to determine whether the injury was one that was within the risk to which a duty was owed, then hindsight must be used to establish what risks were created by the act of the defendant. Otherwise, the test advanced by His Lordship does not work.

[9] The point here is to question whether the purpose of the element which you identified earlier is being carried out following this change.

[10] This ties your answer back to address the suggestion of Viscount Simonds in the quote.

In conclusion, while it was in fact **Donoghue** that caused the problems for **Re Polemis** and not the test itself, the argument has merit: it is clear that with the approach to duty of care firmly established, a test based on foreseeability makes more sense. While this approach does raise questions as to the overall need for such a test, it creates an extra precaution against liability, helping to ensure that liability and the resultant compensation only occurs where justified.

✓ **Make your answer stand out**

- Read the article by Davies, M. (1982) The road from Morocco: *Polemis* through *Donoghue* to no-fault. *Modern Law Review,* 45(5): 535–55 to gain more depth to your argument around *Re Polemis.*

- In particular, expand on the background context to *Re Polemis* and whether, in fact, it could be argued that *Donoghue* was the problem.

- Make sure you use part of your answer to address the point in the quote that hindsight has no place in the test of remoteness.

- Ensure that you consider whether the direct consequence test has merit, as this enhances the overall evaluative nature of your answer.

! Don't be tempted to . . .

- Get too tied down with the facts of either *Re Polemis* or the *Wagon Mound (No.1)*. The key points can be used to illustrate the application of the particular test but you will lose time if you go into too much depth.
- Start a more in-depth account of duty of care and what was said in *Donoghue* and why it was said.

🔖 Question 5

'[There] is a need in the law of tort for a principle which permits judges to deny recovery to a [claimant] on the ground that to do so would undermine the integrity of the justice system.' (*Per* McLachlin J in *Hall* v *Hebert* (1993) 101 *DLR* (4th) 129, 179)

In light of this statement, critically discuss the occasions when negligence denies recovery to a claimant by allowing a defendant a defence to the claim and the extent to which this is justified.

Diagram plan

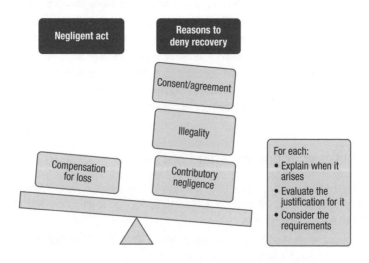

A printable version of this diagram plan is available from **www.pearsoned.co.uk/lawexpressqa**

Answer plan

→ Consider each defence in turn and explain the circumstances in which each operates.

→ Assess whether there is justification for denying recovery by the claimant based on the principles of each defence.

→ Evaluate the requirements of each as you do so.

Answer

As negligence liability is determined by fault, once that is proven, qualifying a person's liability may be difficult to justify. An evaluation of the different defences demonstrates that policy factors provide the justification for their application. However, it is argued that applying contributory negligence more broadly at the expense of the others would produce the fairest outcome in view of the overall principles underlying liability in negligence.

[1] Academically, it is worth acknowledging the debate and assessing the merits of each view, but demonstrate that you are aware of the practical implications of the defence more by highlighting that, in practice, it makes no difference to the individual relying on it. Look to question whether the exceptions undermine the defence or are justified in their own right as this stops your answer just becoming a description of the defence's operation.

[2] As you have set out previously that the defence is a justified means of denying a claimant recovery overall, you need to offer some explanation as to why it is right that it does not apply against all categories of claimant.

The main reason for denying compensation is that, notwithstanding the defendant's fault, the claimant consented to the injury or the risk of it. If one voluntarily invites the risk, they cannot complain if it materialises. Therefore, such a defence makes good sense and is just (**Smith v Baker & Sons** [1891] AC 325). What is unclear is whether the defence operates by removing the existence of the duty or negating liability for the breach. However, in any event, the overall outcome is the same with the courts determining the final issue on the facts of the case before them.[1]

To justify denying recovery, there must be informed consent as to the nature of the risk of negligent injury (**Nettleship v Weston** [1971] 2QB 691). It must be shown that the claimant had full knowledge of the extent of the risk that they faced, and that they agreed to that risk. In the absence of an express agreement, it can be implied through a deliberate course of conduct (**Smith**). Secondly, the legal consequences of the risk must be assumed voluntarily (**Nettleship**). Therefore, the defence generally has no applicability in cases involving employees and rescuers, on the basis they act out of compulsion, not their own volition. This is justifiable on policy grounds, as otherwise employers would never be responsible for the safety of their workplaces and rescuers may be deterred from acting.[2] Perhaps more controversially, the defence does not apply to suicides. While seemingly a clear, voluntary act of risking death, applying the defence hollows the specific duty owed by the defendant (**Reeves v Metropolitan Police Commissioner** [2000] 1 AC 360). This might seem strange in light of the defence denying the existence of a duty and, as Weir (2006) notes, it is at odds with the concept of personal autonomy. Yet, the non-application of the defence is justified, as the duty is to prevent that very outcome from occurring and the negligence allowed it to in fact occur.

The defence is further limited by statutes.[3] First, section 149 of the Road Traffic Act 1988 provides that a passenger does not consent to the risk of injury by entering a vehicle. As the driver must have insurance for this scenario, it is fair to leave the burden of liability there.[4] The Unfair Contract Terms Act 1977 (UCTA) also limits the defence's application for liability arising out of things done, or to be done, in the course of a business, and on business premises. Liability for negligently caused death or personal injury can never be excluded or limited (s. 2(1)); however, other injuries can be if the relevant clause is reasonable (s. 2(2)). Further, under section 2(3), agreement or awareness of a term purporting to exclude or limit liability for negligence is not to be taken as voluntarily assuming the risk. Policy underlies this; the consent cannot be said to be voluntary as it is extracted from the person who needs to enter the contract and as such lacks equality of bargaining power to negotiate the term.

Illegality by the claimant is another reason for denying them recovery. While there is seemingly an obvious public policy justification to the defence, the claimant was injured engaging in criminal activity,[5] the rationale has not, however, always been clearly and consistently explained, and applied. This led the Law Commission to seek parliamentary clarification for many years. However, following **Grey v Thames Trains Ltd** [2009] UKHL 33 they now believe the law has been clearly explained.[6] The defence has two forms with each having a differing policy basis. The narrow form is where the claimant seeks to avoid a penalty imposed on him by the criminal law due to his illegal act; such as compensation for lost earnings, damage to reputation and general damages for imprisonment. The wider form is where the claimant seeks to recover compensation for the consequences of his criminal act; such as compensation to cover their liability for unlawfully killing someone. This latter form was explained by Lord Hoffmann

[3] The logical place for you to discuss these is after the main discussion on consent, as they restrict the situations when that defence could be said to operate.

[4] Make sure you offer some form of explanation as to why the defence is limited by the statute when at a first glance it appears it should apply. The same applies to UCTA.

[5] While your answer will go on to explore how the defence operates and on what basis, make sure you explain why it is needed. This is particularly important with this defence, which has been criticised historically for its lack of coherence.

[6] The purpose here is not to provide the whole history of the defence, but to show that you are aware of its development and the concerns over it which have fuelled that. Keeping this brief allows you to focus on what the law is now, and whether it is justified now, while benefiting from knowing its past.

as being justified on the ground that compensating the claimant for the consequences of his criminal behaviour would offend public notions of the fair distribution of resources. Alternatively, the narrower form is based on the idea that it would simply be inconsistent to compensate someone for the losses incurred by their going to prison for their criminal behaviour. In the wider sense, the issue becomes one of causation and the question is: was the damage caused by the criminal act; or while the criminal act provided the opportunity for the damage to occur, the tortious act was the immediate cause? This focus on whether the criminal act was incidental to the accident helps retains the legitimacy of the defence while providing a better rationale for cases such as *Revill* v *Newbery* [1996] QB 567 where a burglar received compensation for having been shot.[7]

The final way of denying recovery is through the principles of contributory negligence. Following the Law Reform (Contributory Negligence) Act 1945, this is now a partial defence.[8] Damages are reduced to reflect the amount that the claimant contributed to their injury through their negligence; three factors must be proven (*Fookes* v *Slaytor* [1978] 1 WLR 1293). First, the injury must result from the claimant exposing himself to a particular risk. Secondly, his negligence contributed to his injury; and finally that there was fault on the claimant's part. A reduction will be made regardless of the difficulty ascertaining the exact scope of the contribution (*Capps* v *Miller* [1989] 1 WLR 839). In *Vellino* v *Chief Constable of Greater Manchester* [2001] EWCA Civ 1249, Sedley LJ dissenting, considered that applying this defence is a far more appropriate tool for ensuring justice than applying a full defence to deny liability completely.[9] While perhaps no longer needed in light of the changes to the illegality defence in *Grey*, this view has force as if the defendant is not liable for the full extent of the injury, it is justifiable to limit damages to the extent to which they are, but the fault of the defendant is still recognised by still requiring compensation.

In conclusion, even though the injury may be the defendant's fault, it is right that defences are applied to deny the claimant compensation. However, relying more on contributory negligence at the expense of the full defences would better strike the required balance between recognising the defendant's fault while also taking account of the claimant's own role in events.

[7] This is a good example to use as it is a case which was hard to explain previously as the claim seemed to be founded on the illegal act which used to be the stated basis for denying recovery.

[8] This shows that you are aware of the change brought about by the Act more succinctly than giving a fuller account of the background to the defence. You can then get on more quickly to how the defence operates.

[9] Include this as an option for the purposes of assessing whether the justice system could be better served in this way rather than having the current different defences. If you agree with the proposition it will allow you to bring your answer together nicely and flow into your conclusion. If you don't agree, mention this at the beginning of this section before explaining why it is not a better approach.

Make your answer stand out

■ Explore in more depth whether contributory negligence is a more justified approach to the issue of denying recovery than the other defences. In particular, explore the dissent of Sedley LJ in more detail.

■ Compare the approach and use of defences in this country to other jurisdictions to lend depth to your evaluation.

■ Draw on academic writing to substantiate the points that you are making.

! Don't be tempted to . . .

■ Just describe each defence; offer some evaluation of why each is needed if liability is based upon the defendant's fault and whether it is justified.

■ Discuss the requirements for establishing liability in negligence, it is not needed and will use up time better spent evaluating the merits of the defences.

www.pearsoned.co.uk/lawexpressqa

 Go online to access more revision support including additional essay and problem questions with diagram plans, You be the marker questions, and download all diagrams from the book.

Negligence: Combined issue questions

5

How this topic may come up in exams

In the previous chapters we looked at how the aspects of negligence may arise individually as essay questions. Here we combine all of these aspects for problem scenarios. In such a question all aspects of the tort will need to be addressed and skill is needed in identifying the weight which should be given to each aspect. As this is a way of testing your knowledge and understanding of the entire tort they are very common but, provided you work through the tort logically, they should not be feared. Don't forget questions may be focused on the restricted duty situations; some examples are also included here.

■ Before you begin

It's a good idea to consider the following key themes before tackling a problem question that combines various aspects of negligence.

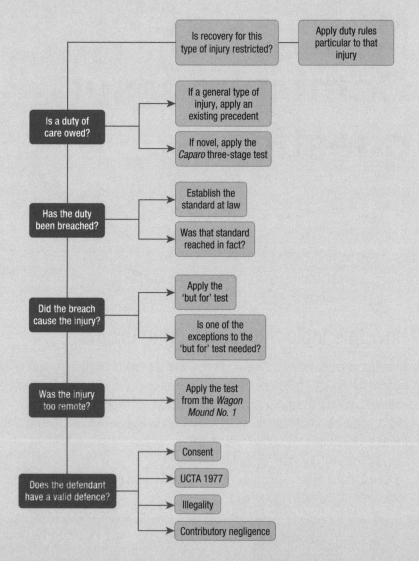

A printable version of this diagram plan is available from **www.pearsoned.co.uk/lawexpressqa**

❓ Question 1

Mick had recently purchased a new sports car and, feeling excited, took it out to see how fast he could get it to go. Having got the car up to 90 mph, he saw something in the road and slammed on the brakes. Unfortunately, he lost control and hit the central reservation.

An ambulance arrived and rushed him to Keefstone Hospital where his condition was stabilised. However, following the operation, a nurse from the hospital failed to rehydrate Mick sufficiently, which left him weaker than he would have been.

Subsequently, because of a pre-existing condition which Mick had, a complication developed which required further major surgery. Owing to his increased weakened state, Mick suffered a heart attack. The evidence shows that the heart attack could have been naturally caused because of the trauma of the second surgery but this is inconclusive; in any event, his weakened state would have heightened the risk of this occurring.

Advise Mick as to whether he has a claim in negligence for his injuries.

Answer plan

→ Confirm the existence of a duty of care owed by the hospital.

→ Explain whether, and if so how, it has been breached.

→ Evaluate the difficulty Mick may face with regard to causation and the non-applicability of the 'but for' test.

→ Discuss whether regardless of the lack of firm evidence Mick could still prove causation.

→ Consider whether the heart attack is too remote from the breach.

→ Discuss whether there is a possible defence because of Mick's own negligence in speeding initially.

Diagram plan

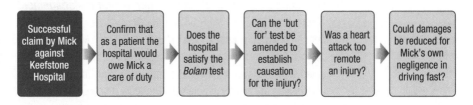

A printable version of this diagram plan is available from **www.pearsoned.co.uk/lawexpressqa**

Answer

In advising Mick on his action for negligence, the rules relating to causation will need particular focus as, on the traditional rules, it seems as if the hospital's act is not the factual cause of his injury.[1] However, it will be argued that Mick's case may warrant a relaxation of these rules and he is likely to be successful in his claim.

[2] The *Caparo* test only applies to novel situations and, therefore, you should not mention it when you have a scenario which is covered by precedent, as it suggests you do not fully understand its operation. While there are more long-standing authorities for the point, factually the situation is the same as *Bailey* so you can justifiably use *Bailey,* which is then easier when you refer to it again.

The first aspect of negligence which needs to be satisfied is that the hospital must have owed Mick a duty of care. As this is not a novel situation, precedent must be relied on to determine the matter, which clearly shows in this situation a duty is owed: for example, ***Bailey* v *Ministry of Defence*** [2008] EWCA Civ 883 which is factually similar to Mick's case.[2] Therefore, the hospital can be said to have owed Mick a duty of care in relation to his operation and the subsequent treatment which would follow.[3]

[3] Make sure that you explain what the duty of care in the instant case is and the extent of that duty, because this will be relevant in terms of determining breach and whether the damage is too remote.

Once a duty is imposed, it then needs to have been breached. This occurs when the defendant's conduct falls below a reasonable standard. Here it will need to be shown that the standard of the operation and aftercare was unreasonable owing to a failure to sufficiently rehydrate Mick following the operation.[4] Mick should be advised that there are two legal questions to ask: what is the required standard and, on the facts, does the conduct fall short of the standard? In terms of the first question, the legal standard is normally to take such care as is reasonable in the circumstances (***Paris* v *Stepney BC*** [1951] AC 367) and determined objectively. However, when the issue is one of professional negligence, as is the case here in dealing with a surgical operation, the standard is altered to take account of the professional status of the defendant (***Bolam* v *Friern Hospital Management Committee*** [1957] 1 WLR 582), regardless of their level of experience (***Wilsher* v *Essex AHA*** [1988] AC 1074).[5] Mick should be advised that the standard required becomes whether the defendant acted with the level of skill and competency expected of someone undertaking the activity in question. Therefore, the question is simply whether a reasonable nurse would have provided the level of rehydration which was given to Mick. While we are not told whether others would have provided the same level of rehydration, owing to the risks brought by the level provided and following a major operation, it is unlikely to be the standard of a reasonable nurse.

[4] So that you can fully explore whether there has been a breach, you need to highlight, out of the facts, what the potential act is which breached the duty.

[5] Even though the question does not mention the extent of the nurse's experience, show that you are aware of the potential issue by advising Mick briefly how this will not affect his claim.

[6] As this part of the claim is inconclusive at this stage, and you are offering advice, emphasise that this aspect is conditional on the previous requirement. This will also illustrate your understanding by showing that you are not making firm opinions when the evidence does not necessarily confirm the view.

[7] This is the main focus of this question so you should factor in most time for this part of your answer.

[8] Even if you recognise straightaway that this is not a 'but for' scenario, you should follow a logical progression through what the law requires. Therefore, set out how this normally applies first rather than jumping to the relaxed rules.

[9] As there have been two operations, identify which one is in issue here, particularly as the first operation appeared successful.

[10] Quoting the facts will strengthen the suggestion that the principle applies.

[11] By stating this, you allude to knowing the issues around the overlap between duty and damage since they are both based on foreseeability following the *Wagon Mound (No. 1)* case.

If a breach is found,[6] the next issue to advise Mick on is whether this left him so significantly weakened as to cause or materially contribute to his heart attack[7] (***Bailey***). Normally, causation is determined on the balance of probabilities by reference to the 'but for' test[8] (***Cork v Kirby Maclean*** [1952] 2 All ER 402): 'but for' the negligent rehydration would the injury have been suffered? On the facts this cannot be said to be so, as the heart attack may have been caused through non-negligent means, the trauma of the second[9] operation. However, this is a cumulative cause scenario whereby, because of evidential difficulties, the 'but for' test is not applied. Under ***Bonnington Castings Ltd v Wardlaw*** [1956] AC 613, provided there is a negligent contribution which is more than negligible, it will suffice as a causative factor. While the hospital may claim that the evidence here does not even show that the lack of hydration made any contribution to the heart attack, this may not matter. The ***Wardlaw*** principle was developed in ***McGhee v National Coal Board*** [1973] 1 WLR 1 so that causation can be satisfied where the evidence shows the negligence caused a material increase in the risk of the harm suffered. This is the situation here as we are told that the risk of the heart attack was 'heightened'[10] by Mick's increased weakened state which resulted from the rehydration failure. It was doubted, following ***Wilsher***, that this relaxation of the causation rules would apply to medical negligence cases and instead was limited to industrial cases. However, following ***Bailey*** the distinction is between distinct, independent causes as in ***Wilsher***, or cumulative causes as in ***Wardlaw***. It was held that there was no sufficient policy reason for not applying the relaxed rules for the latter scenario even where it is medical negligence. On the authority of ***Bailey***, and especially in light of the similarities, it would appear that there is sufficient factual causation.

Even if the breach was the factual cause of Mick's injury, it must also be the legal cause. This means that the injury suffered must be of a type which was reasonably foreseeable (***Wagon Mound No. 1*** [1961] AC 388) and not too remote. Arguably this is satisfied here as a heart attack is a foreseeable occurrence in such incidents and could be said to show that a duty is recognised in this situation.[11] The fact that Mick was suffering a pre-existing condition which necessitated the second operation will also not matter as an 'eggshell' skull rule applies in negligence (***Smith v Leech Brain & Co. Ltd*** [1962] 2 QB 405), meaning that the hospital must take Mick as they find him.

[12] Demonstrate that you appreciate this by stating it as you introduce it.

Therefore, it appears that Mick would have a valid claim for negligence; however, he should be advised that the hospital may seek to rely on the partial[12] defence of contributory negligence; if successful, this would mean any compensation is reduced to take account of his own negligence. They may argue that the only reason Mick was in hospital was through his own negligence: speeding, which caused the initial crash. However, while Mick may satisfy the first requirement of **Fookes v Slaytor** [1979] 1 All ER 137 that the injury resulted from a risk which Mick exposed himself to, his negligence needs to contribute to the injury suffered. The evidence does show that the heart attack was contributed to by his non-negligently caused weakened state following his operation and this could be traced back to him crashing his car. Therefore, this could be a contributing factor to his injury; however, Mick should be advised that as the injury occurred following the negligence and the second operation, not the operation following the crash, a contributory finding may be unlikely. Finally, the hospital must show negligence on Mick's part which, as noted, is easily satisfied as he was speeding.

[13] Remember to use consistent wording: earlier it was couched in less than absolute terms so do not make it concrete now.

To conclude, Mick was owed a duty of care by the hospital which seems[13] to have been breached; this is likely to be deemed to have caused the injury under the principle from **McGhee**. As this injury is not legally too remote, Mick is likely to succeed in his claim; however, this would be subject to a possible reduction for his own negligence in crashing his car initially.

 Make your answer stand out

- Explain how, even though the negligence was the act of an individual nurse, the hospital will be vicariously liable (*Cassidy* v *Ministry of Health* [1951] 2 KB 762).
- Discuss the issue of the skill and experience of the nurse.
- Consider the potential counter to the *Bolam* principle which the hospital could make under *Bolitho* v *City & Hackney Health Authority* [1997] 3 WLR 1151.
- Evaluate the policy factors flowing from the decision in *Bailey* and its potential impact on the health service.

> **!** **Don't be tempted to . . .**
>
> - Just list the different factors.
> - Demonstrate that you know about the *Caparo* three-stage test and mention the aspects. You will show that you understand it better by not referring to it.
> - Mention *Donoghue* v *Stevenson* [1932] AC 562 as it has no relevance to the question.
> - Cover all of the factors considered by the courts in relation to breach.
> - Discuss in length the facts of *Bailey* to show how it is similar. Your examiner will know the facts and know that the question is similar, but by all means offer a brief outline.

? Question 2

Alf and Bert are a pair of low-level criminals who specialise in home break-ins and car jackings. One day the pair had planned to steal a car by staging an accident. Alf pretended to collapse in the road as Eddie was approaching, and made out that he was having a heart attack. Panicking, Eddie slammed on the brakes, stopped and rushed out to help. As he did, Bert rushed out from behind a parked car and bundled Eddie over. Alf and Bert then jumped into the car. As Alf had recently learned to drive they had agreed that he would be the getaway driver. However, just as this was happening P.C. Wedgewood drove around the corner on patrol. Seeing as Eddie appeared OK, he gave chase after Alf and Bert.

Realising that the pair were being followed by the police Bert starting yelling at Alf, 'Drive faster and lose the copper you idiot!' Alf sped up, but the pair started to bicker as to the best way of escaping and so neither was looking at where they were going. As such Alf did not see that he was coming up to a pedestrian crossing and sped through one without stopping. Reg was crossing the road at that point and dived out of the way. However, he landed awkwardly on his shoulder and elbow and due to an unknown condition suffered multiple fractures and permanent loss of mobility. A person without the condition would just have suffered bruising.

Eventually Alf took a corner at too much speed and lost control of the car. The car slid off the road and crashed into a lamppost on the near-side pavement. The lamppost made impact with the front passenger door causing severe injuries to Bert.

Advise Alf as to his liability for the injuries suffered by Reg and Bert.

Diagram plan

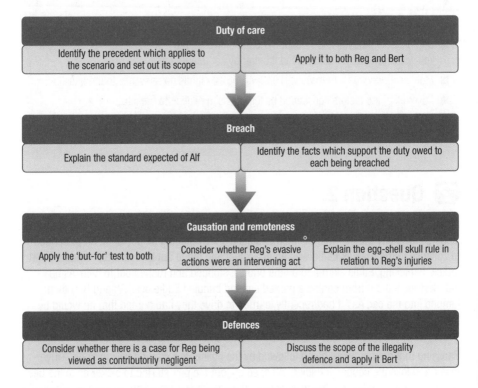

A printable version of this diagram plan is available from **www.pearsoned.co.uk/lawexpressqa**

Answer plan

→ Confirm that Alf, as the driver, owes a duty of care to other road users as well as his passengers.

→ Establish that even though he is an inexperienced driver he is judged to the same standard as a normal driver and so there were breaches of his duty to both Reg and Bert.

→ Apply the 'but-for' test in order to identify the causes of each injury and consider whether Reg's actions were an intervening act.

→ Consider the principle of remoteness and draw on the eggshell skull rule to explain how Reg's injuries will still be considered legally caused by Alf.

→ Evaluate what defences could be relied on by Alf.

Answer

The issue involves advising Alf on his potential liability in negligence (as the driver) for the personal injuries suffered by Reg and Bert following each incident. This will involve looking at the standard of care required by drivers and the impact on liability of the fact the injury occurred involving a stolen car.[1] It will be argued that Alf has clearly breached the duty of care owed to Reg and Bert, and that this has caused each one injury. However, while he may have a defence against Bert due to the illegality of incident he will still be liable to Reg as the injury will not be deemed too remote.

As the car's driver, Alf owes a duty of care to all other road users who may be reasonably foreseeably injured if care is not exercised (*Langley v Dray* [1998] PIQR P314).[2] This duty covers both passengers and pedestrians and so the first element of negligence is satisfied.

The key question, however, is what standard is expected of Alf in order to discharge his duty, especially considering he has only recently passed his test and so has less experience than most drivers.[3] Under *Blyth v Birmingham Water Works Co.* (1856) 11 Ex 781 the expected standard is determined objectively by assessing what the reasonable man would do in the situation; and the reasonable man possesses the standard of foresight which eliminates the idiosyncrasies of the person whose conduct is in question. This means Alf's inexperience is irrelevant and he will be judged by the same standard expected of someone with more experience (*Nettleship v Weston* [1971] 2 QB 691). This may seem unjust on inexperienced drivers; however, it necessary in order to overcome the difficulties of determining an individual standard for each and every driver.[4] Therefore, as held in *Langley*, Alf is expected is to drive with such care and skill so as to avoid exposing other road users to unnecessary risk of injury. By speeding, not looking where he is going, driving through a red light and generally not paying attention; it is clear that Alf has not met the standard of a reasonable driver.[5] As such, Alf has breached the duty owed to both Reg and Bert.

The next consideration is whether each breach of duty was the cause of each injury. Causation is a question of fact whereby it is asked whether, on the balance of probabilities, the injuries would have happened 'but for' Alf's breach (*Cork v Kirby Maclean* [1952] 2 All ER 402).

[1] When faced with a question which just says 'Advise X', it is worth spelling out in your first line that you have correctly identified the exact thing that you should be advising the person on.

[2] As there is a precedent regarding the duty in this situation, there is no need to talk about *Caparo*.

[3] While perhaps not the key question for liability in the question, it would be the key question for Alf personally, as for someone unfamiliar with the law; a natural response would be to highlight their lesser experience than the average motorist. This is why it warrants a bit more treatment than you might otherwise be inclined to give.

[4] As this standard is detrimental to Alf's chances of defeating the claim, you should advise him why this is the situation and, in doing so, you will show that you have more than a superficial knowledge of the law.

[5] It is useful here to briefly remind the marker that you know what the scope of the duty owed is; you then need to draw on the facts to illustrate how it was breached. You can save time and not compromise your structure by dealing with duty and breach in relation to both Reg and Bert at the same time.

[6] Take them in this order as Bert is a more clear-cut situation whereas there is a bit more to say on Reg.

This seems satisfied as if Alf was not speeding and was paying attention he would not have lost control of the car and hit the lamppost thus injuring Bert. In relation to Reg, Alf could argue that his injuries were caused by Reg jumping out of the way.[6] However, as jumping out of the way of an oncoming car is reasonably foreseeable, Alf should have sought to prevent Reg needing to do it, and clearly Reg would not have needed to if Alf was driving to a reasonable standard. As such, Reg's actions will not be considered an intervening act.

[7] Normally, because this is only a partial defence, it should be dealt with last; however, as there is no question of the full defences applying it makes sense to deal with it first as it follows on from the previous paragraph and allows you to finish with Reg. There will be more success against Bert so you can then clearly focus on that in detail.

[8] We do not have much detail in the facts to support this discussion so take care to read what you have been given and draw on what you can to construct as good an argument as you can.

[9] Obviously, there are other actions which Alf may face to which the following may not apply so it is worth clarifying the scope of the application of the defences.

[10] As the section will bar the application of the defence, there is no more that needs to be said other than this. Do not go on and explain what the defence involves, let alone apply the requirements to the scenario, as it will be a pointless exercise.

The breach also needs to be the legal cause of the injuries meaning that the injuries were of a kind, type or class that were reasonably foreseeable (*Wagon Mound (No. 1)* [1961] AC 388). Again there is no issue with this in relation to Bert's injuries; these were clearly foreseeable due to how Alf was driving. However, Reg's injuries were worse than would be expected due to an unknown condition. This means Alf needs to be advised of the 'eggshell skull' rule. This provides that the defendant must take the claimant as they find them and they will be liable for the entire harm caused, even where it is greater than expected owing to a particular condition of the claimant. This might seem at odds with the principle from *The Wagon Mound (No. 1)*, but it has been held to still apply (*Smith v Leech Brain & Co. Ltd* [1962] 2 QB 405). As the injury was a type which was still foreseeable, the fact that Reg's condition meant the injury was far more severe will not limit liability.

In relation to Reg's claim, the only possible defence that Alf could rely on would be the partial defence of contributory negligence.[7] This reduces the amount of damages payable where just and equitable to reflect the level of negligent contribution to the injury made by the claimant (Law Reform (Contributory Negligence) Act 1945, s. 1). For Reg to be negligent using the pedestrian crossing he would need to have been forbidden to cross at that time due to, for example, pedestrians having a red light. However, the facts suggest that Alf should have stopped and if that was the case, on top of his speeding, it would seem unlikely that Reg was negligent here.[8]

Alf should have more chance avoiding liability in negligence[9] against Bert. Under section 149 of the Road Traffic Act 1988, Alf will not be able to claim that Bert voluntarily assumed the risk of such injury by getting in a car which was being used as a getaway vehicle.[10] However, where Alf may have success is in relying on the full defence of illegality which absolves Alf of all liability. The wider form of the defence, as identified by ***Gray* v *Thames Trains Ltd*** [2009] UKHL 33, applies where the compensation is sought as a consequence of the claimant's own illegal act. The question is whether the criminal act caused the injury; or simply provided the opportunity for it occur with the tortious act being the immediate cause. This seems more of a case of the former and this is supported by ***Ashton* v *Turner*** [1981] QB 137 which also concerned an injury suffered by the passenger in a getaway vehicle. As Lord Hoffmann noted in ***Gray***,[11] allowing recovery in such circumstances would offend public notions of the fair distribution of resources. Even though Alf lost control and was at fault for the injury it would be permissible to deny recovery by Bert. If a court were to hold that the claim was not substantially based on the crime, Alf should be advised that he may be successful in pleading contributory negligence on the part of Bert.[12] In terms of what reduction would be made, Alf should be advised that under the Act damages cannot be reduced by 100 per cent even if it was Bert's idea to take the car and drive in that way (***Pitts* v *Hunt*** [1991] 1 QB 24).

In conclusion,[13] Alf should be advised that he owed both Reg and Bert a duty of care which was clearly breached. As those breaches caused the injuries, he would be liable notwithstanding that the extent of Reg's injuries were worse than could have been foreseen. However, owing to the illegality of the situation, Alf will have a defence against Bert.

[11] Try always to be specific as to who said what you are about to advance from the case as it shows greater knowledge.

[12] Even if you think that the illegality defence would certainly apply, you should still discuss this, as there is a possibility the other defence would not be applied. Further, by doing so you show that you know not only about this issue, but also how it relates to the other defences.

[13] While you will always have a conclusion, in negligence problem questions, as there are several issues, sum up events by recapping what you have discussed throughout.

✓ Make your answer stand out

- Read *Langley* v *Dray* [1998] PIQR P314 and draw on the judgment of Stuart-Smith LJ to support your discussion of the nature of the duty owed by motorists and the reasons for it.
- Consider the validity of the 'eggshell skull' rule.
- Explain the policy factors which justify defences to an action for negligence when liability has been made out.
- Mention how Alf could also face a claim from Eddie for trespass.

! Don't be tempted to . . .

- Show your wider knowledge of the tort by raising aspects which are not applicable to the scenario. For example, there is no need in relation to causation to discuss anything more than the 'but for' test.
- Repeat things you have already discussed by taking each claim independently of each other from the outset and, therefore, having two paragraphs on duty and breach.
- Explain in detail why there is illegality at the heart of the issue.

? Question 3

Paddy Chandler was a long-term alcoholic and was recently told that, owing to his lifestyle, he only had about a 45 per cent chance of living more than three years. After an unexpected bet came off, he decided to check himself in to the Ladbroke Hills private medical centre for a liver transplant in order to prolong his life expectancy. Prior to the operation he had spoken to Dr Done who talked him through the procedure that would be used. Reflecting the seriousness of the situation, a new and innovative procedure was to be used which, while not having wide-scale endorsement, has been supported by a leading expert in the field in a national medical journal.

However, because he believed that Paddy really ought to have the operation, Dr Done chose not to inform Paddy that the operation carried with it a 5 per cent risk that the new liver may not be accepted by his body, which could result in death.

Following the operation, it became apparent that the new liver had not been accepted and Paddy was informed that with some medication the condition could be managed, but he would only have a 20 per cent chance of living longer than three years. Paddy has indicated that, if he had been informed, he might not have gone ahead with the operation.

Advise Paddy as to whether he has a successful negligence action against the medical centre.

Diagram plan

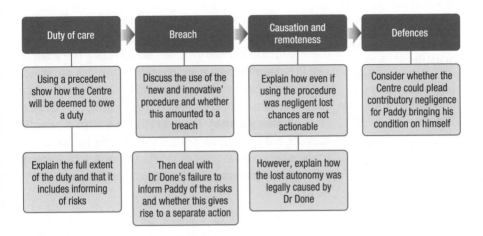

Duty of care	Breach	Causation and remoteness	Defences
Using a precedent show how the Centre will be deemed to owe a duty	Discuss the use of the 'new and innovative' procedure and whether this amounted to a breach	Explain how even if using the procedure was negligent lost chances are not actionable	Consider whether the Centre could plead contributory negligence for Paddy bringing his condition on himself
Explain the full extent of the duty and that it includes informing of risks	Then deal with Dr Done's failure to inform Paddy of the risks and whether this gives rise to a separate action	However, explain how the lost autonomy was legally caused by Dr Done	

A printable version of this diagram plan is available from **www.pearsoned.co.uk/lawexpressqa**

Answer plan

→ Explain quickly how a duty of care is owed by the Centre in this situation and set out the full scope of the duty.

→ Identify the two potential breaches and deal with each, assessing whether they were breached.

→ Explain how, even if the duty with regard to the operation procedure was breached, it is non-actionable.

→ Apply the causation rules to the personal autonomy breach and explain how the approach is taken by the courts.

→ Address any appropriate defences that the Centre may have.

Answer

In advising Paddy as to whether he has a claim against the Centre in negligence, the full extent of the duty owed by the Centre will be established and then the two possible ways any action may take will be considered. It will be argued that while it would appear that he has not suffered any actionable injury, merely a lost chance of living more than three years, the presence of the issue of personal autonomy in

[1] It is important to highlight early that you have spotted that this is not simply a loss of chance problem scenario and that in fact it is arguably more to do with *Chester* v *Afshar* [2004] UKHL 41. To avoid your answer getting messy, clearly separate out the two issues and then explain to the reader this is what you are doing so they know and thus do not lose track of what you are saying by trying to work out why you are saying it.

[2] By inserting this word, and after citing *Cassidy,* you show that you are aware of the applicability of the doctrine of vicarious liability to this situation, without getting sidetracked by a fuller explanation of it.

[3] Even if you strongly conclude that the use of the procedure was non-negligent, it is worth adding an additional paragraph on this point – to show that you have recognised that there is a similarity here to *Gregg,* but that you understand the legal position and, therefore, that an action by Paddy on this basis would not work.

the matter means that he should have some basis for succeeding in any action.[1]

The first point to establish is that authorities such as **Cassidy v Ministry of Health** [1951] 2 KB 343 clearly show that through the doctor–patient relationship the Centre will vicariously[2] owe a duty of care to Paddy when treating and operating on him. It is also important to advise Paddy that there is an additional aspect to the duty which is to warn Paddy of the risks involved even though they were small (**Chester v Afshar**). This gives effect to a person's personal autonomy and forms the basis of their consent to the treatment. This has been recognised as being an important principle since **Sidaway v Board of Governors of the Bethlehem Royal Hospital** [1985] AC 871.

The next issue, therefore, is whether the duty owed to Paddy was breached by the Centre. In taking the duty covering the actual performance of the operation, the standard must be that of the level of skill and competency expected of a person undertaking that activity and with the level of skill that the defendant professes to have (**Bolam v Friern Hospital Management Committee** [1957] 1 WLR 582). While Paddy may argue that the new procedure is not widely endorsed, this is not necessary. Provided the Centre can show that Dr Done acted in accordance with a respectable body of medical opinion, which can withstand logical scrutiny (**Bolitho v City and Hackney Health Authority** [1997] 3 WLR 1151), this standard will be deemed to have been reached. The fact that a leading expert has supported the procedure in a national journal would suggest that the procedure was in line with a respectable body of opinion.

Paddy would have a problem though in that, even if it is accepted the use of this new procedure was negligent, he has suffered no actionable injury. Prior to the operation, he only had a 45 per cent chance of living over three years. After the operation he had a 20 per cent chance. Therefore, this makes his position near identical to that in **Gregg v Scott** [2005] 2 AC 176 where the House of Lords held that the claimant in fact lost nothing as, on the balance of probabilities, the outcome in question would not have happened, there was no chance to lose. Further, it was held that a reduction in the chance itself should not be an actionable head of injury.[3]

However, as explained, the scope of the Centre's duty was wider than merely carrying out the operation in a non-negligent manner. It extended to warning Paddy of all the risks which the operation entailed. While Lord Templeman in **Sidaway** accepted that a doctor may, in light of their training and experience, determine what needs to be said to a patient, he also stated that enough information must be given so as to enable the patient to make an informed decision whether to consent to the operation. Therefore, in light of the importance attached to an individual's personal autonomy, it appears that this aspect of the duty was clearly breached, as no information regarding the risk was provided.

[4] By highlighting this you further distance this part of your answer from the previous discussion, as it shows that passing the *Bolam* test has no bearing on this aspect of Paddy's situation.

[5] Professor Honoré was cited by both Lord Steyn and Lord Hope in the majority in *Chester* in support of their opinions; therefore, a small reference such as this allows you to demonstrate your knowledge of their opinions and the wider academic thinking on this issue.

[6] In the latter part of this sentence, use the facts from the question to identify Paddy with the reasoning of Lord Hope, to make your application stronger as well as, again, showing an in-depth knowledge of the judicial reasoning which impacts on this point.

[7] Refer to *Chester* to reinforce your argument that legally the breach should be seen as the cause of an actionable injury, i.e. the lost autonomy.

Paddy should then be advised that the breach of the duty to inform must then be deemed to have caused the injury suffered. This is where any action becomes complicated. As stated previously, his injury simply amounts to a reduction in his chance of survival, which is non-actionable. Even proceeding on the basis that the lost ability to make an informed choice was the injury has some difficulties. This is because on conventional principles it must be shown that, on the balance of probabilities, 'but for' the negligence, the injury would not have occurred. The issue here is that Paddy may well have proceeded and, therefore, the risk for which the duty was to inform Paddy about would still have materialised, and thus this breach was not the factual cause of the injury. Even if he would not have proceeded, the risk here was not created by the breach but was present regardless and notwithstanding how the operation was performed.[4] However, as Lord Steyn accepted in **Chester** after referring to the academic work of Professor Honoré,[5] situations which Paddy finds himself in cannot be fitted within normal causation principles, but policy and corrective justice support vindicating his personal autonomy. Otherwise, the duty owed would be stripped of its content and would, in Lord Hope's view in **Chester**, be particularly useless for a patient like Paddy who cannot say what they would have done if they had been properly advised.[6]

Therefore, while it could be argued that factually the injury was not caused by the breach of the duty to warn, as Lord Hope highlighted, the injury was caused in the legal sense. It is on this basis that there would not appear to be any issues regarding remoteness of damage, namely that the injury was a kind, type or class that was reasonably foreseeable (**Wagon Mound (No. 1)** [1961] AC 388). The injury suffered was the failure of the new liver to be accepted by Paddy's body, the risk of which, as in **Chester**,[7] was exactly what he should have been informed of by Dr Done.

[8] Your aim here is to just briefly raise the possibility, reflecting your awareness of the similar facts between Paddy's situation and that in *St. George*. This also shows that you understand the point by applying it in dismissal of the potential argument by the Centre.

Finally, Paddy should be advised that there does not appear to be any defences which the Centre could rely on to counter any claim. The only possible argument[8] would be that his alcoholism put him in a position whereby he needed treatment and therefore, this behaviour makes him contributorily negligent. However, following ***St George v Home Office*** [2008] EWCA Civ 1068, as this was a lifestyle choice made prior to the creation of the duty of care, it cannot be considered for the purposes of reducing any compensation.

[9] Make sure that you reinforce that the success of any action brought by Paddy would be solely for this injury.

In conclusion, while there may be causation issues in Paddy's situation, there has been a clear breach of the Centre's duty to inform Paddy of the operation's risk. This denial of personal autonomy should, on the basis of cases such as ***Chester*** and ***Sidaway***,[9] mean that Paddy would have an action for this loss.

✓ Make your answer stand out

- Explain in a bit more detail the issue of vicarious liability.
- Make sure that you clearly distinguish the two potential breaches by the Centre of their duty of care to Paddy.
- Make more reference to academic opinion on the issue of causation and informing patients of risks. A selection of academic articles can be found in the opinion of Lord Steyn in *Chester*.
- Draw on the dissenting opinion of Lord Hoffman in *Chester* to give balance to your argument. He expands on this in Hoffman, L. (2005) Causation. *Law Quarterly Review*, 121: 592–603, which is also worth reading in relation to wider issues of causation.
- Add some of the reasons why loss of chance as in *Gregg* is held to be non-actionable.

! Don't be tempted to . . .

- Get into too much of an in-depth discussion on whether a lost chance should be an actionable claim. As the law stands it is not; show that you are aware of the differing views in cases such as *Gregg* but remember that this is a problem question on the whole of negligence and not an essay on that specific issue.
- Explain the history of the development of the duty of care.
- Gloss over aspects of negligence which are not in issue, all must be referred to.

❓ Question 4

Owing to a recent flurry of burglaries in the area, a group of local residents decided to form a neighbourhood watch team. The purpose of the team was to set up a patrol around the area to act as a deterrent by approaching people who looked up to no good and to contact the police at the first hint of any criminal activity.

One of the members, Brandon, had that day gone away for the night and, having realised he had left a downstairs window open, sent a text to Mac, a friend but non-member, asking him to close it for him. However, Mac was busy getting ready to go out and thought there would be nothing to worry about as the neighbourhood watch patrol would go past Brandon's house regularly and it was only one night.

That evening, it was Keith's turn to do the patrol. Keith had already worked a long day at the factory where he was employed and so was tired. As he approached Brandon's house he saw someone climbing through the window but just wanting to get home to watch TV he did nothing, thinking it was just someone who had locked themselves out.

The next day, Brandon returned home to see his house had been burgled with all of his belongings taken. The burglar has never been caught.

Brandon now seeks your advice as to whether he could bring a claim against Mac or Keith as he holds them responsible for what happened.

Diagram plan

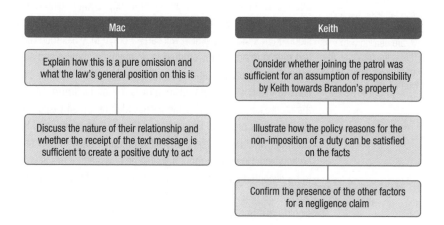

A printable version of this diagram plan is available from **www.pearsoned.co.uk/lawexpressqa**

Answer plan

→ Set out the general position regarding omissions and deal with Mac's potential liability first.

→ Consider if there is an assumption of responsibility by Mac towards Brandon which warrants imposing a positive duty to act.

→ If so, assess whether the duty was breached and confirm the other elements of negligence.

→ Assess the potential liability of Keith on the same basis.

Answer

The issue to determine is whether Brandon has a claim in negligence even though Mac and Keith have not performed any positive acts. This is important, as usually the law only permits this in limited situations and thus, if they do not fit those, Brandon will be left without redress for his loss. It will be argued that Mac does not owe a duty but Keith may well be held liable.

[1] The point here is to show that you are aware of the distinction between the two, and using the facts to confirm what we are dealing with here. This is important as the law does impose duties in the latter type of situation.

As indicated, the general position in negligence is that a duty of care will not be imposed in relation to omissions (***Smith v Littlewoods Organisation*** [1987] 1 AC 241). It is clear that in relation to Mac that this is a case of a pure omission as opposed to being a failure to act as part of a wider positive course of conduct, such as not stopping at a red light, which will carry a duty.[1] Mac has received the text message but clearly omitted to do anything about it and so this is the former category and within the general rule. However, exceptions to this position were outlined by Lord Goff in ***Smith***. Of these, the most likely to be applicable is that Mac assumed responsibility for Brandon's property. Brandon could argue that by asking Mac to close the window and highlighting the present danger a duty should be imposed. However, Brandon should be advised that this is unlikely to be accepted as there was no confirmation by Mac that he would do so. Had Mac done so, then a duty would be present, as Brandon would have had trust and confidence in Mac's words, which would justify a finding of an assumption of responsibility. In the absence of a reply confirming he would act, the political reason given by Lord Hoffmann in ***Stovin v Wise*** [1996] AC 923 for not imposing a duty for omissions is not addressed. The reason is that it is a greater

[2] At this point you are explaining why Brandon is unlikely to succeed in making a claim against someone. As the point of the question is to advise him on the law, you have to make sure you state the reasons why he would not have a claim. If you imagine him in front of you, he would be asking why not, so tell him.

[3] Whereas before you were highlighting how the reasons were not satisfied, now you need to use the facts to show how they have been overcome, as this is what will justify the courts imposing a duty on Keith.

[4] The presence of an assumption of responsibility will generally warrant imposing a duty of care; however, the same facts would also generally satisfy the *Caparo* test. A negative finding of an assumption of responsibility does not preclude reference being made to *Caparo* and so it is worth you highlighting it here to reinforce why you feel Keith is likely to owe a duty in this situation.

[5] The duty of care is only one part of negligence and, while this is the focus of the question, it is important that you cover all the aspects, although naturally these will not need as much depth.

invasion of a person's freedom to compel them to act than it is to require them to take care of others when they have chosen to embark on a course of conduct.[2] This can only be justified when there is an element of proximity between the parties which their friendship alone is unlikely to create.

Brandon should be advised, however, that he may be more successful in a claim against Keith. While, again, this is a case of a pure omission, the reason for the greater likelihood of success is that Keith is a member of the neighbourhood watch patrol and was meant to be keeping an eye out for burglars that night. By accepting this role, Keith assumed responsibility towards those residents who are covered by the patrol, which includes Brandon. As such, the political reason stated above is overcome; he has volunteered to act and failed to do so.[3] The moral reason advanced by Lord Hoffmann for not imposing a duty is also satisfied. This is based on the idea that there could be an indeterminate class of potential defendants in an omission situation, raising the question of why it is justifiable to pick out the actual defendant for liability. However, here, as Keith was performing the patrol that night, it is morally right to pick him out for liability over others.

Those factors which suggest an assumption of liability also suggest that the tripartite *Caparo* test[4] for imposing a duty is satisfied here. It is clearly foreseeable that, if Keith omitted to approach the person climbing through the window, at the time of widespread burglaries, harm could be caused to the property in question. While it was stated in *Smith* that mere foreseeability is not sufficient to create a duty to prevent criminal acts by a third party, the facts indicate that the key requirement of proximity exists between Brandon, as a resident under the patrol's remit, and Keith who was undertaking the patrol. These factors combined, by addressing the policy concerns for imposing a duty, mean that it would be fair, just and reasonable to impose a duty on Keith.

As it seems likely that Keith will owe duty of care, Brandon now needs advising as to whether the rest of the elements for a claim in negligence are satisfied.[5] By not doing anything when he saw the person climbing through the window, it would seem apparent that Keith failed to reach the standard of care expected of a reasonable man: the likelihood of harm was increased and thus Keith should have approached the person, or at least contacted the police, as that was part of the patrol's remit.

'But for' this breach, Brandon's loss of property would also not have occurred. If he had approached the person and/or called the police, the incident would have been prevented or the person apprehended and, therefore, the causal link required is established. While usually the deliberate wrongdoing of a third party will be deemed an independent cause of the loss (***Weld-Blundell* v *Stephens*** [1920] AC 956) exceptionally, where for example the duty in question is to prevent that third party from doing the wrong, as here, it shall not be classed as an intervening act (***Dorset Yacht Club* v *Home Office*** [1970] AC 1004). The scope of the duty also means there is not any issue of remoteness. Here the loss suffered by Brandon is stolen property and so it is of a type that was reasonably foreseeable as required by the ***Wagon Mound (No. 1)*** [1967] 1 AC 617.

[6] By this stage of your answer, if you have time, you could name the defences but it is not necessary. As they are clearly not applicable to Keith, there certainly is no need to discuss them in detail. Therefore, by treating them like this, you show that you understand the full extent of them, which is more important than showing that you simply know them.

However, Brandon should be advised that, if successful, any compensation received may well be reduced on the grounds of contributory negligence. This is because he was aware of the danger of being burgled by leaving his window open, as shown by his text to Mac. However, it is unlikely that any of the full defences[6] to a negligence claim can be relied on by Keith.

In conclusion, Brandon should be advised that he is unlikely to succeed with any claim against Mac, as this is a situation of a pure omission which the law does not generally impose duties for. Owing to the lack of proximity between the two, the policy reasons for the law's approach are not surmounted. However, Keith's position in the patrol is likely to have created an assumption of responsibility which justifies a duty being imposed on him. As the other negligence factors are present, this means that a claim against Keith should succeed.

✓ **Make your answer stand out**

- Expand on the why the law is reluctant to impose duties of care for pure omissions.
- Read Markesinis, B. S. (1989) Negligence, nuisance and affirmative duties of action. *Law Quarterly Review*, 105: 104 and refer to this in support of your arguments.
- Explain in more depth, drawing on the cited case, the issue of intervening acts and why they will not break the chain of causation.
- Discuss more fully the partial defence of contributory negligence and apply the elements of it in more detail to the facts.

! **Don't be tempted to . . .**

- List every exception to the rule; just highlight the ones which are most applicable. Otherwise you risk indicating that you do not fully understand them.
- Focus entirely on the duty issue because of the prominence of the omission issue in the question. To obtain the highest marks you will need to address the question in full which, here, is to advise Brandon on a claim in negligence as a whole.

Question 5

Morris had been unemployed for several months and has recently passed his driving test in order to aid his chances of finding a job. Subsequently, he obtained an interview which he had to drive to. The mixture of driving and the prospect of the interview made Morris feel quite nervous. On his way there he suffered a large anxiety attack during which he overran a red light and struck Siobhan at high speed as she was crossing the road using a pedestrian crossing. Siobhan was rushed to St Leonard's Hospital where her condition was stabilised after being diagnosed with internal bleeding, a collapsed lung and multiple bone fractures. Part of her post-op care was undertaken by a junior nurse, Rebus, who was working his first shift and forgot to check the records to establish whether Siobhan was allergic to anything before administering any medication. As a result Siobhan was given medication which she was highly allergic to and she consequently suffered a massive heart attack and ended up paralysed.

Advise Morris and the hospital as to their respective liability, if any, for these injuries.

Answer plan

→ Discuss how Morris owes Siobhan a duty of care.

→ Consider the impact of the anxiety attack and whether this was breached.

→ Highlight how, if Morris's duty was breached, there would be no causation issues for the initial injuries.

→ Evaluate whether the actions of Nurse Rebus constitute a *novus actus interveniens* and give rise to a separate action against the hospital.

→ Explain how any compensation will be quantified.

Diagram plan

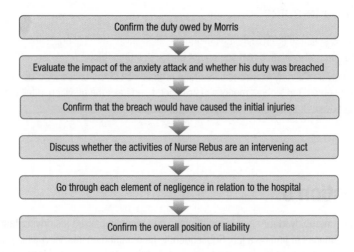

A printable version of this diagram plan is available from **www.pearsoned.co.uk/lawexpressqa**

Answer

The issue regarding Siobhan's situation concerns the interrelationship between Morris's acts and the hospital's and the concept of new intervening acts. This is important to determine as it will impact on the level of liability which may be imposed on both parties. It will be argued that, as the action of Nurse Rebus was an independent event, it will break the chain of causation with regard to Morris's liability.

[1] Remember; as with previous answers, where a precedent exists, there is no need to talk about *Caparo*.

Firstly, as a motorist, Morris owes a duty of care to pedestrians such as Siobhan (***Bassett v Victoria Wine Co.*** (1958) WL 18557).[1] The question is whether this duty to Siobhan was breached. The standard of care to be exercised is that of the reasonable competent driver regardless of their level of experience and, therefore, it is irrelevant that Morris was newly qualified (***Nettleship v Weston*** [1971] 2 QB 691). The fact that Morris hit Siobhan 'at high speed'[2] after going through a red light suggests a clear breach. However, Morris's situation is complicated by his anxiety attack before the accident, as this could be classed as a disabling event affecting his level of care and skill. Reference should, therefore, be made to ***Mansfield v Weetabix Ltd*** [1998] 1 WLR 1263, where a driver suffered a medical condition which impaired his driving ability and led to a crash,[3] which is arguably[4] what happened here. The court held that there was no reason in principle why a person should not be deemed negligent where the disabling event was gradual, as opposed to a sudden event, provided they were unaware of the condition. Therefore, if Morris's attack was a sudden condition which came out of the blue and which he was unaware that he might suffer, he would not have breached his duty. However, this is likely to rest on the speed of the attack and its duration with regard to the impact with Siobhan. At the onset of the attack, it is likely Morris would have realised that something was happening and so should have pulled over. Obviously, if he was speeding prior to the attack and before he went through the lights, he would be in breach notwithstanding how sudden it was.

[2] Make sure that you highlight that you are using the facts of the question to substantiate your point.

[3] State enough of the facts, to highlight the connection with Morris's situation, but do not go into a full-blown account.

[4] Strictly speaking, from the facts we do not know for certain that this was definitely the case and so you should not write this sentence as if it was.

[5] As you have identified two scenarios, split them up into separate paragraphs in order to maintain the clarity of your answer.

Morris should be advised that he may be deemed to have been negligent if the anxiety attack happened gradually.[5] Ultimately, to determine this issue, more information would be required. If Morris knew he suffered from such attacks, particularly as we are told he was feeling nervous while driving, and he felt one coming on yet continued to drive, then on the basis of ***Mansfield*** he would be negligent. If on the other hand, the attack slowly built up, gradually impairing his driving and he had no reason to suspect he suffered such attacks then, again on the basis of ***Mansfield***, it is unlikely he will be held negligent. Although, again as with a sudden attack, this may well rest on the issue of duration as even if Morris had never suffered an attack, once it gradually started he should have appreciated some danger and pulled over. Morris should be advised that, depending on the full facts, it is quite likely he will be held in breach of his duty.[6]

[6] When you have given a range of potential options remember to give some indication as to which is the likeliest from the known facts. Remember the essence of the question is to advise someone as to what is likely to happen.

[7] As there is an element of doubt as to whether there was a breach, reflect this in your choice of words.

If Morris is held in breach of his duty,[7] he should be advised that it is clear that the breach caused the initial injuries suffered by Siobhan. Applying the standard 'but for' test from **Cork v Kirby Mclean** then, on the balance of probabilities, 'but for' Morris's negligent driving, he would not have hit her and caused those injuries. These injuries are also of a type which was reasonably foreseeable (**Wagon Mound (No. 1)** [1961] AC 388) thus not too remote. Further, as we are told Morris went through a red light at a pedestrian crossing which Siobhan was crossing, he would seem to have no valid defence.

[8] By calling it 'alleged', you maintain consistency with your previous discussion.

[9] This is obviously the language to be used when discussing breach. You need to use it here because it is only a highly negligent breach of duty by the hospital which will break the chain of Morris's liability.

[10] You could use the Latin phrase if you know it but this will suffice.

[11] This should be an obvious and on the facts unarguable point, but remember to address it for completeness. Part of your advice should be to advise against whom any claim will be made.

The issue, however, is the extent of Morris's liability and whether he will be liable for the subsequent injuries. In negligence the defendant is liable for the damage caused by his breach. While it could be said Siobhan was only in the hospital because of Morris's alleged[8] negligence, an act by a third party can be said to break the chain of causation. For the court to find this, the third party act must not be a natural and probable consequence of Morris's own act (**Knightly v Johns** [1982] 1 All ER 851) or a foreseeable act (**Lamb v Camden LBC** [1981] QB 625). In applying this we are told that the heart attack was caused by an allergic reaction to medication administered by Nurse Rebus and, therefore, from the injuries sustained in the collision. Medical negligence could be said to be a foreseeable occurrence but does not automatically break the chain of causation. It can do so, though, where the treatment was so grossly negligent so as to be an irresponsible treatment to the injury initially caused (**Webb v Portsmouth Hospitals NHS Trust** [2002] PIQR P8). Failing to check a patient's allergies before administering treatment is far below the standard of care to be expected by a medical professional[9] because of the obvious danger of a reaction, as in Siobhan's case. Morris should, therefore, be advised to argue that Nurse Rebus's actions were a new intervening act[10] and thus he is not liable for these subsequent injuries.

[12] Normally, you would establish the duty first but in this instance it makes sense to show the negligence on the part of the hospital, as this is crucial to there being an intervening act for the purposes of Morris's liability.

Naturally, a hospital vicariously[11] owes a duty of care to all patients for the acts of its staff (**Cassidy v Ministry of Health** [1951] 2 KB 343) and, as discussed above,[12] this seems to have been breached. The facts also indicate that this breach caused the allergic reaction to occur and thus there appear to be no issues surrounding causation or remoteness. Therefore, the hospital, which has no defence, would be liable in negligence for Siobhan's paralysis.

To conclude, Morris should be advised that he faces being held liable for damages reflecting the initial injuries suffered by Siobhan. The chain of causation regarding Siobhan's condition was broken by the intervention of Nurse Rebus and so the hospital should be advised that they would be liable for the subsequent injuries. As these acts and the resulting injuries are more independent than concurrent, the Civil Liability (Contribution) Act 1978 will not apply (***Rahman* v *Arearose Ltd*** [2001] QB 351) and each party will be liable for the amount of compensation quantified to reflect the harm that they individually caused. However, Morris should be advised that the quantification of his amount of compensation will not be curtailed by the subsequent tort if it would have resulted in any future, ongoing losses by Siobhan (***Baker* v *Willoughby*** [1970] AC 467).

✓ Make your answer stand out

- Support your discussion of whether Morris breached his duty to Siobhan with reference to academic articles such as McDonald, B. (2005) Blameless? *Public Interest Law Journal,* 35: 15–17.

- Indicate how the junior status of Nurse Rebus and his inexperience is irrelevant on the basis of *Wilsher* v *Essex Area Health Authority* [1988] AC 1074.

- Explain more why on the basis of *Rahman* the Civil Liability (Contribution) Act 1978 will not apply.

- Discuss in more detail the issue of quantification of damages and mention the criticisms of the approach in *Baker* by the House of Lords in *Jobling* v *Associated Dairies* [1982] AC 794.

! Don't be tempted to . . .

- Get into a full discussion of cases such as *Bolam* and *Bolitho,* despite this question involving medical negligence. By this stage of your answer, your time is likely to be nearly up and so you should concentrate on completing the answer, which you risk not doing by going into those cases. The breach is quite evident here and so such a discussion is not really necessary.

- Explain at length how a duty is owed in both cases; simply state one is owed on the facts, and provide an authority to support the point.

❓ Question 6

One afternoon, Henry, a delivery driver for Agnew Petroleum plc was driving his petrol tanker in rush hour traffic. Henry was tired and just wanting to get to his last stop and get home. Ignoring the extreme weather conditions and a recommendation that high-sided vehicles not use the motorway, Henry took the motorway as it was only one junction, driving over the speed limit to get off the motorway quicker. However, a gust of wind blew the tanker over resulting in a multi-car pile-up, and the petrol caused a massive fire.

Geoffrey was watching the news at home. His nephew Monty, who Geoffrey has raised from a young boy, uses that road to drive home. Geoffrey thought he saw a car similar to Monty's on the screen. After not hearing from Monty, Geoffrey rushed to the hospital to see if Monty was there. Two hours after seeing the incident on TV, Geoffrey is informed that Monty has been killed and is asked to identify the body. Owing to the number of patients, Monty's body has not been cleaned up. Upon seeing Monty, Geoffrey suffers a nervous breakdown. Agnew Petroleum Plc has admitted liability to anyone that they owed a duty to.

Sachin is a staff nurse at the hospital where the victims of the crash were brought. Although having a history of work-related stress, he has never been offered any counselling services since his return to work. On the day of the crash, having complained of already being on duty for 20 hours due to a previous emergency, Sachin was told he had to stay on shift and help with the accident victims. However, after working several more hours in such difficult conditions, Sachin collapsed and has been signed off work since with a stress-related mental illness.

Advise Geoffrey and Sachin whether they could make a claim in these circumstances.

Diagram plan

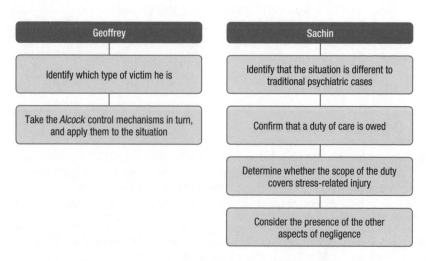

Answer plan

➡ Geoffrey – establish that he is a secondary victim for the purposes of negligently inflicted psychiatric injury, and then work through each control mechanism in turn and apply it to the facts of the question.

➡ Sachin – identify that this is a different situation, being a stress-related illness, and work through the legal principles set out in *Hatton* v *Sutherland* [2002] EWCA Civ 276 which apply for this type of injury.

Answer

The issue to advise Geoffrey and Sachin about is whether they have satisfied the criteria that the law requires in order to bring a claim for negligently inflicted psychiatric harm. They should be advised that this is a policy-influenced area, and control mechanisms are usually imposed to limit when a duty of care will be owed by the defendant, especially in Geoffrey's situation. It will be argued that, whilst being a secondary victim and facing evidential difficulty in his claim, Geoffrey may still succeed on the facts. Sachin is also likely to be successful in his claim on the basis of the facts provided.

[1] In order to show the full range of your knowledge, you need to highlight the two types of victim and then establish which one Geoffrey will be. However, it is important to remember to highlight the significance of having each type of victim status, as this will demonstrate a greater level of knowledge and add structural sense as to why you have explained both.

In regards to Geoffrey's claim, he should be advised that he will need to show that he was owed a duty of care. Following **White v Chief Constable of South Yorkshire Police** [1999] 2 AC 455, in order to be owed a duty as a primary victim of the alleged negligence, which has less restrictive requirements to satisfy,[1] he must have been placed in physical danger through the defendant's negligent act or at least have had grounds to reasonably fear for his physical safety. As Geoffrey was not involved in the crash himself, this is not satisfied, therefore Geoffrey should be advised on the restrictive law for secondary victims governed by **Alcock v Chief Constable of South Yorkshire** [1992] 1 AC 310. Geoffrey must first have suffered a medically recognised injury which occurred despite his being of 'customary phlegm' (**Bourhill v Young** [1943] AC 92). A nervous breakdown would satisfy this requirement although we do not know if he is of reasonable fortitude.[2] However, on the basis that he is, Geoffrey requires advice as to the **Alcock** control mechanisms.

[2] Although 'customary phlegm' has been used before, phrasing it in this way for the second time will help demonstrate your understanding of what is meant.

First, the claimant needs a close tie of love and affection with an immediate victim of the incident, which is Monty here. This is required, as the claimant's injury must be reasonably foreseeable to

[3] It is vital that you do not just assume that simply because Geoffrey is not within the categories identified by the court as having a close tie of love and affection, he has no chance of claiming as that is not what the court actually determined in *Alcock*. You need to draw on the facts to support why he still may be able to satisfy the requirement.

[4] Because we cannot conclusively establish whether the necessary closeness is present, you will need to phrase your next sentence in this way to explain why you are proceeding to the next control mechanism when the claim may well have already failed.

[5] A brief account of the facts is required to lay the basis for arguing that Geoffrey's case is more like *McLoughlin* than *Alcock*.

[6] It is vital to use the facts within the question to support the argument being advanced.

[7] Although there is the option of discussing the *Alcock* mechanisms in any order, it is advisable here (as opposed to, say, after the point of medically recognised injury), to deal with this one following the proximity in time and space, as the question suggests that the injury was caused by the shock of seeing the unclean body in the hospital and, therefore, it follows better from discussing how he needs to be at the scene or immediate aftermath.

the person who caused the primary incident to warrant liability. The aim is to prevent an excess of claims and liability which is disproportionate to the conduct concerned. Geoffrey should be advised that such closeness is presumed between spouses and parent/child, but under *Alcock* other types of family relationships will not automatically be regarded as being sufficiently close. Therefore, Geoffrey will have to show evidence that he was sufficiently close to Monty, which may be difficult. However, Lord Ackner acknowledged that such closeness will be determined on a case-by-case basis and, therefore, the fact that Geoffrey is only Monty's uncle may not prevent Geoffrey successfully claiming.[3] That Geoffrey has raised Monty since he was young suggests the absence of Monty's parents, and that Geoffrey has more of a parental relationship with Monty.

On the basis that Geoffrey satisfies the court of his closeness to Monty,[4] the next issue is whether he has sufficient proximity in time and space to the incident. This means that Geoffrey must have personally been at the incident. This may be an issue here as initially Geoffrey only sees the crash on TV, which is not sufficient (*Alcock*). However, Geoffrey should be advised that coming across the immediate aftermath of the incident with one's own senses is sufficient (*McLoughlin v O'Brien* [1983] 1 AC 410). Although in *Alcock* the claimant who identified his brother-in-law at the mortuary some eight hours after the incident was held not to have witnessed the immediate aftermath, Geoffrey should be advised that his situation is more analogous to the actual case of *McLoughlin*. In that case the mother was told at home of a crash involving her family, two hours after it had happened. Upon arriving at hospital, she was informed that one of her children was dead, which, together with seeing the extent of the injuries to the rest of her family, caused her to suffer psychiatric illness.[5] Therefore, as Geoffrey saw Monty in the state that he would have been in at the roadside as in *McLoughlin*, and this was only two hours after the actual incident,[6] Geoffrey should have the necessary immediacy to overcome this mechanism.

The final requirement of *Alcock* is in relation to the means with which his breakdown was caused.[7] Psychiatric injury must be caused by perceiving the incident or the immediate aftermath through one's own senses, rather than merely being informed by a bystander. Although Geoffrey learned of Monty's death from another party, we are not told

[8] Again, you need to draw on the facts to support your argument here as without the point about 'upon seeing' there is not a lot to substantiate the satisfaction of this requirement.

exactly when the breakdown occurs. It appears to have occurred from the sudden shock of seeing Monty dead, as we are told he suffered the breakdown 'upon seeing' the body.[8] Therefore, on the basis that he can satisfy the court that he had a sufficiently close tie of love and affection with Monty, Geoffrey should be able to make a successful claim.

Sachin's situation is different, as are the legal principles governing it. Sachin should first be advised that psychiatric injury resulting from workplace stress is actionable, and is simply part of the employer's normal common law duty of care to their employees (*Walker v Northumberland County Council* [1995] 1 All ER 737). As an employee, Sachin is owed this duty. Even if the stress results from the strain of simply doing the job Sachin is employed to do, provided that the stress was foreseeable, there are no special control mechanisms and the injury is within the scope of the duty.[9]

[9] Take some time at the start of this section of your answer to set out the background of claims for stress and demonstrate that you appreciate that it is a different regime from the traditional claims for psychiatric injury.

The case of *Hatton v Sutherland* [2002] EWCA Civ 76 provides the governing principles for this situation. First, as noted above, the stress-related injury must be foreseeable. Importantly for Sachin, the injury need not be foreseeable in a person of ordinary fortitude, but foreseeable within him. This reflects that the duty is owed to the individual employee, and therefore, the employer should know about any particular vulnerability (*Paris v Stepney BC* [1951] AC 367). As Sachin has a demanding job, both intellectually and emotionally the hospital should already be more alert to the signs of stress (*Hatton*).[10] Here, Sachin has also been complaining and has already had a period of leave owing to stress. Therefore, there are lots of signs pointing to this outcome, and in light of Sachin's history this appears even more a foreseeable injury. As nothing seems to have been done to support Sachin since returning from the first injury, and on the basis that the injury was the result of stress at work, the issues of breach and causation appear satisfied. There can be no suggestion of contributory negligence from Sachin carrying on his work (*Young v Post Office* [2002] IRLR 660).[11]

[10] Raise this point from *Hatton* in order to lay a solid foundation as to why this injury was foreseeable. The facts of Sachin's personal situation will build on this and provide a strong case overall.

[11] Include these points just to round off your discussion as the question does not simply limit you to whether a duty is owed, but whether the claim can actually be made.

To conclude, both parties appear on the facts to have actionable claims, and a chance of succeeding in them. However, more evidence is likely to be required to fully determine that a duty of care was owed in each instance.

Make your answer stand out

- Highlight your knowledge of cases by relating the facts of the question to what actually happened in particular cases; this will then strengthen your various argument as you will have actual authority for applying the legal principles in that way.

- Demonstrate the policy rationale underpinning the law on psychiatric injury during your answer. Advise the parties not only as to what the law is but also why, as in this area of law a person, such as Geoffrey, may not be successful in a claim simply on the grounds of policy. This will also demonstrate that you have a deeper understanding of the topic.

- Demonstrate from the start that you are aware of the distinction between the two types of psychiatric injury that we are dealing with in the question and consider why the distinction exists and consequent approach to the injuries differs.

- The question does not ask for any comment as to reform of the law, and in seeking advice an individual will be more concerned with what the law currently is. However, as this area has been heavily criticised, both by academics and the judges themselves, it is beneficial to touch on the issue, at least in your conclusion as this will show that you are aware of the debate. References to academic opinion will also have the benefit of adding depth to your level of analysis and evaluation.

! Don't be tempted to . . .

- Assume that, as Monty was only Geoffrey's nephew, there could not be a close tie of love and affection.

- Go over the other aspects of negligence in relation to Geoffrey as we are told that it is only the duty of care which is questioned by Agnew Petroleum Plc.

- Provide a detailed account of all of the different categories of claimant in psychiatric injury cases; just keep to those that are directly applicable.

❓ Question 7

Henry, a financial adviser, undertakes work for Clown's Bank plc, although he also does independent work for himself. When he is doing work for Clown's Bank, he is provided with an office and administrative staff; the bank also has control over the range of financial products he may offer and provides him with a basic wage plus bonuses. However, he does have the opportunity to make extra profits from any non-investment products that he sells to the customer and he can determine the level of risk to expose the customer to.

One night in the Ducker and Diver Arms public house, somewhere Henry is known to work out of when he is working late, Henry is approached by Gideon, whom he met through his work with the bank. Gideon explains that he has inherited £1 million and requires investment advice. Henry explains that he has had six pints of strong Belgian lager and so is not really in the right frame of mind and tells Gideon to come to the bank tomorrow. As Henry leaves he shouts back: 'Royal Bank of Wales – that's a company on the up; we'll discuss them tomorrow.'

Thinking that this was Henry's investment advice, and as he has always acted on his advice and never lost out, he decides to save time and rather than see Henry went online and invested the whole sum in Royal Bank of Wales. Two weeks later the Royal Bank of Wales received an urgent government bailout and their shares became worthless, with Gideon losing his investment.

Gideon now seeks to sue Clown's Bank for his economic loss, owing to what he feels was a negligent misstatement by Henry. Advise the bank.

Diagram plan

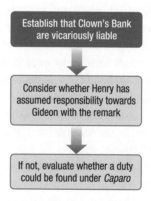

A printable version of this diagram plan is available from **www.pearsoned.co.uk/lawexpressqa**

Answer plan

➜ Determine whether Henry is an employee acting in the course of his employment for vicarious liability purposes.

➜ Evaluate whether there is an assumption of responsibility towards Gideon by Henry, by him making the statement that he did.

➜ Consider the social environment in which the statement is made.

➜ Discuss whether, in the event there is no assumption of responsibility, a duty towards Gideon may be found under the *Caparo* tripartite test.

Answer

The issue to be determined is whether Clown's Bank vicariously owed a duty of care towards Gideon in relation to his economic losses. Such a finding would be financially significant and, despite the law's reluctance to find such duties on policy grounds, there are instances where one will be found.[1] However, it is argued that, while it is possible that they have responsibility for Henry, the situation is not such as to overcome the law's policy concerns and warrant finding a duty.

Firstly, it needs to be established whether the bank are in fact responsible for Henry's acts if a duty of care is found. The bank should be advised that they will be vicariously liable if it can be shown that Henry is an employee and was acting in the course of that employment when he made the statement. Henry's employment status is blurred by the fact that he works independently of the bank as well as acting for them. Historically, whether a person was an employee was determined by reference to the level of control that he was under.[2] However, this did not fully reflect emerging employment relationships, so an economic reality test was developed. This requires looking at the overall situation for evidence of a contract of service (***Market Investigations Ltd v Minister of Social Security*** [1969] 2 QB 173). This case proposed a non-exhaustive list of factors to consider, with control just being one. Others were whether the person provided his own equipment and hired his own staff and their degree of responsibility. Applying the factors to Henry, they suggest that he is likely to be classed as an employee. While Henry has some individual responsibility, he is provided with an office and administrative staff by the bank who also dictate what he can offer clients; significantly, they pay his wages and bonuses. Therefore, overall, this suggests that there is a contract of service.

Henry, though, must have been in the course of his employment when he made the statement. However, it occurred in the evening, in a pub, after Henry had been drinking. The test to apply is the close-connection test from ***Lister v Hesley Hall*** [2002] 1 AC 215. This requires the tort to so be closely connected with the employment that it is fair and just to hold the bank vicariously liable. Henry met Gideon through his employment with the bank and the tort is allegedly[3] in making a negligent misstatement to a client regarding a financial investment which is what he is employed to give; the fact that Gideon was told to visit the bank also suggests that the advice was given in his role as an employee. All of this, together with the fact that Henry is known to work late and uses the pub for work, suggests that he could have been in the course of his employment.

On the basis that the bank could be deemed vicariously liable for Henry's statement, it is important to advise the bank now as to whether a duty of care was owed to Gideon.[4] Generally, there is reluctance to find duties for economic losses. Partly this is because, as Lord Reid observed in *Hedley Byrne* **v** *Heller* [1964] AC 465, people will often express definite opinions in informal settings, even though recognising that people may be influenced by them, but they do so without the same level of care as if it was a professional setting. As words can spread far and be relied upon by people of whom the maker has no knowledge, it can lead to indeterminate liability to an indeterminate class. Therefore the House of Lords held a duty could, in principle, exist but more was needed than for normal negligent injuries. There would need to be an assumption of responsibility by Henry towards Gideon, and then reasonable reliance by Gideon on the statement.

A duty can occur outside of contractual and fiduciary relationships (*Hedley Byrne*) as the assumption with the reliance is deemed to create a special relationship which overcomes the law's reservations. The bank should be advised, though, that Lord Reid in *Hedley Byrne* suggested that a special relationship could only arise in a business situation owing to the reasons stated above. Therefore, while the social nature of the incident may still warrant being classed as in the course of his employment, it may negate the imposition of a duty of care. The Court of Appeal has, though, found a duty in a situation of non-business advice between friends (*Chaudhry* **v** *Prabhakar* [1988] 3 All ER 718). In any event the existence of an assumption of responsibility is judged objectively (*Henderson* **v** *Merrett Syndicates* [1995] 2 AC 145), but a divergence of opinion exists as to whether it refers to the task or actual legal responsibility.[5] In *White* **v** *Jones* [1995] 2 AC 207 Lord Browne-Wilkinson felt it referred to the task. If this is the case, by making the statement Henry could be said to have assumed responsibility. However, this is questioned academically by Murphy (1996), who argues it must refer to assuming legal responsibility to the claimant. On this basis Henry arguably fails this requirement.

[6] Insert a reference to causation to show that you are also advising in the wider context of negligence as, if the bank is to be liable, which is what the question asks you to advise them on, this is a factor which would need to be satisfied.

[7] Although you have said this a lot, you want to keep driving home the facts which support the view you are expressing. As long as the context is there, this is fine.

[8] In this part of your answer it is all about the application of the facts, so you do not need to write that much here and you do not need any great reference to case law.

[9] Although the preceding paragraph may read like a conclusion and the end of your answer, you should just draw both strands of potential liability together and conclude by reiterating that both tests are likely to fail.

He has indicated that Gideon should visit him tomorrow in the bank to discuss the investment and also indicates that he has been drinking. These facts could actually also be used to counter any suggestion of even satisfying Lord Browne-Wilkinson's interpretation, as he has not technically given advice.

Gideon obviously relies on the statement, which means that if a duty was found, causation would also be satisfied;[6] however, reliance must be reasonable. The informal context – with Henry leaving a pub, indicating that he has drunk a lot of strong lager,[7] while additionally, only saying they will discuss the investment tomorrow – means it can be strongly argued, especially in light of the sums involved,[8] that Gideon's reliance was in fact wholly unreasonable.

Therefore, while it would seem that the requirements for a duty have not been satisfied, it has been held in ***Customs and Excise Commissioners v Barclays Bank plc*** [2007] 1 AC 181 that the absence of an assumption of responsibility does not prevent resort to finding a duty on the basis of the alternative threefold test. However, while foreseeability is present here and proximity is also arguably satisfied owing to their past relationship, the reasons why Gideon's reliance is not reasonable are also likely to mean that it is not fair, just and reasonable in these circumstances to find a duty towards Gideon.

In conclusion,[9] it appears that on either basis of establishing a duty for economic loss, Gideon is unlikely to be successful and, therefore, the bank will not be liable for Henry's advice.

✓ Make your answer stand out

- Advise the bank on the rationale behind vicarious liability as the doctrine may be used to support why they could end up liable.
- Explain why the law is more reluctant to recognise a duty of care in relation to purely economic losses.
- Relate your discussion of the impact of the statement being apparently made in a social context to the issue of whether Henry is in fact in the course of his employment.
- Include a fuller discussion on whether the other elements of negligence are present to round off your advice to the bank, if the bank was deemed to owe a duty.

Don't be tempted to . . .

■ Spend too long on the vicarious liability element. Show that you have spotted that there is a potential issue there and that you have an understanding of how the law works, but remember that the main thrust of the question is on economic loss. Although at the same time, make sure you do cover all aspects of it.

■ Go off on a long tangent with your discussion of what the phrase 'assumption of responsibility' should mean; remember the question is ultimately about advising the bank of their liability and requires application of the law to the facts.

❓ Question 8

Cogmire Builders Ltd contracted to renovate a sports complex for Quay Borough Council, who had bought the existing premises after the complex had closed down. Under the terms of the contract the shell of the building is to be built by Cogmire Builders Ltd, but certain specialist electrical work was carried out by Peter & Sons Ltd. All building operations were solely supervised by a firm of consulting architects, Cleveland Consultants, who were employed by Cogmire Builders Ltd at the request of the Council as they had previously overseen other Council projects and were specialists in this type of work.

On the day the new complex was due to open, a fire broke out which was caused by the negligent electrical work of Peter & Sons Ltd, and the complex remained closed for a further two months.

Several months after the complex finally opened, cracks appeared in the floor of the gym. Investigations showed that the floor was not laid properly and could not take the weight of the machines. The sports complex was closed for several weeks while the gym floor was re-laid and reinforced.

Cogmire Builders Ltd has now gone out of business; advise Quay Borough Council as to what action, if any, they may take in common law negligence.

Diagram plan

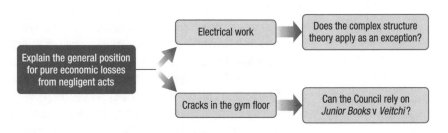

A printable version of this diagram plan is available from **www.pearsoned.co.uk/lawexpressqa**

Answer plan

→ State the law's position on economic losses arising from negligent acts of construction and advise the Council why this is the case.

→ Then take each defect separately.

→ Explain the 'complex structure theory' and whether this may provide the Council with an exception to the general position.

→ Discuss the applicability of *Junior Books* v *Veitchi* [1983] 1 AC 520 in relation to the cracked floor as an option for claiming the losses from that defect.

→ In doing so, explore the ex-post rationalisation of *Junior Books* as an application of the *Hedley Byrne* principle and assess whether this helps.

[1] As the law is quite firm in its reluctance to recognise a duty in such a situation as this, it is perhaps even more beneficial to highlight early on how you are going to go about arguing your case so the marker knows.

[2] It is important early on in your advice to the Council to explain not only what the legal position is, but also to demonstrate that you understand why their situation falls within that position. This sentence shows the marker that you have fully understood the context of the question and grasped the basic principles.

[3] By then going into the rationale for this position and explaining it to the Council, you will reinforce the impression that you fully understand the framework for this area and early on in your answer have obtained a good foundation of marks before you have really got into the question.

Answer

The issue here is whether the Council has any redress for the economic losses which they have incurred through the negligent construction of the new complex. This area of negligence is one which is tightly restricted on policy grounds, meaning there is little scope for a duty of care to be established. However, there are some limited exceptions and the Council will be advised of two which may be applicable to their case: namely, the 'complex structure theory' for the electrics and the case of **Junior Books** in relation to the gym floor.[1]

The Council should be advised that the general position is that where someone negligently performs an act, they will not be liable for any losses which result that are of a purely economic nature. However, economic losses which are consequential to property damage or physical injury can be claimed if a duty was owed and its breach caused such damage or injury. While it may seem that the fire damage and the floor cracks are property damage, they should be advised that the courts see situations such as this as simply a case of purchasing something which is of less quality and, thus, value, than what was expected. Therefore, the actual loss is the financial cost of bringing the premises up to the standard that was expected (**Murphy v Brentwood DC** [1991] 1 AC 398).[2] The rationale for this position[3] was explored in **Spartan Steel & Alloys Ltd v Martin & Co. (Contractors) Ltd** [1973] 1 QB 27 and includes the prospect of indeterminate liability for the defendant, the fact that the nature of the risk being such that precautions could be taken, e.g. insurance, and the need to avoid undermining contract law. Allowing a tortious claim for a defective product would create a transferable non-contractual warranty. It would also duplicate contract law which provides remedies where a product is not of satisfactory quality or fit for purpose.

In relation to the fire damage, if the Council directly contracted with Peter & Sons, a claim under the contract would arise. If not, the Council may still have an exception to the general position under the 'complex structure theory' which would allow a claim against the electricians. The theory suggests that the different elements of a building can be viewed as distinct items of property and thus if one part damages another part, there would be sufficient appropriate property damage on which to base a claim for economic loss. In the Council's case this would mean that the electrical work is distinguished from the rest of the complex which it damaged through its negligent installation.[4] However, the theory, first mooted in **D & F Estates v Church Commissioners for England** [1989] AC 177 as a basis for explaining **Anns v Merton LBC** [1978] AC 728, is not an adopted legal principle. The theory received a closer evaluation in **Murphy**, and notwithstanding academic criticism it received some judicial support for its application in limited circumstances. Lords Keith, Jauncey and Bridge[5] stated that the complex part in question would need to have been installed by a sub-contractor. Here, the Council should be advised that if the electricians were sub-contracted by Cogmire Builders, they would appear to have a claim. This is supported by the fact that all three gave an example of when the theory could apply – negligently fitted electrical wiring which caused a fire.

If a duty is held to exist, as we are told the electrical work by Peter & Sons was negligently fitted and this caused the fire to break out,[6] it appears that the Council would have a claim against them in negligence for the economic losses suffered. The only possible defence they may have is an exclusion clause;[7] however, in view of the danger to life, this is likely to be unreasonable under the Unfair Contract Terms Act 1977.

In relation to the gym floor, as Cogmire Builders have gone out of business any potential claim, in contract or tort, would be futile.[8] This leaves only the consultants as possible defendants. This is complicated by the absence of a contract between them and the Council: they were contracted by the builders. As above, the loss is purely economic but the Council may have recourse to the case of **Junior Books** in any claim.

[4] After explaining the outline of the theory, illustrate how it transfers to the facts to show the marker what you are thinking before you go on to discuss the merits of the theory in full.

[5] By including all three you show that, while not part of the *ratio* of the case, it did have majority support.

[6] As the facts indicate that this is a given, there is no need to go into depth as to what is required in these aspects of negligence, but for completeness you should use the facts as stated in the question to support the proposition that a negligence claim can be supported.

[7] Although there is nothing to suggest this is the case on the facts, you should consider it, as, just because one is not expressly mentioned, it could well be the case and so your advice would be incomplete without assessing the implications of one being present.

[8] This is obviously a practical point but important in the context of giving advice as to what action may be taken. Demonstrate that you have picked up on the fact and understand the implication.

In that case, a specialist sub-contractor, specifically chosen by the claimant to be employed by the main contractor, was successfully sued when their work, defective flooring, turned out to have been negligently performed. There is a slight factual similarity, therefore, between both instances. This is important as *Junior Books* has been subsequently heavily criticised and seems now confined to its own facts (*Muirhead* v *Industrial Tank Specialities* [1986] QB 507). In the case, Lord Roskill outlined several factors which created a sufficient degree of proximity between the parties. These included being nominated and specialists in the role they were contracted for. Further, the sub-contractors were solely responsible for the contracted task and knew exactly what was required. As such they knew that their skill and experience were being relied upon by the claimants. While slightly different, the Council should be advised that there is some correlation here. The consultants were specialists in overseeing this sort of work and hand-picked by the Council for their skill and experience. As such, they were solely responsible for overseeing the construction and would have appreciated this and that their expertise was being relied upon by the Council.

The Council should be warned, though, that while the case has not been overruled, it has been criticised at every opportunity by the House of Lords and, therefore, basing a claim on this authority may not be the best course. As the case has been subsequently rationalised on the basis of the *Hedley Byrne* principle of assumption of responsibility, any claim should perhaps be framed on this basis. This requires the Council demonstrating that Cleveland Consultants, in performing their service, assumed responsibility towards the Council who reasonably relied upon their service. This appears supported on the factors mentioned above in relation to *Junior Books*; however, in *Henderson* v *Merrett Syndicates* [1995] 2 AC 145 this explanation of *Junior Books* was doubted. Therefore, any claim for the losses from the cracked floor may prove futile, no matter how it is framed, for the absence of a duty.

In conclusion, owing to the nature of the losses suffered by the Council, their chances of any actions being successful are remote. However, it may be possible to successfully sue the electricians in relation to the cost of restoring the complex following the fire, but the losses from repairing the gym floor will be harder to recoup.

✓ Make your answer stand out

- Advise the Council as to their position regarding any consequential economic losses and explore further why these are more justifiably recovered.

- Include some explanation as to the merits of the rationale for restricting recovery in this area – would it really undermine contract law?

- Include some comparative analysis with other jurisdictions which have not followed *Murphy*.

- Read O'Sullivan, J. (2007) Suing in tort where no contract claim will lie: a bird's eye view. *Professional Negligence*, 23(3): 165–92 and Hedley, S. (1995) Negligence – pure economic loss – goodbye privity, hello contorts. *Cambridge Law Journal*, 54(1): 27–30 for some academic opinion on this area of law and the cases which you will refer to in your answer.

! Don't be tempted to . . .

- Stray into examining in depth the merits of recoverability for economic losses; remember the question is about whether the Council can establish a duty owed to them by either party.

- Focus heavily on the history of recovery in this area and the merits of *Anns,* as it has been overruled, and as this is a problem question you need to focus on what the law is and how it might be applied.

- Miss out reference to the other aspects of negligence. They are needed briefly for completeness.

www.pearsoned.co.uk/lawexpressqa

 Go online to access more revision support including additional essay and problem questions with diagram plans, You be the marker questions, and download all diagrams from the book.

Product liability

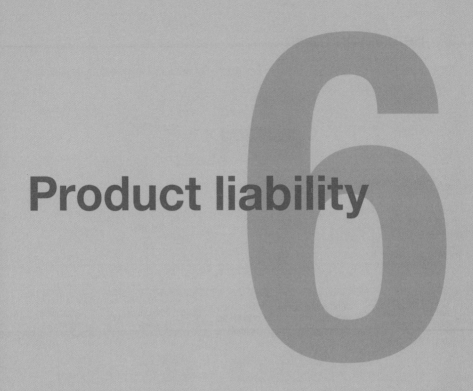

How this topic may come up in exams

This topic is centred primarily on the Consumer Protection Act 1987; however, the Act did not abolish the common law negligence action. Therefore, you also need to be aware of the narrow rule in *Donoghue* v *Stevenson* and how this applies to manufacturers of defective products. The existence of both actions means that a comparative essay is likely, alongside issues of why the Act was needed. However, the differences between the two actions mean that both will have to be discussed in problem questions in order to assess which claim may be best.

■ Before you begin

It's a good idea to consider the following key themes of product liability before tackling a question on this topic.

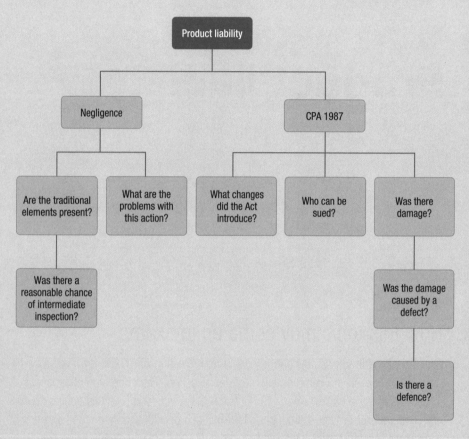

A printable version of this diagram plan is available from **www.pearsoned.co.uk/lawexpressqa**

 Question 1

'In numerical terms the problem of injuries caused by product defects is small when compared with those attributable to other risks and the difficulty of establishing a case under the law of negligence can be exaggerated.' (Rogers, 2010)

In light of this statement evaluate whether the enactment of the Consumer Protection Act 1987 was in fact needed.

Diagram plan

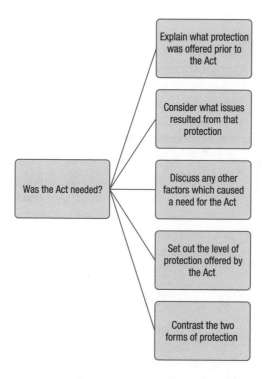

A printable version of this diagram plan is available from **www.pearsoned.co.uk/lawexpressqa**

Answer plan

→ Discuss the level of protection that was historically offered to consumers by the common law tort of negligence.

→ Evaluate the difficulties in establishing such a claim in negligence or whether they are 'exaggerated'.

→ Outline the rationale for passing the Act.

→ Explain the requirements for liability under the statutory provisions, highlighting the difference to the common law.

→ Consider if the Act is needed or whether it has just created more problems in this particular area of tort.

Answer

[1] Always give the name of an academic to support a proposition that you are advancing as this gives it strength. If you just write 'People argue' or 'Academics have suggested' it will raise the question of 'Such as who?' in the reader.

[2] Not only is this factually and legally accurate, but by mentioning it here you demonstrate that you are aware of the Act's background and place in the wider scheme of the law. You will also have shown straight away that you have recognised how this relates to the premise within the question: namely, that regardless of the merits of the protection under the Act, it was required.

[3] The question is predominantly on the need for the Act in light of similar protection being offered by the common law, especially as that claim is not so difficult to satisfy as can be said. You need to set out the basis of the negligence claim, but focus on what the problems were in bringing such a claim. This sets a platform from which you can discuss whether the Act was actually needed in practice.

The issue to assess is whether the common law tort of negligence was satisfactory in protecting consumers from defective products or whether the Consumer Protection Act 1987 was needed to alleviate difficulties which existed. Commentating in 2007, Mildred argues the Act has just created uncertainty.[1] If this is so and the level of claims are only small and easily brought, then the Act can be said to be an unnecessary burden on manufacturers. It is argued though that the Act strengthens consumer protection and was also needed as part of a wider process of EU consumer protection in light of the development of the Internal Market.[2]

Manufacturers have only owed a duty of care in negligence to the ultimate consumer of their product since **Donoghue v Stevenson** [1932] AC 562; provided the product is intended to reach the consumer in the condition it left the manufacturer, with no reasonable chance of inspection by an intermediary. Therefore, if this duty was breached by failing to take reasonable care and this breach caused damage, which was of a foreseeable nature, then the manufacturer was liable unless they had a valid defence.[3]

While significant, there are limitations to the decision.[4] First, there must not have been a reasonable possibility for the product to have been inspected between manufacture and purchase by the consumer. This means that if someone in the supply or manufacturing chain could have inspected the product and found the defect, then the manufacturer avoids liability. As consumers may not know if their product had a reasonable chance of being inspected, something of a lottery is created.

Secondly, **Donoghue** concerned product manufacture and not design defects. Often the design creates the defect rather than the absence of reasonable care when making the product. Further, where a design

⁴ Use the limitations of the negligence action to support why the Act was required, even if there are only a few claims, as these claimants still need adequate protection.

⁵ Use this opportunity to show off your deeper knowledge of tort and its underlying principles in order to support why the idea of a strict liability regime had merit. By relating its implementation to tort principles, you strengthen the argument that it is justifiable.

⁶ Although you are now talking about the Act, make sure you show that you know how the two actions relate to each other, seeing as both still exist.

⁷ Don't worry that you are somehow changing the question with a sentence such as this. The point is to tackle head-on why the Act was passed and refute the implication in the question that the Act was not needed to be passed, as common law negligence could have dealt with what is a relatively small-scale problem.

⁸ By starting this part of your answer like this, it means that you are relating your discussion back to the statement and shows that you are now dealing with the underlying premise within the statement.

defect exists there is a greater potential for harm as all of the products are affected, not just a batch. The importance of causation in negligence deepens this problem, as a claimant must show that the design defect is capable of causing the harm in question, and then did cause that harm. This difficulty is clearly evidenced in relation to medicinal drugs and the Thalidomide cases. In negligence, claimants do not benefit from hindsight (*Roe v Minister of Health* [1954] 2 QB 66) and must show that at the time of the product's circulation the manufacturer acted unreasonably.

Consequently, the idea of a strict liability regime for defective products emerged. Such an idea is consistent with the principles of loss distribution, deterrence and economic efficiency. The manufacturer is best placed to insure the risk and can then pass this cost on to consumers. To ensure their prices are kept low, greater care would be taken to ensure premiums do not rise.⁵ The idea also reflects the viewpoint that it is fair to impose the risk on the manufacturer as they created the product for profit. The EU took the initiative, however, by passing Directive 85/374/EEC which aimed to harmonise the level of protection offered by all member states by implementing a strict liability regime. Therefore, even if it has caused difficulties of its own, the Act needs to exist to give effect to the superseding EU regime.

Notwithstanding the difficulties faced by consumers, the common law action has been retained, though.⁶ The Act's central aim is to impose liability without fault on the producer of a defective product (s. 2(1)). A product is defined in section 1(2) as any 'goods or electricity' and includes a component of a larger product, such as the fan within a laptop, and therefore it has broad scope. The consumer's position is also aided under the Act by the fact that the product's producer also includes the person who imported the product into the EU, which makes bringing an action easier for consumers rather than them having to sue a manufacturer from overseas. Generally, however, suppliers remain non-liable for the defect unless the conditions of section 2(3) are satisfied. The question is whether the Act, while initiating the EU measures, has also resolved the difficulties faced by consumers and so was worthwhile.⁷

If the Act does create a strict liability regime then its enactment was justified.⁸ However, from the Act's wording and the early cases, arguably, liability was not so strict. Section 3 defines 'defect' as being where 'the safety of the product is not such as persons are generally entitled to expect'. Under section 3(2) all circumstances should be taken into account when determining the level of safety that the public can expect. These include the product's marketing and whether any instructions or warnings regarding its use were provided. Further consideration is to be given to how the product may reasonably be expected to be used and the time when the product was supplied. The issue is that, while the Act seeks strict liability, determining whether the product was defective allows for the consideration of fault, and so negligence reappears by the back door. This was seen in ***Worsley v Tambrands Ltd*** [2000] PIQR 95 where a warning placed on the product regarding a small risk of toxic shock syndrome meant that liability was avoided.[9] The courts' assessment of a warning's sufficiency can be said to amount to whether the manufacturer has been at fault. This negates the Act's purpose and supports the suggestion that it was not needed as it does not solve the difficulties of negligence, as establishing a lack of care would still be required, and then that this caused the resultant injury. The use of fault-based reasoning was criticised in ***Abouzaid v Mothercare (UK) Ltd*** [2000] All ER D 2436, with whether the defect had come to Mothercare's attention deemed irrelevant. The lack of negligence was held to not prevent liability under the Act. The emphasis on strict liability was followed in ***A v National Blood Authority*** [2001] 3 All ER 289, where consideration of the care taken by the manufacturer was excluded; what should be assessed are all relevant circumstances, not all circumstances. While perhaps contrary to the wording of both the Act and Directive, ***A*** is defendable for giving effect to the spirit of the legislation and provides a justifiable rationale for the Act.[10]

In conclusion, the Act, especially as interpreted in ***A***, is a needed level of increased consumer protection to that which exists at common law, regardless of EU law compliance issues. Even if the difficulties of negligence claims are exaggerated, they do exist, and the Act circumvents those problems by placing the risk of defective products on the best placed person to carry that risk – the manufacturer. Notwithstanding any difficulties created in turn by the Act, it should be considered to be a welcome addition to the law on product liability.

[9] There are a number of cases that you could use here. It does not matter which you do use, so long as you include one which illustrates the point that the courts were interpreting 'defect' in a way which was akin to looking for fault. This forms the basis of whether, despite the Directive, the Act was worthwhile or just reiterating the common law position.

[10] As it is implied in the question that the Act serves no purpose, make sure that you include an opinion on this issue.

Make your answer stand out

■ Discuss briefly the limited scope for liability prior to *Donoghue*.

■ Expand your coverage of the limitations of the common law action and consider whether the modern developments of the duty concept and negligence generally have had any impact.

■ Read Stapleton, J. (1994b) *Product Liability*. London: Butterworths. This will allow you to incorporate material regarding the theoretical basis for strict liability in this area and why this approach was adopted in the EU in light of American experiences. You can then question the merits of strict liability.

■ Refer to journal articles on *A* as, if this case is wrong to adopt such a strict line in relation to 'defect', then we arguably do have a system which considers fault. You can then consider whether there is still enough distinction between the claims to warrant the existence of both actions. For example, look at Hodges, C. (2001) Compensating patients: case comment on *A* v *National Blood Authority* [2001] 3 All ER 289. *Law Quarterly Review*, 117: 528; and Howells, G. and Mildred, M. (2002) Infected blood: defect and discoverability a first exposition of the EC Product Liability Directive, *Modern Law Review*, 65: 95.

! Don't be tempted to . . .

■ Try to cover all of the provisions of the Act. Remember that the main aspect of the question is that there was no need for the Act to be passed. Therefore, you should weight your answer more in favour of the difficulties under the common law position.

■ Describe in detail the requirements in negligence. Explain what they are but, as above, focus on the problems they caused.

■ Gloss over the influence of European law in this area. Ultimately that was the reason for passing the Act and, so, on a question regarding whether the Act was necessary, it is quite a fundamental point.

❓ Question 2

Nicholas Guy is a brand of luxury hair straighteners which have just released a new product, the fh24/7. A prominent feature was a new safety device whereby the straighteners contained a motion sensor within the heat-plates. The sensor was designed to cut off power to the heat-plates, which could reach 200 degrees Celsius, after five minutes of inactivity. The product is manufactured in the USA, but imported into the UK and sold exclusively by luxury retail chain, Lewis Fraser's, at a cost of £300.

Sunita, who had had several near misses of overheating having left straighteners on, and had been shocked to have read news stories of the damage which could be caused, decided to buy the fh24/7 as soon as it was released. However, having seen the cost she had second thoughts until a shop assistant persuaded her that other features, such as the comfy grip, light weight and overall energy efficiency, were worth it.

However, the fh24/7 had a design fault whereby the motion sensor would not cut off the power supply until after 50 minutes of inactivity. A last minute test by Nicholas Guy identified the fault, but as the marketing materials had already been produced and orders placed, the company did not want to pull the product. Instead they quickly inserted a warning that the product should be used in conjunction with a heat resistant mat and that care should be taken to turn off after use. It was felt that if this was done, no damage should be caused and any complaints could be dealt with on an individual basis.

One morning though, having overslept, Sunita was late for work and forgot to turn off the hair straighteners after using them and left them on the laminated wood floor. The sensor failed to cut off the power despite not picking up movement for over five minutes. Consequently they overheated and caught fire, which then spread throughout Sunita's house. The fire caused such severe damage that the house was totally destroyed.

Advise Sunita as to what action she may take, and against whom, for the losses that she has suffered.

Diagram plan

A printable version of this diagram plan is available from **www.pearsoned.co.uk/lawexpressqa**

Answer plan

→ Outline the purpose and scope of the Consumer Protection Act 1987.

→ Consider whether the Act provides redress for the type of property which has been damaged by the product.

➡ State what role Lewis Fraser's and Nicholas Guy will have in proceedings.

➡ Evaluate the criteria for establishing liability and identify whether there was a defect with the hair straighteners.

➡ Discuss the possible application of any defences.

➡ Consider an alternative claim by Sunita under the rule in *Donoghue* v *Stevenson* [1932] AC 562.

Answer

Sunita requires advice on her ability to recover for the loss of her property resulting from the fire, and who she can recover these losses from. This will involve advising Sunita on the provisions of the Consumer Protection Act 1987 as well as the common law tort of negligence. It will be argued that, while compensation cannot be obtained for the damaged straighteners, any other damaged property will be recoverable under one or both actions.

[1] You could legitimately deal with the common law negligence claim first. If this is the approach that you adopt, use a line such as this one to explain why the Act has come into being to offer a parallel form of protection.

[2] Deal with this before the position of the two possible defendants as if the property is not recoverable under the Act, there is no point bringing a claim against either.

Sunita should be advised that Parliament passed the Consumer Protection Act 1987 so as to give effect to the Consumer Protection Directive. The aim was to better protect consumers from defective products by resolving some of the problems which had existed previously in common law claims for negligence.[1] Strict liability is imposed on producers of products which cause damage owing wholly or partly to defects within the product (s. 2(1)). The hair straighteners will clearly be a product under section 1(2).

The first issue is whether Sunita has suffered actionable damage under the Act in order to bring a claim.[2] Under section 5(2) the loss of the actual straighteners is not recoverable as this is purely economic loss to the product itself. However, under section 5(1), damage is recoverable for any other property, including land. This is important as Sunita's house suffered severe damage so this can be claimed for alongside her personal possessions. The Act restricts the amount of property that Sunita can claim though to that worth over £275 (s. 5(4)). Therefore, it is likely some of her damaged personal goods will not be recoverable.

The question is who is liable for the damage. Nicholas Guy have manufactured the straighteners and so are naturally the producer for the purposes of section 1(2); however, as they are based overseas

[3] You are showing off a touch here, by demonstrating your wider knowledge. However, to do this legitimately you need to include a line such as this to explain why you are exploring the possibility even though it will, ultimately, not apply. Do keep this section brief though, in light of that fact, otherwise you risk looking as if you understand it less than you do.

[4] Explain why the courts take such an approach and comment on the justification for it, particularly as some authorities have tried to incorporate fault.

[5] In light of what you are writing at this point, reiterate what you see as the defect in the straighteners to substantiate the point.

[6] Make sure that you get across your knowledge that it is only a partial defence as this shows you fully understand the nature of the defence.

it may be easier for Sunita to sue Lewis Fraser as the supplier of the straighteners.[3] This is possible as they have imported the product into the EU and section 2(2)(c) provides that liability will apply to such a person. However, as the straighteners identify who the actual producer of the product is, a requirement for imposing liability on a supplier such as Lewis Fraser is missing. Therefore, any action will just be against Nicholas Guy.

Under section 3(1) a defect in the straighteners must then be established. The section makes clear that there will be a defect where the product 'is not such as persons are generally entitled to expect'. Importantly for Sunita, this includes components within the product and safety in the context of risks of damage to property. Guidance is given in section 3(2) as to what the public are entitled to expect, but it is clear from cases such as *A v National Blood Authority* [2001] 3 All ER 289 that a strict line is taken against the producers and efforts are made to remove considerations of fault. This is in keeping with the purpose of imposing strict liability under the Act.[4] Therefore, even though there was a warning of sorts in terms of using the product, the nature of the defect here, overheating and fire risk,[5] coupled with the fact the company knew the sensor did not cut-off the power after five minutes means that the straighteners are certain to be found defective.

It is clear that none of the defences contained in section 4 are applicable, especially in light of their knowledge. However, under section 6(4) contributory negligence can apply to claims under the Act. The product specifies that it should be placed on a heat resistant mat, and should always be unplugged after use. Sunita did neither of these things, yet knew hair straighteners could cause fires. While not capable under the Law Reform (Contributory Negligence) Act 1945 of completely absolving Nicholas Guy, the defence is likely to succeed in reducing part of the damages awarded to Sunita.[6] The reduction may not be large though, as while using a mat may have stopped the fire from starting before the sensor finally worked, Sunita could legitimately counter that the fire may not have started at all if the product had worked as advertised.

Although Parliament sought to better protect consumers, the Act operates complementary to common law negligence which can still be used. There is no value threshold in such actions and so it provides

[7] Include this to show that you are aware of the distinction between the two actions and to demonstrate why you are discussing this when it seems Sunita may succeed under the Act.

[8] By mentioning this at the start, it ties in with your previous sentence about why it may be worth bringing a claim in negligence while also showing that you know the limitations of such an action.

[9] By wording this in this way, you show that you are fully aware of the differing principles which come out of Donoghue, and particularly that you understand its direct application to this issue.

[10] On the facts, there is no real issue of the aspects of causation and remoteness, and there is no real defence available. Therefore, sum these up in the one paragraph, although, if you are faced with a question which does need more detailed discussion of any of these points, then use a separate paragraph.

a useful vehicle to recover for any property damaged by the fire, which is worth less than £275.[7] The loss of the straighteners themselves, though, will still simply be regarded as purely economic and is not recoverable (**Murphy v Brentwood DC** [1991] 1 AC 398).[8]

Sunita must show that she was owed a duty of care in relation to the product. This is easily shown as the actual *ratio* of **Donoghue**[9] is that the manufacturer owes a duty of care to the ultimate consumer of their product. Therefore, Nicholas Guy owed Sunita a duty of care to take reasonable care in the manufacturing of their straighteners to ensure that their use would be safe.

The issue is, obviously, whether Nicholas Guy did take such reasonable care. Even if the faulty motion sensor was sourced from someone else, Nicholas Guy must exercise reasonable care purchasing that part and checking it is suitable (**Winward v TVR Engineering** [1986] BTLC 366). While Sunita should be advised that the principle of *res ipsa loquitur* does not apply (**Donoghue**), the courts have been willing to infer a lack of reasonable care from the presence of a defect (**Grant v Australian Knitting Mills Ltd** [1936] AC 85). The fact that Nicholas Guy knew of the fault and circulated the product would be a strong indication of a lack of care.

Causation[10] is also clearly established here, as 'but for' the fault the straighteners would not have overheated and the fire would not have started. This is especially the case considering that the straighteners would have not gone through any other inspection process between manufacture and purchase by Sunita which could be said to have interfered with the product. It would also seem obvious that fire damage was damage of a foreseeable type which would occur from the fault. The partial defence of contributory negligence would, equally, apply to this claim.

Therefore, in conclusion, Sunita is likely to have a claim under the Act for the damage to her home caused by the fire and any other property of hers, worth over £275, which was damaged in the fire. Alternatively, she could claim in negligence and this may be advisable as an additional claim for obtaining property which is under the threshold value of the Act. However, whichever way the action is brought the loss of the straighteners will not be recoverable owing to this being purely economic loss.

Make your answer stand out

- Explain the rationale and merit for imposing strict liability on producers of defective products.

- Consider the distinction made between manufacturing defects and design defects and discuss the different approach to each by the courts, explaining what sort the straighteners are.

- Explore the problems which exist with each action and make a deeper comparison of the merits of Sunita bringing an action under each.

- Read Hodges, C. (2001) Compensating patients: case comment on *A* v *National Blood Authority* [2001] 2 All ER 289. *Law Quarterly Review* 117: 528 in order to obtain some academic criticism of the judicial interpretation taken to the meaning of 'defect' under section 3.

- Discuss the difference between standard product defects and non-standard product defects.

! Don't be tempted to . . .

- Spend more time on the negligence action at the expense of the provisions of the Act. Remember that this is ultimately a question on product liability and you are likely to have a question elsewhere solely dedicated to common law negligence. If you treat the product liability problem question as an opportunity to repeat your answer from that other negligence question, you risk losing out on marks for not fully appreciating the scope of this question. You will also fail to show the full range of your knowledge.

- Try to show that you have more knowledge than you need by reciting parts of the Act which are not relevant, such as the range of defences within section 4. If you cover these in depth, it will instead show that you have not read the question properly and do not fully understand those provisions.

- Get tied up in the requirements of causation and remoteness unless the facts indicate that they warrant particular discussion. You must mention them, but the weight of discussion should reflect the extent that they are an issue on the facts of the question.

❓ Question 3

Piper and Galbraith plc is a pharmaceutical company and has recently produced a new drug, Fiagera, which is marketed as preventing anxiety attacks. The drug was subjected to trials in the UK in line with industry standards and approved by the national regulator.

Approval, though, was subject to the drug's packaging highlighting that it should not be used by people suffering epilepsy. However, research in Canada indicated that an ingredient of the drug could cause kidney damage if it was taken for a sustained period. This was published in the *Journal of Canadian Medicine,* which is also available globally.

Manisha had regularly suffered anxiety attacks during her first two years at university. As a result, she visited Dr Legg who, having never seen Manisha before, prescribed her Fiagera without knowing that she suffered from epilepsy. After taking the drug for four weeks, Manisha went into an epileptic shock. However, while she was in hospital it was also discovered that Manisha had suffered damage to her kidneys.

Advise Manisha on whether she could succeed in a claim against Piper and Galbraith for her injuries.

Diagram plan

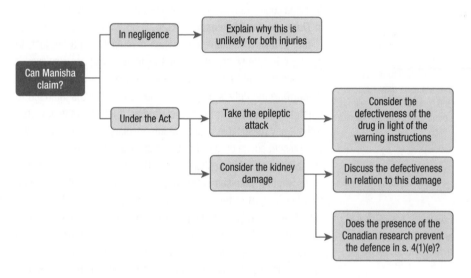

A printable version of this diagram plan is available from **www.pearsoned.co.uk/lawexpressqa**

Answer plan

→ Start with whether Manisha could claim successfully in negligence for her injuries.

→ Discuss the implications of the drug being prescribed by Dr Legg and whether this was a reasonable chance to inspect the product.

→ Advise Manisha as to how she could alternatively claim under the Consumer Protection Act 1987.

→ Deal with the epilepsy injury first and consider whether the drug was defective in this regard.

→ Discuss separately the kidney damage and whether the drug was defective in relation to that injury.

→ Consider the possible defence under section 4(1)(e) and the issue of the state of scientific knowledge at the time of the drug's circulation.

Answer

The issue to advise Manisha about is whether she can successfully sue Piper and Galbraith (P&G) for the epileptic attack and the kidney damage following her taking of Fiagera. There are two options available to her: one in negligence and another under the Consumer Protection Act 1987. It is argued that Manisha may succeed under the Act for the kidney damage.

[1] Owing to the facts of the question and the difficulties of bringing such a claim, deal with common law negligence first. This will allow you to end your answer more strongly by discussing the claim which is more likely to succeed. Your answer will read a bit strangely if you write about the Act first and the argument that Manisha may succeed and then proceed to talk about an alternative claim which is likely to fail.

Manisha could firstly claim in negligence.[1] Following the specific rule in **Donoghue v Stevenson** [1932] AC 562, a manufacturer owes a duty to take reasonable care when manufacturing a product, to ensure it is safe when used by the ultimate consumer. However, it would be very difficult for Manisha to succeed in this claim. Under **Donoghue** the duty is only owed when the product is intended to reach the consumer in the same state as it left the manufacturer, without any reasonable chance of intermediary inspection. Manisha was prescribed the drug by Dr Legg and so arguably there was a reasonable chance of inspection by him. Dr Legg should have enquired as to whether Manisha suffered epilepsy and thus not prescribed it to her in light of the warning. An analogy could be drawn here with **Evans v Triplex Safety Glass Co. Ltd** [1963] 1 All ER 283 where the windscreen was fitted by another party. Manisha should be advised that Dr Legg's failure to do this may mean that she would have a claim in negligence against him under **Bolam v Friern Hospital Management Committee** [1957] 1 WLR 582.[2] Even in relation to the kidney damage, Manisha is likely to have problems in negligence owing to the need to prove that, even if P&G failed to take reasonable care in producing the drug, this breach of duty caused her injuries. There could be various reasons for the kidney damage, such as Manisha's lifestyle or whether she was taking any other medicines. This task is made harder by the fact that this is a design defect rather than a manufacturing defect and the courts have been more ready to infer negligence in the latter (**Grant v Australian Knitting Mills Ltd**

[2] While you have not been asked to advise Manisha regarding Dr Legg, by highlighting this you demonstrate your wider knowledge and understanding of negligence, so it is beneficial but do keep it brief.

[1936] AC 85). Therefore, Manisha is unlikely to succeed in negligence against P&G.

However, in view of the difficulties with a fault-based system of liability for defective products, a strict liability regime has been implemented in addition.[3] The Act implemented Directive 85/374/EEC, which sought to introduce strict liability for defective products as a means of ensuring a level of harmonisation for consumers within the Internal Market.[4] It is clear from section 1(2) and section 45 that the drug will be a product for the purposes of the Act. The fact that Fiagera is made up of different ingredients will not matter as section 1(2) states that a product also includes the component parts within an overall product. It is also clear that P&G will be the producer for the purposes of the Act as they have manufactured the drug (s. 1(2)).

The damage must be actionable under the Act which this is, as under section 5(1) damage means personal injury, which Manisha has clearly suffered. The question is whether the product was defective. Section 3 defines 'defect' as where the 'safety of the product is not such as persons generally are entitled to expect'. Guidance is given in section 3(2) which significantly states[5] that account should be taken of how the product is marketed and the instructions given. We are told that Fiagera was approved and marketed as not being suitable for epileptics. This causes a problem for Manisha as the first injury she suffers is that of an epileptic attack. Therefore, notwithstanding the strict approach taken when interpreting 'defect' in *A v National Blood Authority* [2001] 3 All ER 289, Fiagera was a standard product – meaning it was designed and manufactured as intended. Further, in view of the marketing and that in section 3(2)(b) provision is made as to what may reasonably be expected in terms of the product's use, Fiagera is unlikely to be defective. This is a prescription drug and so it is reasonable for P&G to expect that the drug would not be used by epileptics, especially as this was warned against. Therefore, Manisha is unlikely to succeed for the attack.

However, Manisha has also suffered kidney damage and the likelihood of this was not shown on the product.[6] Therefore, Manisha needs to be advised as to whether Fiagera was defective in relation to this injury. The issue in relation to this is that under section 3(2)(c) the courts should take account of the time at which the product

---

[3] Use a sentence such as this explaining why the Act has come about to link the two sections of your answer. You will show that you are aware of the Act's aim as being a response to the difficulties mentioned, as well as developing a nice flow for your structure.

[4] While perhaps not seemingly directly in issue, highlight your awareness of this briefly to show your depth on the subject. This places your discussion of the Act in context.

[5] When discussing this guidance, focus on the aspects which are most relevant to the facts of the question and ensure that you apply them to the facts. This will keep your answer structured and relevant. If you just spell out all of the points, your answer will become descriptive and not read as well.

[6] As the drug is more likely to be defective in relation to the kidney damage, you should deal with this separately from the epilepsy. This will aid your structure by making it clear that you have identified two separate issues.

was put into circulation. At this time, the trials had not shown that it could cause kidney damage. There was evidence from Canada that this would be the case. Further, this information was available globally and so, as a pharmaceutical company, it is arguable that P&G should have known of this. This is supported by the strict approach endorsed in *A*. The public would expect Fiagera to be safe, especially seeing it had undergone a trial. Therefore, the drug could be said to be defective. Manisha's problem, though, is that even if defective it must, on normal causation principles, be shown to have caused the kidney damage. Therefore, it must be shown that 'but for' the taking of Fiagera Manisha would not have got kidney damage.[7] It is difficult to say whether this was the case and a lot will rest on the conclusiveness of the Canadian research.

[7] If you covered causation in more depth previously when dealing with the action at common law, then you can just refer back to it here. Make sure you do not repeat yourself.

If the drug is deemed defective and causation shown, Manisha should be advised that the Act does contain defences. The most significant is within section 4(1)(e). This concerns development risks. The producer's knowledge must not be such that a producer of the same product might be expected to have discovered the defect while the product was under his control.[8] Therefore, there is some overlap with whether the drug was defective. The question is whether a reasonable producer of the same product would have known that the defect existed at the time. While criticised as diluting the strictness of liability under the Act, it was approved in *Commission* v *UK* [1997] 3 CMLR 923.

[8] You could learn the section in full and quote that, but as it is quite long it may be better to paraphrase it. This will also show that you understand what the section means, as you can write it in your own words.

However, even if generously interpreted, it is unlikely P&G would satisfy this as, arguably, a reasonable producer would keep up to date with the latest scientific research.[9] Further, the journal was published before Fiagera was marketed and as it is a global publication it was accessible, which is what is necessary (*Commission* v *UK*).

[9] Although following *A* the matter is not likely to be interpreted generously; by highlighting that the claim is likely to succeed even on a generous view, it strengthens the argument that the defence will fail.

Therefore, Manisha will be successful in claiming for the kidney damage under the Act provided she can satisfy the issue of causation, which may not be easy, as shown in *X* v *Schering Health Care Ltd* [2002] EWHC 1420. The drug is unlikely to be deemed defective in relation to the epilepsy.

Make your answer stand out

- Explore the debate further around section 4(1)(e) and the corresponding part of the Directive and the extent to which the section is compatible.

- Explain in more depth the distinction made in *A* between standard and non-standard products.

- Consider the merits of strict liability over fault-based negligence and particularly the approach taken in *A* for interpreting the Act. In furtherance of this, look at Hodges, C. (2001) Compensating patients: case comment on *A* v *National Blood Authority* [2001] 2 All ER 289. *Law Quarterly Review,* 117: 528; and Howells, G. and Mildred, M. (2002) Infected blood: defect and discoverability, a first exposition of the EC Product Liability Directive, *Modern Law Review,* 65: 95.

- Discuss the prospect of P&G being jointly liable with the national regulator that approved the drug.

! Don't be tempted to . . .

- Ignore either of the possible claims in favour of solely talking about the other in depth. As the question does not set any limits, you need to discuss both. Even if you do not do so because you feel that claim is futile, it may look like you did not realise there is a chance of the claim. At the very least raise it to dismiss the possibility of success.

- Get into a discussion of loss of a chance and *Gregg* v *Scott* [2005] 2 AC 176 with regards any chance of the kidney damage occurring.

- Merge your discussion as to both injuries, as arguably the outcome will be different and so you may find you compromise the clarity of your argument.

- Set out all of the defences within section 4 unless you can make the case for them being relevant; otherwise you will use up valuable time without gaining any real benefit.

Vicarious liability

7

How this topic may come up in exams

Vicarious liability is an important topic as there could be an element of it in a problem question on any other topic, with varying degrees of emphasis. However, it can also be examined on its own. Where this is the case, it is more likely to be an essay with questions focusing on the justification for imposing liability on a third party who did not commit the tort. Therefore, as well as knowing the mechanics of how the doctrine works, you will need an in-depth knowledge on the policy and theoretical reasons for and against it.

■ Before you begin

It's a good idea to consider the following key themes of vicarious liability before tackling a question on this topic.

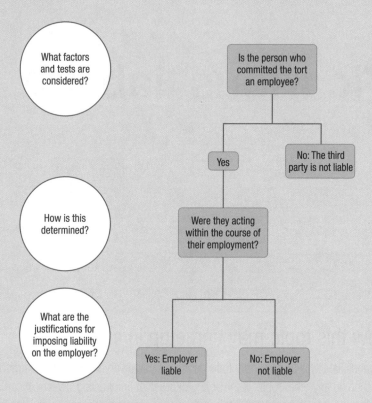

A printable version of this diagram plan is available from **www.pearsoned.co.uk/lawexpressqa**

Question 1

'[the decision in *Viasystems*], accepted as it has been in *Hawley* v *Luminar,* has extended the conventional boundaries and will, I believe, come to be seen as something of a William Ellis moment where, perhaps unwittingly, their Lordships picked up the ball and ran with it thereby creating a whole new ballgame – vicarious liability even if there is strictly no employer/employee relationship . . .'. (*Per* Ward LJ in *E* v *English Province of Our Lady Charity* [2012] EWCA Civ 389 at [60])

Critically evaluate the approach taken by the courts in establishing vicarious liability and whether policy considerations can continue to justify its use.

Diagram plan

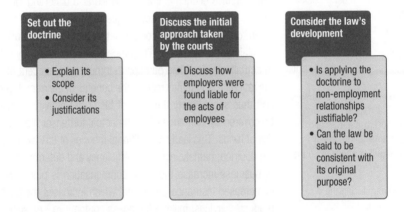

Set out the doctrine	Discuss the initial approach taken by the courts	Consider the law's development
• Explain its scope • Consider its justifications	• Discuss how employers were found liable for the acts of employees	• Is applying the doctrine to non-employment relationships justifiable? • Can the law be said to be consistent with its original purpose?

A printable version of this diagram plan is available from **www.pearsoned.co.uk/lawexpressqa**

Answer plan

→ Explain the doctrine and assess the justifications for shifting liability in this way.

→ Discuss the court's initial approach in finding an employer vicariously liable for the acts of their employees.

→ Evaluate the merits of the law's development so the doctrine applies even where there is no employer/employee relationships.

→ Consider if the doctrine can still be said to be giving effect to its original purpose.

Answer

The issue is whether the 'new ballgame'[1] that the doctrine finds itself in due to judicial development is such as to call into question the validity of the doctrine itself. This matters as its operation can lead to those not at fault being held liable. However, it is argued that the current application has achieved a desirable level of flexibility which still correlates to the doctrine's original justifications.

The doctrine has historically shifted liability from an individual tortfeasor to their employer, even in the absence of direct fault or breach of duty by the latter. Therefore, it provided a form of strict liability and places a burden on business, which could prove unduly restrictive, with negative economic impacts, while also distorting ideas of corrective justice. However, several justifications exist. First, effect is given to the principles of compensation and loss distribution in that the claimant is able to obtain compensation from a party with funds to actually pay it. While perhaps detrimental to innocent employers, the rationale is that they receive the benefits of their employee's work and thus should carry the risks of his or her activity. They will also be covered by insurance while the actual tortfeasor may have insufficient funds. This leads to additional theories of tort[2] which underpin the doctrine: namely, economic efficiency and deterrence. The costs of business increase the more compensation is paid, even if only in increased insurance premiums, which increases the cost of their products/services, making them less competitive.[3] As such, there is a strong deterrent factor in ensuring injury is not caused by their employees. Overall, the doctrine is based on 'social convenience and rough justice' (Lord Pearce, *ICI Ltd v Shatwell* [1965] 656 AC 686), and in light of these factors a clear justification exists.[4]

Notwithstanding these justifications, liability is not automatically imposed.[5] Two stages are considered: whether (1) the tortfeasor is an employee; and (2) acting in the course of their employment. The first reflects the justifications discussed above.[6] Initially it was determined in light of the level of control the employer had over the tortfeasor, but as employment practices changed alongside technological developments, an economic reality test was applied which, while still considering control, required an assessment of factors which could illustrate an employment relationship (*Market Investigations Ltd v*

Minister of Social Security [1969] 2 QB 173). This overcame the problem around control, while giving a fair assessment of who should be considered an employee, and justifies shifting liability.

However, as the question demonstrates, employment is no longer needed. The doctrine will be applied to relationships akin to employment when close enough in character to make it just and fair to do so (*E*). This raises questions as to doctrine's validity as the initial justifications for it would seem inapplicable.[7] However, Ward LJ reiterated the doctrine's fluidity and opined it should not be constrained by concepts arising from different contexts. What matters is whether, in the interests of justice, the 'employer' should be responsible for the tortious acts of those authorised to act on its behalf. Acting under a common purpose would suffice (***Various Claimants v Catholic Welfare Society*** [2012] UKSC 56). Otherwise the principles of compensation and loss distribution would be undermined in such situations.[8]

The focus of stage 2 of the doctrine has also changed following ***Lister v Hesley Hall*** [2002] 1 AC 215. Now, a 'close connection' test determines whether the tort was so closely connected with the employment relationship (or equivalent) as to make liability fair and just. This has resulted in questionable instances of vicarious liability being imposed, particularly in cases of clearly illegal and prohibited conduct where it is harder to see any connection. In ***Lister*** the employee warden had sexually abused children in his employer's care. Liability was imposed, however, because as Lord Millett[9] highlighted, the warden had been given responsibility for discharging the duty of care owed by the employer to the children, which he clearly failed to do. Further, as Lord Steyn stated, the tort was 'inextricably interwoven' with his duties. This link warranted liability and not simply the fact that the employment created an opportunity for committing the tort; which is why it was stated that liability would not have arisen if the tortfeasor had been the gardener.

The test offers no exact guidance on what is a sufficient connection (***Dubai Aluminium Co. Ltd v Salaam & Others*** [2003] 1 AC 366) and so can lead to seemingly inconsistent results, as seen in the factually similar cases of ***Weddall v Barchester Healthcare Ltd; Wallbank v Wallbank Fox Designs Ltd*** [2012] EWCA Civ 25. Arbitrary operation raises questions as to the doctrine's rationale,

[7] You need to set up a discussion as to the merits of this development, but in a way which identifies what the issue is in light of what you have mentioned previously.

[8] Remember to come down on one side or other of the argument. To strengthen your position wed your mini-conclusion here back to the principles which you used to discuss the doctrine's historical justification.

[9] In *Lister* no test of uniform language was adopted, so it is important that you identify which judge you are referring to as this can help show that you are aware of that fact.

as seen in *Maga v Birmingham Roman Catholic Archdiocese Trustees* [2010] EWCA Civ 256 where Longmore LJ queried whether it is simply to ensure someone can pay or to encourage employers to exert more vigilance over employees. From a practical perspective, employers cannot obtain adequate insurance to pay compensation when they do not know the scope of the cover needed. This could cause significant economic difficulties for firms as they may end up uncovered or the premiums become too expensive, reducing their competitiveness and their financial health: all for an act which was not of their doing and even expressly prohibited. This is hard to defend and arguably goes against the doctrine's rationale.

[10] Never be afraid to take an opposing view to that in journal articles that you have read or that of the judges; provided that you substantiate your answer and show why your view has strength, you should gain more marks.

However, these concerns suggest that the justifications are at odds and require one overarching justification when in fact, as *Salmond and Heuston* argues (Heuston and Buckley, 1996), there never has been. The stronger view[10] is that while terms such as 'fair and just' are vague they allow for flexibility and the doctrine's applications to new situations, while being mindful of the need for fairness to both parties. Assessing all of the facts of each situation and weighing them against the doctrine's justifications ensures liability is justly shifted when necessary so as to ensure appropriate compensation for claimants. Any uncertainty could instead be viewed positively,[11] as it forces employers to ensure employees are competent and to undertake appropriate and regular checks, which strengthens the deterrence principle through principles of economic efficiency. While employers may be unable to foresee all acts of employees, they do have a degree of control on events by employing the individual. This simply requires them to perform adequate risk assessments, which is surely good practice.

[11] As above, have the courage to consider whether the issues that are suggested as being detrimental are in fact so. This allows you to really evaluate the merits of the arguments relating to the doctrine's justification.

In conclusion, the move away from an employment relationship as seen in *E* and *Various Claimants* simply illustrates a synthesis of the doctrine's two requirements and does not detract from the merit of the doctrine's operation. The current approach still gives effect to the underpinning principles of tort upon which the doctrine was founded by ensuring that, on appropriate facts, tortious conduct is corrected through compensatory payments and spreading losses to those who are most able to bear them. Further flexibility is retained to aid its future use.

✓ Make your answer stand out

- Draw on the judgment of Ward LJ in *E,* which has been widely commended by members of the judiciary, to gain a full overview and understanding of the issues.

- Make sure that you have an understanding of the underlying principles of tort so as to be able to draw on them in this area in support of the argument that you advance.

- Consider whether any issues regarding the justification of the doctrine are theoretical or merely concerned with its practical implementation by the courts.

- Read Morgan, P. (2013) Vicarious Liability on the Move. *Law Quarterly Review*, 129: 139 and assess whether the changes at stage one will require further development of stage two.

- Look at the following articles in order to see the extent of the expansion of the doctrine and obtain some academic criticism of these developments:

  - Gilliker, P. (2006) The on-going march of vicarious liability. *Cambridge Law Journal,* 489;

  - Hope, Lord (2013) Tailoring the law on vcarious liability. *Law Quarterly Review*, 129: 514.

! Don't be tempted to . . .

- Refer to vicarious liability as a distinct tort: this will simply suggest that you do not understand the basis of the concept.

- Try to establish a definitive explanation and justification for the doctrine. Simply outline the basic premise and highlight some of the various factors advanced in support of it.

- Gloss over the need to discuss the need for an employment relationship. Even though this has now seemingly been reduced in importance, it is this change which really raises questions as to the ongoing purpose and merit of the doctrine.

- Overlook the close-connection test just because the quote does not expressly refer to it. It is an integral part of the doctrine, arguably even more so now in light of *E* and similar cases.

Question 2

'This "close-connection" test focuses attention in the right direction. But it affords no guidance on the type or degree of connection which will normally be regarded as sufficiently close.' (*Per* Lord Nicholls in *Dubai Aluminium Co. Ltd* v *Salaam & Others* [2003] 1 AC 366 at [25])

Evaluate the extent to which the 'close-connection test' is appropriate for determining when the doctrine of vicarious liability should apply.

Answer plan

➜ Outline what the purpose of the doctrine is and why it is warranted.

➜ Briefly mention within that context the need for an employee–employer or analogous relationship.

➜ Evaluate what the 'close-connection' test is and the purpose it serves.

➜ Consider the effectiveness of the test and whether it has distorted the role of the doctrine.

Diagram plan

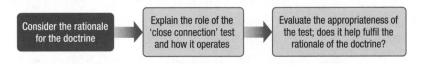

A printable version of this diagram plan is available from **www.pearsoned.co.uk/lawexpressqa**

Answer

Vicarious liability is the vehicle tort uses to transfer the cost of compensating injured parties from the tortfeasor to their employer. While there are long-standing justifications for this, the issue is whether once a relationship of employment, or equivalent, is established, the close-connection test is appropriate to conclude the matter, or damages the rationale for the doctrine.[1] It is argued that, while lacking definitive clarity, the test is effective and allows the doctrine to fulfil its purpose in a justifiable manner.

The doctrine imposes strict liability on the employer, irrespective of the fact that they have not directly inflicted the claimant's injury, it being caused solely through the actions of an employee. It acts as a form of distributive justice ensuring compensation is forthcoming, but spreading the loss onto shoulders which are more able to bear the loss. This is justified by the courts[2] as the employer should be protected by insurance and can also absorb costs by passing them on to consumers through price increases. This provides, therefore, a deterrent factor in ensuring staff are competent and continually trained to remain so, as this will make the employer more economically efficient with better quality products/services and thus more competitive in the market place. Another justification is that as the

[1] As the question focuses on this specific aspect of vicarious liability, make sure that you highlight in your introduction that you appreciate this. The task is to stay disciplined and not stray into a broader-based answer.

[2] If the doctrine does not have a justified theoretical basis, then there really is no argument that the test should not apply. Therefore, this is the foundation upon which you must build your answer. Briefly set out why the doctrine should apply and then you can concentrate on the merits of the practical application of it.

employer is taking the benefit from the conduct underway when the tort was caused, morally they should also carry the risks.

The doctrine operates in two stages. First, the tortfeasor must be an employee of the defendant or be in an equivalent relationship (**Various Claimants v Catholic Child Welfare Society** [2012] UKSC 56). However, the second stage has arguably proved the most controversial. Historically the stage required the employee to have been in the course of their employment when they committed the tort.[3] The purpose of the requirement is to support the rationale for the doctrine by providing justification for the shift in liability.[4] Otherwise the doctrine itself would fall into disrepute if employers have responsibility for acts done outside of their time or for their benefit (**N v Chief Constable of Merseyside Police** [2006] EWHC 3041). Previously, judicial consideration focused on[5] whether the act was authorised or not and, if it was an authorised aspect of their employment, whether it was performed in an authorised manner. This was based on the proposition that acts relating to the scope of employment which were prohibited would not carry liability, but a breach of a prohibition as to the manner of performing an authorised act would be within the scope of the doctrine (**Plumb v Cobden Flour Mills Co. Ltd** [1914] AC 62). This caused complications over what was the actual scope of employment and whether the specific act fell within it, notwithstanding that the scope of employment should be looked at broadly (**Rose v Plenty** [1976] 1 WLR 141). Such a determination was particularly difficult to make with regards to intentional wrongdoing.[6]

In **Lister** a children's home was held vicariously liable for the sex abuse by a warden who was an employee. Clearly, he was not even performing his authorised employment in an unauthorised way, let alone under express permission.[7] It was a clearly illegal act. Lord Steyn[8] felt that his duties as a warden were 'inextricably interwoven' with what he did; there was an undertaking by the employer to care for the boys and they were abused in the employer's time, and on their premises, creating a close connection. The questions was whether it was 'fair and just' to impose liability on that basis. It was not the opportunity given by the employment that warranted liability but, as Lord Hobhouse stated, a relationship had been assumed between the claimant and the employer which imposed duties on the latter. The warden had been entrusted to perform that duty of care and instead breached it.

[3] By starting this section with a sentence such as this, you reinforce and justify why you have just briefly discussed the issue of the need for the tortfeasor to be an employee.

[4] By stating the purpose of the requirement at the start, you tie this part of your answer to your earlier section and you have the foundation for assessing the merits of the test.

[5] While the test is the current authoritative approach to the issue, you should consider what it replaced in order to assess whether the move was justified.

[6] By ending with this statement, you highlight one of the problems with the old approach and flow straight into explaining what happened in *Lister,* a case on intentional wrongdoing.

[7] This links the case to the problems identified in the previous paragraph.

[8] All the judges gave opinions, so clearly identify whose analysis you are explaining.

[9] The point here is to reiterate your understanding of the principal issue of the question and signal, therefore, the key stage of your discussion.

The question is whether the close-connection test achieves its purpose or whether its formulation in *Lister* is detracting from the justifications of the doctrine.[9] Giliker (2006 and 2010) has repeatedly argued that the lack of definitive formulation of a test is causing problems for lower courts, a view seemingly reflected by Lord Nicholls in *Salaam*. Giliker suggests this allows the doctrine's application in inappropriate areas. Clearly, the test is vague, and legal uncertainty is rarely useful. Employers are left not knowing what acts will result in their liability and increased litigation could result as parties feel they have an equal chance of success, particularly when intentional illegal acts are involved. At the very least it affects the employers' ability to obtain insurance, which removes one of the factors which is said to make the transferring of liability fair.

However, taken collectively the opinions in *Lister* are reconcilable. Lord Hutton agreed with Lord Steyn, and there is little difference in the language used by Lords Hobhouse and Millett. Although, strictly speaking, adopting a different language, they can be reconciled: by entrusting the performance of the duty to the warden, it created a sufficient connection to make it fair and just to impose liability. All emphasised the need for a causal link which, as Lord Clyde noted, went back to Salmond's first account of the doctrine. Further, the test provides flexibility, allowing a full consideration of the facts and an evaluative judgment made as against the underlying principles of compensation, deterrence and loss distribution while drawing on precedent where applicable. Indeed, this approach was accepted by Lord Nicholls in *Salaam* owing to the wide variety of situations in which the doctrine may operate. He therefore saw an appropriate way through the issue highlighted by the question.

[10] It is important that you reconsider this point as it was advanced as one of the objections to the test. You need to consider whether the clarification given by the Supreme Court in the case has alleviated the problem or not.

Further clarification has also been given in *Various Claimants*. Where, as traditionally has been the case, tortious acts are clearly committed within the course of employment, liability will still result. Beyond that, however, when the acts are clearly not part of the tortfeasor's job, liability will arise where it is fair, just and reasonable in light of how closely connected the relationship between the defendant and the tortfeasor is with the commission of the tort, as that closeness will provide the necessary causative link. The creation of risk was said to be an important factor and bearing that in mind, employers should be able to make a reasonable enough assessment in order to facilitate insurance cover which may have been a problem post-*Lister*.[10]

Therefore, Giliker's concerns regarding the lower courts can be overcome. Lower courts are arbiters of fact. Once they have established the full facts of what the employee's duty was and how the tort was committed they have the scope to determine, in light of the doctrine's purpose, whether the two are sufficiently close. If they are, the requirement maintains the necessary justifiable link to the employer to give effect to the doctrine's rationale.

 Make your answer stand out

- Learn each opinion in Lister and quote the different judges' reasoning to support the argument that they are reconcilable.

- Consider some of the arguments used in the Canadian case of *Bazley* v *Curry* (1999) 174 DLR (4th) 45, SC (from which the House of Lords took the test) to show a broader understanding of its merits in applying to situations such as *Lister*.

- Ensure that you always relate your arguments in relation to the test back to the theoretical purpose that this aspect of the requirement for vicarious liability is meant to serve.

- Consider the case of *Allen* v *Chief Constable of Hampshire* [2013] EWCA Civ 967 where there was not deemed to be a sufficiently close connection. This will allow you to demonstrate that increased expansion of the doctrine does not automatically lead to liability on the part of the employer.

! Don't be tempted to . . .

- Broaden your answer to deal in detail with the wider aspects of vicarious liability; stay focused on the 'close-connection' test as the question requires. You will not impress the marker with this wider knowledge and it will suggest that you do not understand the main issue of the question.

- Avoid coming down from the fence and making a decision as to the appropriateness of the test. You will have stated arguments for and against and your answer will end weakly if you do not conclude on the ultimate point.

❓ Question 3

Brett is an uninsured plumber who gets his work from Brogan Construction. Brett is always instructed on what is required for the job and how it should be carried out by the Brogan foreman, although he must supply all his own tools, including a van to get to each job; he can bring his own labourers to a job but he must pay them out of his wages. Brogan pays Brett a daily rate for any jobs but he receives no other benefits.

Recently, owing to a shortage of plumbing work on offer, Brogan arranged for Brett to do some work with Hacker Heating Ltd in return for a fee. The job involved fitting a new boiler in a residential property, owned by Ted. However, owing to a part turning up late, Brett rushed the installation as it was already past his normal finish time with Brogan Construction and he had a hangover from the night before and wanted to get to bed. The boiler subsequently exploded, killing Ted.

It has been accepted that the boiler was installed negligently and that this caused the explosion; however, Brett has argued that as an employee he should not be held personally liable, while Hacker Heating Ltd argue he was certainly not their employee.

Advise Brogan Construction on whether they could be held vicariously liable for Ted's death.

Diagram plan

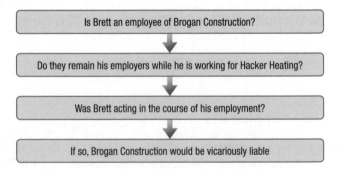

A printable version of this diagram plan is available from **www.pearsoned.co.uk/lawexpressqa**

Answer plan

➜ Explain what the doctrine of vicarious liability is and why it is important to this situation.

➜ Establish whether Brett can be considered an employee of Brogan Construction.

➜ Discuss whether Brett is in the course of his employment.

➜ Evaluate the implications of the work being for Hacker Heating Ltd.

Answer

¹ Although it is not going
to need discussing as the
doctrine can apply to all torts,
it is worth confirming that
you are aware of what tort
Brogan Construction could be
vicariously liable for.

² As you have to advise on
their potential liability, you will
be referring to them a lot, so
abbreviate the name.

³ This means that straight
away you have identified the
key aspect of the topic to be
addressed without straying
into irrelevant material.

⁴ BC would naturally argue
they did not do anything
wrong so why should they
be liable. Therefore, in a
question such as this explain
why the issue of liability even
arises to illustrate that you
understand the theory behind
the doctrine.

⁵ You need to state enough to
show that you understand the
basis for the doctrine, while
not deviating from a structure
which the question warrants.

⁶ The point here is to show
that you know what the
purpose of the requirement
of employee status is, but
you need to remember to
frame your explanation in the
context of giving advice to a
lay party, i.e. BC.

There is no issue that compensation for Ted's death is due under the tort of negligence;[1] the matter to be resolved is simply whether Brogan Construction (BC)[2] will have to pay this under the doctrine of vicarious liability. This rests on whether Brett is actually an employee of BC.[3] It is argued that while they may have some liability they should be able to successfully argue that Hacker Heating (HH) should be the predominant contributor of any compensation.

BC should be advised that the reason they face potential liability is that the doctrine operates[4] to shift losses so that they are borne by those who are best able to do so. As employers will have insurance and also benefit from their employees' actions, it is deemed acceptable for them to run the risk of their malfeasance and compensate any injuries caused through the work.[5]

This explanation forms the basis of the requirements which need to be met for an employer to be liable. The first is naturally that the tort-feasor is an employee. If they are not, there is no justification behind the transferring of liability.[6] Traditionally, this is determined applying the control test (***Short* v *J & W Henderson Ltd*** (1946) SC (HL) 24). This is significant as the factors considered are the employer's power to select who does the work, their right to control the method of work, the paying of wages and their right to suspend or dismiss the individual. Applying this to Brett, we can see that BC do choose what work he does and dictate how it is performed. While we do not know the details regarding the last point, they do pay Brett his wages. Therefore, in all, Brett would seem to be their employee.

However, the control test is no longer the sole factor to determine a person's employee status. Reflecting changes in working practices and technological developments, it was felt that simply looking at the level of control was not appropriate. Instead a range of economic factors are also considered – the economic reality test (***Market Investigations Ltd* v *Minister of Social Security*** [1969] 2 QB 173). This requires, among other factors, an assessment of who provides the equipment and whether the person can hire helpers. On these factors, Brett seems more of an independent contractor, as we are told he brings his own equipment and pays labourers from his own

131

[7] While the issue may be
unclear, you do need to
offer some advice on Brett's
status; otherwise you are
not really answering the
question, which is to advise
BC. Highlight what you feel
is the key factor which may
swing a decision to support
your opinion.

[8] Reflect the fact that it is
uncertain by framing the
opening sentence like this.
Even if you do not feel Brett is
an employee, you still need to
continue to this section on the
transfer issue as clearly this
is a key part of the question;
if you just stop with the
previous section, there will
be significant aspects of the
question and topic which you
will not have demonstrated
any knowledge of.

wages; contractors are also quite common in this field. If Brett is a contractor, the doctrine would not apply and BC would avoid liability, but there are other economic factors which suggest Brett is an employee. Although not told definitively the facts regarding these, it seems Brett has no management responsibility and other than wages has no opportunity of profiting from the sound management of his task. Therefore, while it is possible Brett is not an employee, taken as a whole, particularly the element of control exerted over his work, it is quite likely that he is.[7]

On the basis that Brett is an employee,[8] the next issue to advise BC on is the fact that at the time of the tort Brett was working for HH. Under *Mersey Docks & Harbour Board* v *Coggins & Griffith (Liverpool) Ltd* [1947] AC 1, the permanent employer of the employee remains liable even after lending them to another firm. From the case, the decisive factors will be whether BC still pays Brett's wages and can still dismiss him, as well as how long Brett was sent to HH and how complex any machinery to be used is. In relation to the latter two points, Brett was only there to install a boiler and this was within his usual work for BC. As HH paid BC a fee for Brett's services, it is unlikely that they paid him as well; in view of the short duration and nature of the job BC should be advised that the facts suggest that they would remain liable for Brett's work.

However, BC could benefit from *Viasystems (Tyneside) Ltd* v *Thermal Transfers (Northern) Ltd* [2006] QB 510 where the Court of Appeal held dual vicarious liability could exist in a situation such as this. Liability could be joint or several, with the contributions to be made by each side being determined by the Civil Liability (Contribution) Act 1978. Indeed the facts are similar to those that Rix LJ gave for when liability is likely to be shared. However, *Viasystems* maintained that, where one party has absolute control of the employee, they will remain solely liable. Here, while we are told Brett was always told how to perform each job by the BC foreman, they would not have been present at Ted's house. Further, HH are a heating firm and so would have detailed knowledge of how to install boilers. This would suggest that any control over how Brett performed the job was more likely exerted by HH. Ultimately, Brett rushed because he was hung over and wanted to get home; HH let Brett work hung over, and therefore, it was within their control to prevent Brett working that day on the boiler regardless of whether BC's foreman instructed Brett on how to install it. Therefore, it can be strongly argued that while Brett may have been an employee of BC, if indeed he was, HH had the sole control of him while he was lent to them for that job. This would mean that BC avoid liability, or at the very least have a much reduced share, with HH being liable for the remaining compensation.

[9] Do not forget this aspect of vicarious liability, as without it the previous discussion is irrelevant. While it seems apparent it will be satisfied, you do still need to touch on it to firmly show that you do in fact know it and can apply it.

However, in any event Brett needed to act in the course of his employment.[9] Clearly, as a plumber engaged to install a boiler, the negligent act was within his employment. The installation took place after Brett's normal finishing time, but while the tortious act must be performed within the authorised employment time, it is clear that Brett extended his day in order to finish the job and so will be classed as still within his employer's time (***Ruddiman & Co. v Smith*** (1889) 60 LT 708). The fact that Brett would not be authorised to install a boiler negligently will also not suffice as there is clearly a close connection between the act and his employment (***Lister v Hesley Hall Ltd*** [2002] 1 AC 215).

Therefore, the potential vicarious liability of BC will turn on firstly whether Brett is deemed to even be an employee of theirs. Even if he is, owing to the fact that at the time of the act some, if not all, control of his work was in the hands of HH, BC should only, at most, be liable to contribute a part of any compensation under the Act, with HH contributing the rest.

✓ Make your answer stand out

- As control is still a significant factor for cases of transferred employees, cover the control test in a bit more depth than you would other vicarious liability problem questions.
- As there are not as many concrete facts to definitively apply in this question, draw on facts from similar cases and judicial reasoning from those cases to support the arguments that you do advance.
- Explain, using the judgment of May LJ in *Viasystems*, why dual vicarious liability had not been used previously and consider its merits.

! Don't be tempted to . . .

- Make a definitive statement of fact as to Brett's employment, as the facts are not definitively conclusive; do assert a reasoned opinion, though, as to whether he is likely to be an employee.

- Get into a full discussion as to the 'close-connection' test. You will need to reference this but remember the focus of the question is on the employee part of vicarious liability.

- Set out a full account of the tort of negligence, as the presence of the essential requirements are not an issue in the question. The issue is vicarious liability.

www.pearsoned.co.uk/lawexpressqa

 Go online to access more revision support including additional essay and problem questions with diagram plans, You be the marker questions, and download all diagrams from the book.

Employers' liability

How this topic may come up in exams

Although this is another offshoot of negligence, it is again a specific application covering injuries caused by the claimant's colleagues, equipment or the system of work imposed by the employer. Naturally, there is an overlap with vicarious liability but this area is distinctive in its own right. Problem questions are more common than essays but you should check carefully how this area is dealt with on your course in relation to vicarious liability and the extent that breach of statutory duty is covered alongside the common law duties.

Before you begin

It's a good idea to consider the following key themes of employers' liability before tackling a question on this topic.

Common law duty

- Were there competent staff employed?

- Were the workplace and associated tools and equipment reasonably safe?

- Was a safe system of work in operation?

- If no, was the breach the same as the cause of the injury?

Employer's liability

Are any defences applicable?

Statutory duty

- Does the statute expressly permit or exclude damages in tort?

- If silent, can the court construe the wording as giving a remedy in tort?

- Is the duty owed to the particular claimant?

- Was the statutory duty breached?

- Was the breach the cause of the injury suffered?

- Is the injury one which the statute intended to prevent occuring?

A printable version of this diagram plan is available from **www.pearsoned.co.uk/lawexpressqa**

❓ Question 1

Hobletts Building Services Ltd is a manufacturing company which produces tools for builders and other tradesmen. One morning Charlie was sawing wood on an electric saw, bought from a reputable firm, in a loud part of the factory; thinking he heard someone call him, he looked up. As he did this, the wood came away from the saw, which should have resulted in the machine stopping. Unbeknown to Charlie, the machine had an electrical fault which meant it did not do this. As Charlie went to resume his work his hand made contact with the saw causing a major laceration. The machine had recently passed a routine safety inspection by a licensed external individual, but it transpires the defect was too latent to be picked up in a basic check.

Awaz has worked for the company since he turned 16, three years ago, and is a very competent and skilled worker, with all of the necessary qualifications and top marks on a course for workplace safety. Awaz has always had a reputation, though, for conducting practical jokes around the factory. Whilst no one has ever suffered an injury, people have regularly complained to all levels of management, but Awaz has never been reprimanded for his behaviour. However, one day as Gina was showing a potential new customer around the factory, Awaz dropped a banana skin on the floor. Not seeing it as she walked, Gina slipped and twisted her knee in the fall.

Advise Wendy, the sole owner of company, as to her liability for these injuries.

Diagram plan

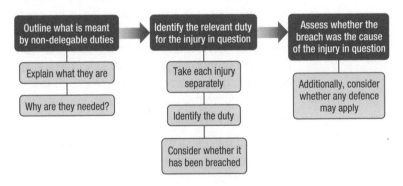

A printable version of this diagram plan is available from **www.pearsoned.co.uk/lawexpressqa**

Answer plan

→ Explain what the non-delegable duties are and why they exist.

→ Identify which duty is in issue with regards to Charlie's situation.

→ Assess whether this has been breached.

→ Consider the possibility of contributory negligence reducing any potential liability.

→ Repeat points two to four with regards to Gina's injury.

Answer

The issue to advise Wendy on is whether her company will be held liable in negligence even though not directly at fault for the injuries. This will involve considering the non-delegable duties an employer owes to all staff, which ensures that they cannot escape liability by insisting that responsibility for the duty of care in question had been delegated to another to discharge.[1] It is argued that the relevant duties of providing adequate equipment and competent staff[2] have been breached.

Wendy should be advised that a series of non-delegable duties were developed by the case of **Wilson and Clyde Coal Co. v English** [1938] AC 57. These include providing competent staff, adequate plant and equipment, a safe place of work, and a safe system of work, and apply to each employee personally (**Paris v Stepney BC** [1951] AC 367). These were required to reflect the socio-economic and technological developments of the industrial revolution and the increasing use of potentially dangerous machines in the workplace.[3] The historic absence of insurance meant the courts were reluctant to burden emerging businesses with civil liability claims. However, as insurance systems developed, and ultimately became compulsory (the Employer's Liability (Compulsory Insurance) Act 1969), in light of the increased dangers it became untenable for employers to simply claim they had delegated their duty to a competent member of staff whom they had hired with care.

The first issue to advise Wendy is that an employer has a duty to provide adequate machinery and equipment for their employees. This requires reasonable care to ensure that reasonably safe equipment is used and kept in reasonable condition. Wendy may argue that she has discharged this duty as best she could in relation to Charlie's injury. The machine was purchased from a reputable source and had recently been inspected by a licensed external person with no defects found. Under **Davie v New Merton Board Mills** [1959] AC 604 no liability would arise, as it seems that the latent nature of the defect meant there was no way of noticing the development of the fault.

[1] By discussing this in your introduction, you show that you have correctly identified what specific issue of tort the question is addressing and have not mistakenly read the question as one on vicarious liability.

[2] Identify what specific non-delegable duties are in issue. This, and the previous point, will help create a sense of anticipation in the marker that they are about to read an answer which is on the right track.

[3] What you want to do here is to show that you know the duties and understand why they are needed. This will allow you to explain to Wendy why the law may see it as justifiable that the company be held liable.

Therefore, even if Wendy, or someone that she is responsible for, did reasonably inspect the machine as well, the defect was unlikely to be discovered, especially as it went unnoticed during the external inspection. However, this position has been overturned by the Employer's Liability (Defective Equipment) Act 1969.

The statute provides in section 1 that any negligence is attributable to the employer, where they have provided equipment for the purpose for their business and a defect in the equipment causes injury to an employee operating the equipment in the course of their employment, where the defect is in fact the fault of a third party.[4] The section was designed to address the perceived imbalance resulting from *Davie* and make it easier for employees to obtain compensation, as otherwise their only route was a claim against the manufacturer, who may be out of business or, increasingly, based overseas.

Section 1 does not automatically impose liability on Wendy though.[5] It seems clear that the injury was caused by the defect, as if the saw had stopped as it should have, it would not have occurred. However, on the balance of probabilities the defect must still be due to the fault of the manufacturer. We are told there was an electrical fault in the machine, as opposed to an electrical fault in the factory, and therefore this suggests a manufacturing fault.[6] Naturally, this will need to be proved: and if it cannot, Wendy would avoid liability but if it can, as is more likely,[7] Wendy would be liable for Charlie's injury. Wendy may have a partial defence based on contributory negligence by Charlie which would reduce the amount of compensation owed. Charlie has not looked before continuing sawing, which would be unreasonable in the circumstances, especially if he has moved when looking up. Further, notwithstanding the background noise, the noise of this saw would arguably have still been noticeable. This would mean that under the Law Reform (Contributory Negligence) Act 1945 any compensation would be reduced to reflect Charlie's contribution to his injury. Whilst the courts have been reluctant to find contributory negligence against employee factory workers (*Caswell* v *Powell Duffryn Associated Collieries Ltd* [1940] AC 152) this was in relation to a breach of statutory duty, and at a time when contributory negligence was a full defence. As a common law duty is breached here, and the defence's harshness has eased, some reduction is quite likely.

---

[4] Clearly you need to learn this section; however, rather than learning it word for word, learn it in your own words. This will allow you to write the provisions more quickly while also demonstrating that you have understanding of the section as well as knowledge.

[5] As you are now moving into some specific application of the requirements under the section, put these in a separate paragraph in order to add some clarity to your answer and ensure the answer is easy to read.

[6] This is quite an important fact in the context of the question so make sure you utilise it to support your argument on this point.

[7] Remember you are advising Wendy of the company's potential liability; while you need to give the possibilities, she would expect an indication of what is the likeliest scenario, so offer one.

[8] This allows you to show not only that you have knowledge of vicarious liability but also that you have an understanding of the relationship of the two and when each is more applicable.

[9] As such you should just say this clearly and concisely. Do not go through the motions of showing that there are no issues on this point. Save your time for those points which are more in issue.

[10] This allows you to show that the defence has applied in the past and can still be used in some circumstances, but illustrate your understanding of the area by using the theory you discussed earlier to show why it would not succeed here.

[11] There is a slight difference here to the causation point above. There is nothing necessarily wrong in throwing a point out if only to immediately dismiss it. Here, at least, the point is arguable albeit weak. You are at least advising Wendy of the full range of possibilities, whilst advising her as to their strengths, and at the same time showing you fully understand the defence by recognising its limitations to this scenario.

The other duty which the company will be alleged to have breached is in not providing competent staff. Although we are told Awaz is skilled and competent in his work, the duty extends further than just employing people who are competent at doing the actual work. As such, it covers situations falling outside the 'course of their employment' requirement of vicarious liability.[8] This can be seen in **Hudson v Ridge Manufacturing Co.** [1957] 2 QB 348, where an employee with a history of conducting practical jokes tripped another up, causing injury. That is a similar situation to that of Awaz. Significantly though, in **Hudson** the employee had been reprimanded several times and the company was held liable for not exercising reasonable care to bring the jokes to an end, which is slightly different to Awaz. The fact he has never been reprimanded for his jokes could be because he has never previously caused injury, and could support an argument that Wendy has not breached the duty. It will depend on the nature of the previous jokes and the risk that they posed to his colleagues, as simple banter in the workplace is permissible.

From the facts there are clearly no causation issues.[9] Historically, the defence of *volenti* may have applied in that Gina assumed the risk of working alongside Awaz, but this defeats the modern thinking regarding employer's liability and thus would not succeed.[10] It could possibly be argued that Gina was contributorily negligent by not looking, but in the circumstances this will be hard to argue and is unlikely to succeed.[11]

To conclude, Wendy should be advised that duties are imposed on employers to ensure the safety of those carrying out work for them, and thus from whom they are benefiting. While not her fault, there is defective machinery in use in the factory, and so she would be liable for Charlie's injury, albeit with some reduction likely for contributory negligence. As regards Gina, by not preventing Awaz's practical jokes, Wendy may have failed to employ competent staff. This may rest on whether his other jokes have at least risked injury even if none materialised. If so, in line with **Hudson**, Wendy is likely to be liable.

✓ Make your answer stand out

- Draw on the opinion of Lord Sumption JSC in *Woodland* v *Swimming Teachers Association* [2013] UKSC 66 in order to consider in more detail the theoretical justification for imposing such duties on employers.
- Expand slightly more on the difference between liability under this area and vicarious liability. On this point see again Lord Sumption's opinion in *Woodland* and also Murphy, J. (2007) The juridical foundations of common law non-delegable duties in Neyers *et al.* (eds) *Emerging Issues in Tort Law*. Oxford: Hart Publishing.
- Highlight possible statutory duties which Wendy's company may be in breach of, and indicate that you are aware of that aspect of the area (but see below).
- Discuss how Wendy could seek a contribution from the manufacturer of the machine if her company is found liable in relation to Charlie, and also how in the future she could seek an indemnity clause from suppliers.

! Don't be tempted to . . .

- Turn the question into one on the standard negligence duty: it is specifically about the non-delegable duties that an employer has. So the focus needs to be on those duties which are relevant to each situation.
- Go into detail about the non-delegable duties which are not within the focus of the question, as you will merely be describing everything you know and not advising Wendy on the specific issues which she is faced with.
- Go into great depth on potential liability for breach of a statutory duty, as no statute is present in the question. You will have no grounding to base your discussion on, so again it will detract from the analysis of your answer. Just raise it briefly as a possibility but no more.

? Question 2

Fleetwood Mechanics Ltd is a garage providing mechanical repairs for all types of automobile. As such, they are subject to the (fictitious) Automotive Engineering (Protection of Workers) Act 2012, which was passed after a series of accidents involving mechanics. This provides in section 1 a list of safety equipment which must be supplied to mechanics and includes eye goggles. Section 2 also provides that all safety equipment supplied to any workers must comply with British safety standards and have an appropriate safety certificate. Section 3 simply states that a breach of sections 1 and/or 2 will result in a fine. Due to a parliamentary oversight, the Act, and the consequences of a breach, are not mentioned in any other legislation.

However, at the time the legislation was passed the garage was struggling financially so Otis, the company owner, chose not to purchase goggles with a British safety certificate as these were more expensive. Instead, he purchased some from another country with less rigorous safety standards. One day, Ray, wearing the goggles supplied by Otis, was working on an engine fitting a new mount; however, when taking out the old bolts, one became lodged in the mount. Ray managed to force it loose but in doing so it flew up striking him in the eye. As the goggles Otis had bought were not of sufficient safety strength, the bolt cracked the lens and blinded Ray.

Also that day, Dobie was working near the entrance of the garage sorting out a tyre delivery. However, the way he had stacked the tyres meant he had narrowed the entrance. Booker was driving a car into the garage for a service but the entrance was now too small and tight to enter so he hit the tyres which fell onto Dobie leaving him with broken ribs.

Advise Otis of his company's liability for the injuries to Ray and Dobie.

Diagram plan

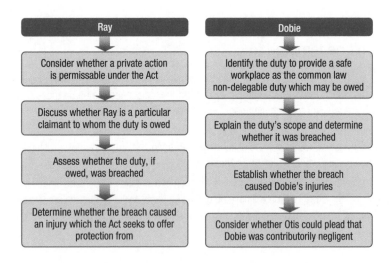

A printable version of this diagram plan is available from **www.pearsoned.co.uk/lawexpressqa**

Answer plan

→ Consider whether the Act may give rise to damages in tort.

→ Discuss how this statutory duty was breached and assess causation.

→ Evaluate whether Otis has also breached his non-delegable duty to Dobie regarding a safe place of work.

→ Determine whether Dobie has been contributorily negligent for his injuries.

Answer

[1] This indicates that you have identified the area of tort covered by the question.

[2] This shows that you have seen that both aspects apply and in relation to which injury.

[3] While the main point to discuss is the Health & Safety at Work etc. Act 1974, by referring to this legislation you show you are aware it is a recent change in the law.

[4] Make sure you use the facts you have been given to explore all possibilities rather than making assumptions based on the presence or absence of certain information.

[5] Structurally, it is always important to state and explain the general rule first and then explain how there may be exceptions to it. Then, as you go on to state the factors which create the exception, ensure that you apply them to the facts.

Although Otis was not the direct cause of both injuries, the issue which arises is whether he will still be liable as their employer[1] for breaching a statutory duty to Ray and a common law duty of care to Dobie.[2]

The first issue is whether a civil remedy is permitted. If so, it is simply a case of establishing whether the elements of negligence are satisfied. Alternatively, the Act may expressly exclude civil liability. Either way, we are not expressly told. Following the Enterprise and Regulatory Reform Act 2013[3] civil liability for breaches of health and safety duties provided by 'existing statutory provisions' will not arise unless expressly provided for in regulations under the Health & Safety at Work etc Act 1974, section 47(2A). As there does not appear to be any such regulations providing for civil liability Otis is seemingly without redress. However, the absence of the 2012 Act from any other legislation means it would not feature in the list of 'existing statutory provisions', contained in Schedule 1 of the 1974 Act, meaning the 2012 Act is outside the scope of section 47(2A) and civil liability may be possible.[4] However, Otis should be advised that there is still no general notion that civil liability arises (***Lonrho Ltd v Shell Petroleum Co. Ltd (No. 2)*** [1982] AC 173). Instead the courts exercise their discretion in interpreting the Act to determine the matter.

Lonrho held that if the Act provides for penalties, this should generally be construed as not conferring a right. However, Lonrho identified exceptions to this general proposition,[5] one being where the Act was passed to protect a particular class. We are told that the Act's purpose was to protect mechanics after a series of accidents, therefore the exception appears applicable. ***X v Bedfordshire County Council*** [1995] 2 AC 633 supports this; although it also stated that Parliament must additionally have intended to grant a private right of action on members of the protected class. Where the Act is deemed to have 'social welfare', the intention to create a private right will not exist (***Phelps v Hillingdon LBC*** [2001] 2 AC 619). In relation to this Act, while it is aimed at the welfare of mechanics this is a far narrower class than society at large, as in ***Phelps***. Arguably, it is unjust if an Act aiming to prevent injury to a class did not allow injured class members to seek a civil remedy.

6 This naturally follows on from the preceding sentence, but deal with this aspect in a new paragraph to enhance the clarity of the arguments. Simply use a sentence such as the preceding one to create a flow from one paragraph into the next.

7 Don't dwell on this point as it is not of primary relevance, but provide an example to illustrate your point.

8 Be careful not to sound repetitive. You are just building on the general point that you made earlier. You could alternatively deal with this point at the time of first raising the general proposition.

9 While this aspect of the question is the subsidiary issue, do not miss the opportunity to earn more marks by providing some evaluation and showing an insight into the depth of your knowledge.

One reason why the Act may do this is if it expressly provides for an alternative remedy, or a better alternative exists elsewhere.[6] The latter could be where the duty is placed on local authorities whereby the claimant would have recourse to administrative law remedies.[7] This is not the case for Otis, and the more significant issue is the fact that section 3 states that a breach will result in a fine. This shows a remedy is within the Act; however, as *Lonrho* states, if the Act is specifically for the protection of a class, a civil action may still arise.[8] A fine is unlikely to go to the injured mechanics unless it goes to a central fund akin to the Motor Insurance Bureau to pay victims. If this is not the case, then the mere imposition of a fine would not mean it is inappropriate to give rise to a civil action, and indeed where the situation relates to workplace safety a more generous approach is adopted (*Ziemniak* v *ETPM Deep Sea Ltd* [2003] EWCA Civ 636). Notwithstanding these considerations, the process has been criticised for ultimately coming down to the courts making a policy decision on the merits of the case. However, there would not seem to be any policy reasons for denying a claim and, on balance, it is likely that the duty would give rise to a civil action.

If the matter is actionable in tort, several other requirements must be satisfied. However, it is clear that Ray is certainly, as a mechanic, owed the duty; and that this was breached, as we are told that Otis bought cheap goggles that were not compliant with British safety standards. Causation appears satisfied as we are told that the bolt cracked the goggles because they were of insufficient strength. On the basis that a British standard pair would not have cracked, it is clear that 'but for' failing to supply the right goggles, as the duty requires, the injury would have been avoided. Finally, as the Act specifically mentions supplying goggles, it is clear that eye damage was an injury which the Act sought to protect mechanics from. Otis should be advised that he will not have a defence as even if the Act is not construed as strict liability, Ray cannot be said to have assumed the risk or contributed to the injury in any way himself as he was wearing what was supplied.

In relation to Dobie; while the Act does not deal with his situation, Otis should be advised that as an employer he also has a series of non-delegable, personal duties towards each of his employees (*Paris* v *Stepney BC* [1951] AC 367). These are non-delegable in the sense that responsibility for discharging the duty owed cannot be delegated to someone else.[9] They ensure that the claimant is able to prove an action against someone and thus receive compensation (which is also aided by compulsory insurance under the Employer's Liability (Defective Equipment) Act 1969). The duties were set out in **_Wilson and Clyde Coal Co._ v _English_** [1938] AC 57 and are to reasonably ensure competent staff, adequate plant and equipment, a safe place of work and a safe system of work.

[10] As previously, create a flow between the paragraphs: separate out this aspect of your question into one paragraph on the nature of the duty and a second on the application of the duty to facts.

The relevant duty here[10] is the provision of a safe workplace, as Dobie was injured after the entrance to the garage was narrowed by the tyre wall. The duty requires the employer takes reasonable care to create a safe environment, and this extends to entrances[11] (**_Ashdown_ v _Samuel Williams & Sons Ltd_** [1957] 1 QB 409). From the facts, Booker crashed through the tyres because the entrance was narrowed, which suggests a breach. It is apparent that if the duty was breached it did cause the injury, as the falling tyres broke Dobie's ribs as they hit him. While seeming harsh as the danger was created by Dobie himself, the Law Reform (Contributory Negligence) Act 1945 means a reduction in Dobie's compensation may be possible to reflect any contributory negligence on Dobie's part. By stacking the tyres in the entrance so as to restrict it and then continuing to work behind the stack, Dobie has indeed been negligent.

[11] On these facts this is highly relevant, so make sure you explain the scope of the duty's application.

[12] As you will have already concluded each injury as you dealt with it, you just need a short overall conclusion here to round off your answer.

Therefore, in conclusion, Otis should be advised that he is likely to be found liable for both injuries as he breached his duties owed, although the compensation payable to Dobie could be reduced.[12]

✓ Make your answer stand out

- Consider, briefly, the wider implications and merit of the changes to section 47 of the Health & Safety etc. at Work Act 1974.

- Consider whether the injury to Ray may also be a breach of the common law duty to provide reasonably safe equipment and/or a safe system of work, particularly if you feel the injury may not be actionable in tort under the Act.

- Discuss in a bit more depth why Ray could not be said to have voluntarily assumed the risk of injury.

- Give some explanatory comment as to the policy behind the non-delegable duties in order to justify Otis being found liable for Dobie's injury, notwithstanding the probable application of the contributory negligence defence.

- Include a bit more on the difference between liability under this area and vicarious liability.

Don't be tempted to . . .

- Turn the question into one on standard negligence, or vicarious liability: it is specifically about employer's liability for breach of statutory duty and one specific non-delegable duty.

- Go into detail about the non-delegable duties which are not within the focus of the question, as this will just make your answer come across as a description of everything you know and you are not advising Otis on the specific issues.

Question 3

'The statutory right has its origin in the statute, but the particular remedy of an action for damages is given by the common law in order to make effective, for the benefit of the injured plaintiff, his right to the performance by the defendant of the defendant's statutory duty. It is an effective sanction.' (*Per* Lord Upson in *London Passenger Transport Board* v *Upson* [1949] AC 155, 168)

Discuss the approach taken by the courts to determine when a tortious remedy will be permitted to redress a breach of a statutory duty when the statute itself does not expressly provide for one.

Diagram plan

A printable version of this diagram plan is available from **www.pearsoned.co.uk/lawexpressqa**

Answer plan

→ Outline the leading case of *Lonrho Ltd* explaining its importance.

→ Discuss the general rule from the case.

→ Analyse the exceptions that exist to the general rule.

→ Comment on the merits of the current position.

Answer

The issue to analyse is the manner in which the courts will determine when someone will be burdened with tortious liability towards another private individual when they have breached a statutory duty. This involves exploring the rules of statutory interpretation used by the courts as the approach taken in interpreting a statute and the factors the court considers when doing so is vital to any outcome.[1] These rules are important because quite often statutes are not clear on the matter and do not expressly provide for a common law remedy. However, as Lord Upjohn suggests, it is common law damages which provide the most effective sanction for a claimant injured by a breach of a statutory duty. While the courts have consistently held this to be a matter of construction, it is argued that the actual decision in each case is, in fact, influenced by policy considerations.

The leading case which sets out the framework of how the courts will approach this issue is ***Lonrho Ltd v Shell Petroleum Co. Ltd (No. 2)*** [1982] AC 173. The case concerned losses suffered by Lonrho arising from compliance with a sanctions regime created by the Southern Rhodesia Act 1965. The subsequent legislative orders made it a criminal offence to supply oil to Rhodesia and outlined the punishment for non-compliance.[2] However, as Lonrho's competitors did not comply with the order, Lonrho lost out financially. The question was whether, in the absence of an express provision of a civil remedy, the legislation could be construed as providing one.[3] Lord Diplock, giving the opinion for the House, noted it had been held since ***Cutler v Wandsworth Stadium Ltd*** [1949] AC 398 that the matter was one of construction of the legislation. His Lordship then proceeded to set out the process for undertaking such construction.

The starting point is always what the legislation states; however, the problem is that Parliament regularly fails to expressly cover the issue when drafting legislation. Consequently, the courts have developed a general rule whereby if the Act creates an obligation and specifies how it will be enforced, the obligation cannot be enforced in any other way. Therefore, where criminal sanctions are provided in the legislation, a tortious sanction cannot also be applied to enforce the duty. The rationale for this is that Parliament has clearly considered the issue of enforcement and remedies for a breach and, while not

[1] By setting out the specific issue in full here; not only do you immediately show your marker that you understand the question, you also save having to repeat it again, such as in paragraph 2, and can simply refer to 'the issue' or 'this issue'.

[2] Include this point in your outline of the facts, as the presence of the criminal sanctions was a factor which influenced the court's decision. Mentioning it now will tie in with your discussion of this factor later.

[3] Do not go into the exact details of the case. Remember: your aim here is just to set out the fact that this is the leading case and introduce the starting point for the court's approach.

[4] It is important to explain the reasoning behind this. Use this reasoning as the basis of your analysis as to whether it is right for the courts to deny a party the chance of obtaining compensation.

[5] Include a discussion of this, as not all statutes will provide for criminal sanctions and so it is a different factor within the debate. This also allows you to get into the treatment of public authorities and discuss whether they should be protected from tort actions because of the possibility of administrative law remedies.

[6] Don't be afraid to demonstrate your knowledge of other branches of law when there is link to the area being discussed, provided you keep it to the context of the discussion you are having. This will show that you have a broader level of knowledge of the issue and the arguments.

[7] Using an example at this point demonstrates your knowledge of that case but also strengthens your explanation of how the exception operates and what is required for it.

[8] By stating that the previous material applies here, you will not need to repeat that part of your answer. The marker will already have read your points on the matter. This allows you to then focus on additional points which relate directly to this exception.

expressly ruling out a tortious action, has expressly opted for another form of enforcement.[4] The same is also true where a breach of the statutory duty will give rise to remedies in administrative law.[5] For example, where the duty under the legislation is placed on a public authority, an action in judicial review will exist. The courts have preferred this action rather than subjecting the public authority to a tortious action which would reduce the funds available for the operation of that authority; at the very least operational costs will rise through insurance premiums to cover any potential actions against it in tort. This threat of litigation can stifle the operational performance of the authority and so is considered against public policy. However, this approach perhaps needs reconsidering in light of the restrictions now placed on judicial review applications.[6]

However, *Lonrho* provided for two exceptions to the general position. The first is where the statute is passed to protect a specified limited class, as opposed to the public generally. In determining this, it is important to consider the purpose of the statute as just because a specified class is referred to, it does not automatically follow protecting them was Parliament's intention. *Cutler* is a good example:[7] the Betting and Lotteries Act 1934 provided that bookmakers must be given space at dog tracks. However, it was held that the purpose of the Act was not to protect the livelihood of bookmakers, but simply to regulate proceedings at dog tracks. Therefore, as explained in *X v Bedfordshire County Council* [1995] 2 AC 633, for the exception to apply it must be shown that the statute imposed a duty on someone for the protection of limited class and that Parliament intended to give members of that class a tort action for a breach of the duty.

The second exception is where the statute creates a right to be enjoyed by the general public. While seemingly contrary to the first exception, it is the essential that one of the public then suffers 'particular, direct and substantial' damage (*per* Brett J in *Benjamin v Storr* (1874) LR 9 CP 400), which is different from the public generally. However, where these are welfare statutes implementing social policy, the duty is naturally going to be placed on a public authority. This brings into play the considerations discussed above regarding whether another branch of the law already provides a more suitable remedy, such as administrative law.[8] The right conferred under the duty is part of a wider public policy and not simply a private matter between the authority and the individual, and this is why there is a strong requirement to show damage beyond that suffered by others before the individual tortious right will arise. In ***O'Rourke* v *Camden LBC*** [1998] AC 188, Lord Hoffmann also noted that the wide discretion given to authorities under such social welfare legislation means that Parliament would have been aware there could be errors of judgment and thus unlikely to see these lead to tortious liability.

[9] It is beneficial to highlight this, particularly if you are adopting the argument that this answer does. If you have time before you start your conclusion, you could use this point as the basis of a penultimate paragraph and explore the positive impact that policy can have in more detail.

Therefore, while there is a clear general rule, uncertainty is created by the presence of exceptions. This uncertainty arises because there is no set formula as to when a case will be deemed to be within an exception and the heavy influence of public policy factors. This is why the likes of Williams (1960) dismissed the process undertaken as a fiction of looking for something which is not there. While this has helped employees in industrial situations, it could be said to have been unfair on the employer by increasing costs and creating an artificial liability.[9] Parliament has responded with section 69 of the Enterprise and Regulatory Reform Act 2013 which removes all civil liability for breaches of all health and safety duties. Regardless of the particular merits of that decision, the approach is in line with reform proposals by the Law Commission; namely that a presumption of a civil right will exist unless the contrary is clearly expressed in the statute. This is a better overall approach.[10] Parliament would at least be required to fully contemplate the implications of any proposed statutory duty, following a debate as to the merits of permitting civil liability, and clearly decide what the consequences of a breach should be. This would create certainty and reduce the financial burdens of litigation and insurance, particularly in light of the growing number of regulatory statutes which create duties on parties.

[10] Obviously, if you are criticising how something works, you should offer an opinion on how it can be rectified. This is particularly important if there are published proposals for reform, as otherwise it may indicate your lack of knowledge.

✓ Make your answer stand out

- Read academic articles such as that by Williams, G. (1960) The effect of penal legislation in the law of tort. *Modern Law Review*, 23: 233 to obtain some depth as to the criticisms of the current process.
- Look at Law Commission (1969) Report No. 21, The interpretation of statutes, to be able to provide a fuller explanation of what the Commission proposed and contrast them with the counter arguments by Buckley, R. A. (1984) Liability in tort for breach of statutory duty, *Law Quarterly Review*, 100: 204.

Make your answer stand out

■ Explore further how policy can be seen as the basis for finding a civil action and whether this is fair. Consider where the abolition of civil liability for breaches of health and safety statutory duties by section 69 of the Enterprise and Regulatory Reform Act 2013 leaves the scope of this tort.

❗ Don't be tempted to . . .

■ Spend too long on the facts of *Lonrho*, you just need to set up the issue you are discussing.

■ Similarly, when considering the impact of the new parliamentary approach to civil liability for breaches of health and safety duties, do not get tied down in a detailed examination of the merits of that decision. Stick to the overall approach that the courts should adopt if Parliament's intention is unclear.

■ List a series of case examples where a tort action was found to exist or not. Focus on the rules for dealing with the issue and what factors are considered. Just draw on case examples where necessary to support your argument. An excessive amount of fact from cases will have a negative impact on your structure.

■ Go into detail regarding what else the court must consider after determining whether the Act in question permits a civil action in tort. The question is focused on the issue of construction of the statutory wording.

www.pearsoned.co.uk/lawexpressqa

 Go online to access more revision support including additional essay and problem questions with diagram plans, You be the marker questions, and download all diagrams from the book.

Occupiers' liability

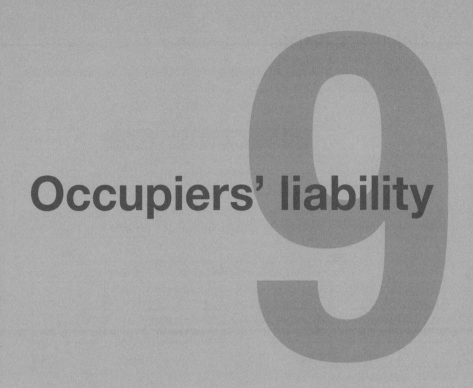

How this topic may come up in exams

This topic is an extension of the tort of negligence. However, it has its own self-contained statutory framework governing when a duty will arise, and so you need to be careful to recognise whether a problem question is concerned with normal negligence or occupiers' liability. In the question, look for premises which are controlled by one of the parties. Although the situations when the duty of care arises differ, some aspects are the same, notably causation and remoteness. The Acts do not have many sections, but what is needed is located in specific subsections so ensure you know these. Problem questions are more common than essays. However, when the question is an essay, it tends to focus on whether the legislation is necessary and/or whether it achieves the right balance between the parties in terms of burden and protection.

Before you begin

It's a good idea to consider the following key themes of occupiers' liability before tackling a question on this topic.

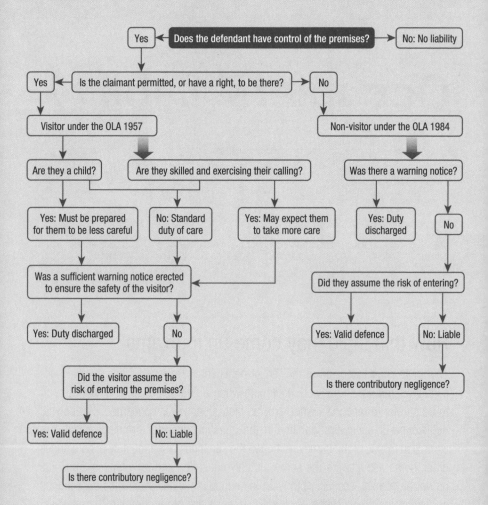

A printable version of this diagram plan is available from **www.pearsoned.co.uk/lawexpressqa**

? **Question 1**

Hubert has gone to his council-owned local park with his seven-year-old brother, Cornelius. One of the main attractions of the park is an outdoor swimming pool at its centre.

Owing to the hot weather, and the fact that it is quiet, Hubert decides to have a swim; as children are not allowed in the pool, he tells Cornelius to wait where he is while he does so. However, after five minutes, Cornelius becomes bored and, noticing a newly installed playground, goes off to play on the slide.

Owing to financial restraints, the council had to build the slide cheaply. They employed the firm who tendered the lowest amount – Cowboy Construction Ltd. Because of the financial restraints, the council did not check to see the quality of their previous work and took at face value their claim that they had in fact undertaken such a project. Cowboy Construction Ltd had actually never built children's playgrounds and so made up what they were doing as they went along. This meant the slide was very unstable, which an adult would have appreciated. When Cornelius reached the top, the extra weight sent the slide crashing down, resulting in Cornelius suffering a broken leg.

Advise the council as to their potential liability under the occupiers' liability legislation.

Diagram plan

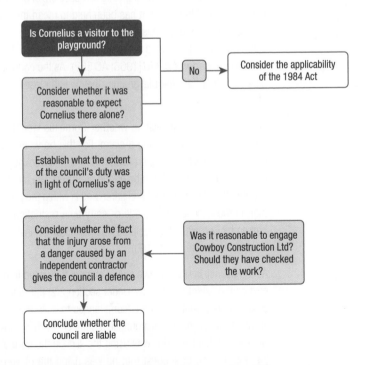

A printable version of this diagram plan is available from **www.pearsoned.co.uk/lawexpressqa**

Answer plan

→ Identify the status of Cornelius and which Act applies to him.

→ State what the extent of the duty of care is under the Act.

→ Consider whether this is modified owing to Cornelius's age.

→ Evaluate the significance of the danger being created by an independent contractor.

→ Consider if the council may have any other defences to Cornelius's claim.

Answer

[1] Do not wait to show that you have identified which Act is most relevant to the facts.

[2] Show early on that you appreciate the purpose and the scope of the Act and use this to provide the context to the issue which you have identified.

[3] Similarly, show that you know what the key issues in the Act are in relation to the question.

[4] While this may seem an obvious point, it is important that you advise the council on it and establish that they will be the occupier for the purposes of any claim. By doing so you also show that you have knowledge of the point.

The council requires advice as to the applicability of the Occupiers' Liability Act 1957[1] to the current situation. The applicability of the Act is important as it imposes liability for controllers of premises towards those who are injured while on those premises, and provides for greater care towards children.[2] It will be argued that the council will have owed Cornelius a duty of care and that they are unlikely to be able to rely on the work of the contractors[3] to discharge this duty.

Liability under the Act is only imposed on occupiers of premises. While not defined within the Act, it has been held to mean the person who has such control of premises that they should realise that want of care on their part may lead to injury to those coming to the premises (*Wheat v E Lacon Co. Ltd* [1966] AC 552). As the council owns the park, and therefore the playground, they would clearly have control of the premises.[4]

The first issue to establish is whether Cornelius would be owed a duty under the Act, creating a claim. For this he would need to be classed as a 'visitor' to the premises. This term covers anyone who is permitted by the occupier to be on the premises. The fact that we are told that the playground is for children and is within the park suggests that, in the absence of any age or entry time restrictions which are broken by Cornelius, he would be deemed to be an invitee and thus a visitor under the Act (s. 1(2)).

As the council is likely to owe a duty of care, they need to be advised next on the extent of that duty. Under section 2(2) this is to take such care as is reasonable in the circumstances to ensure that Cornelius is safe while using the playground in a manner which is permitted. As we are told that Cornelius was using the slide in the normal manner, there is nothing to suggest that he was using the playground in a

[5] It is important that you illustrate this; otherwise, your argument is unsubstantiated on what could be a key point in assessing the council's liability.

way which would take him outside of his permission for being there.[5] Therefore, as the slide was unsafe for normal usage, it is clear that the council have breached their duty to ensure Cornelius's safety while using the playground.

The council might argue that the danger of the slide would have been noticeable to an adult and that Cornelius should not have been there alone. However, two points can be raised against this assertion. First, following ***Phipps v Rochester Corp*** [1955] 1 QB 450, in such a situation it must be determined whether the council could reasonably have expected Cornelius's unaccompanied presence. More information is needed here and evidence will need to be gathered as to the extent that children did use the playground unaccompanied.[6] If this was the case, the council would need to demonstrate that they took steps to prevent it from occurring. However, displaying notices saying that children must be accompanied at all times may not suffice, as the playground could be deemed an allurement[7] to children. This would mean that Cornelius would remain a visitor and thus owed a duty through implied permission (***Jolley v Sutton LBC*** [2000] 1 WLR 1082), even if certain entry requirements were displayed but not complied with. This is because the issue must be viewed in light of section 2(3)(a) which provides that the council must be prepared for children to be less careful than adults. This would relate to not only spotting dangers but also appreciating any warnings. Therefore, they should expect Cornelius, as a seven-year-old,[8] not to have noticed that which an adult would. In view of Cornelius's age and the nature of the premises in question, it would seem likely that the council not only owed a duty, but breached it, particularly if there were no entry restrictions. In light of the playground being new, guardians are less likely to anticipate any danger as it would be reasonable to expect it would be safe before opening it to children.

[6] Where the facts are too vague to give a more concrete answer as here, discuss both possibilities and if need be tell them that more information is needed. Remember they are your client, so this would be a valid comment rather than giving them an inaccurate picture. You should give them some idea, though.

[7] You could discuss this above when you discuss whether Cornelius is a visitor. If you do, then take care to ensure that you do not repeat yourself.

[8] You have been given Cornelius's age in the facts for a reason, so use them to build up the strength of your argument.

[9] Show your understanding of the subsection by paraphrasing the wording, and then to aid your structure break it down into the individual components and apply them to the council in turn.

However, the council should be advised that they may have a defence of having discharged their duty because the injury resulted from a danger caused by an independent contractor. Under section 2(4) the occupier is not to be treated as answerable, without more on their part, for a danger where it is caused by the faulty construction work of an independent contractor and it was reasonable in the circumstances to use the contractor.[9] The council should be advised that where the work, here the construction of the playground, requires special skill and equipment which they do not possess, then it will be reasonable to engage the contractor (**Maguire v Sefton MBC** [2006] EWCA Civ 560). This would seem applicable to the situation here; however, the council should be advised that the subsection goes on to state that the occupier may also have to have taken reasonable steps to ensure that the contractor was competent for the task, and the work was properly done. This would be a reasonable step here, as it would be clear that failure to check the quality of the work would pose a danger to users of the playground. As we are told that an adult would notice the slide was dangerous and yet the playground was open, it is clear the work was not checked upon completion by the council. This, when combined with the fact that, although the council inquired as to their competency, they did not verify the information, would suggest that the council will probably be held to have not discharged their duty.

In conclusion, the council will have owed Cornelius a duty of care, and their failure to check the competency of Cowboy Construction Ltd and the quality of the work upon completion will result in them being in breach of that duty. There do not appear to be any issues of causation or remoteness[10] and, therefore, the council should be advised that they will be liable for Cornelius's injury. They should be further advised that even if Cornelius was not deemed to be a visitor under the 1957 Act, they could well be liable under the Occupiers' Liability Act 1984 as a non-visitor.[11] The slide was in a dangerous state and they arguably had reasonable grounds to know this, as it had been constructed by a firm whose work had not been checked. There would also be reasonable grounds to believe that unaccompanied children might go on the slide and, owing to the nature of the danger, it was a risk which was reasonable for them to protect against.

[10] As this is still an aspect of negligence, do not forget to touch on these issues.

[11] Depending on how long you have left, you could include this within your main body and expand upon it.

✓ Make your answer stand out

- Highlight the possibility of a claim against the council in common law negligence.
- Explain why children are afforded more protection, using some of the judicial comment in *Phipps*.
- Use the facts of the question as much as possible to build and support your argument.
- Use academic opinion from your reading as well to support your interpretation of the facts, particularly where you do not have a case authority, such as with regard to the need for the council to check the work of Cowboy Construction Ltd.

! Don't be tempted to . . .

■ Discuss section 2(3)(b) and the issue of the duty owed to skilled workers; it is not relevant to the specific issue of the question and you would just be indicating that you have not fully understood the question.

■ Alternate between the Occupiers' Liability Acts. If you think that the 1984 Act may be applicable, or want to discuss it for completeness, do so at the end once you have advised the council fully on the 1957 Act, or you will lose your structure.

? Question 2

Noel is a saxophone player who has a licence to practise in the hall of the pub which his friend Paul owns and runs. Recently Noel has had his 10-year-old brother, Liam, stay with him and so he had to bring Liam with him one night. The entrance to the pub has a large notice stating that no children are allowed inside due to renovation work, although they are usually allowed in. Noel saw the sign and thought that it would be alright as it would be quiet and he would keep an eye on Liam. As they entered, Noel said hello to Paul, who greeted Noel in return, but, not having seen Liam as he was busy, said nothing about his presence.

During Noel's practice, the fire alarm sounded and Paul shouted for everyone to leave immediately. Noel quickly got his things together before heading for the exit at the end of the corridor. However, Paul, who had been carrying out some refurbishment work in the corridor when the alarm went off, had left some tools on the corridor floor. Noel did not notice and slipped on a screwdriver, severely injuring his back to the extent that he could not get up. As the alarm was still going off, Liam panicked and ran for the door to get help, but Paul had locked it to stop people going back inside until it was time. Remembering a fire exit in the hall, Liam ran to that exit, but as he got to the door fell through some rotten floorboards and ruptured his ankle ligaments.

Advise Paul about the two injuries.

Diagram plan

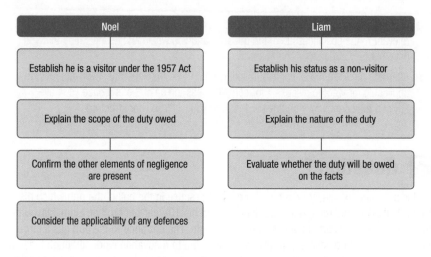

Noel
Establish he is a visitor under the 1957 Act
Explain the scope of the duty owed
Confirm the other elements of negligence are present
Consider the applicability of any defences

Liam
Establish his status as a non-visitor
Explain the nature of the duty
Evaluate whether the duty will be owed on the facts

A printable version of this diagram plan is available from **www.pearsoned.co.uk/lawexpressqa**

Answer plan

→ Take Noel first, and establish whether he is a visitor under the 1957 Act.

→ Explain the extent of the duty under the Act.

→ Assess Paul's liability and the applicability of any defences.

→ Highlight how Liam is a non-visitor under the 1984 Act.

→ Consider the scope of the Act and whether Paul will owe Liam a duty under it.

Answer

[1] Abbreviate the name of the statutes to save yourself time, but make sure you shorten them to something which still distinguishes the two Acts.

[2] This sentence indicates to your examiner that you have identified the specific area of tort which the question is concerned with straight away, particularly as the question does not highlight this for you.

The issue to be determined is whether Paul will be liable to Noel and Liam for the injuries that they have suffered while on his premises. He will need advice as to potential claims under both the Occupiers' Liability Act 1957 (the 1957 Act)[1] regarding lawful visitors to premises, and the Occupiers' Liability Act 1984 (the 1984 Act) which governs injuries to non-visitors.[2] Which Act applies is important, as the law provides far greater protection for visitors. It will be argued that, despite being told to leave, Noel is still likely to have been owed a duty as a visitor and be successful in a claim, whilst Liam will be a non-visitor and is less likely to be successful.

First, it should be established that Paul will face any action as the occupier of the premises. Whilst 'occupier' is not defined in either statute, it was stated in **Wheat v E Lacon Co. Ltd** [1966] AC 552 that occupiers are those with such control over the premises that they should realise that want of care on their part may lead to injury to those coming to the premises; as the owner of the pub, Paul would have such control.[3]

[3] Make sure that you use the facts of the question to illustrate, and support, your argument as to the position of the parties.

In advising Paul about Noel's injuries first, it must be confirmed whether Noel was a 'visitor' for the purposes of the 1957 Act. This term is also not defined in the Act; however, section 1(2) does provide that it covers the common law terms of 'invitee' and 'licensee'. Therefore, anyone who is lawfully on the premises will be a visitor. As Paul had given Noel permission to use the hall, Noel will satisfy the definition of a visitor. This is significant for Paul as any duty owed under the 1957 Act is more rigorous and increases his chances of being liable for Noel's injuries.[4]

[4] When you have reached a definite position such as this, make sure you explain what the significance of that position is. This will show that you have fully understood the legal principles and the consequences of them, rather than just luckily applying some law that you have learned, and reached the right answer.

The extent of the duty Paul will owe to Noel as Paul's visitor is provided by section 2(2),[5] and it is to ensure that he takes such care in all the circumstances so that Noel is safe while using the premises for the purposes for which he is allowed. Significantly, this indicates that the duty only extends to ensuring safety during permitted activities. However, Noel suffered his injury after having remained on the premises after he had been told to leave because of the fire alarm. Therefore, Noel was not technically permitted to be there at that time. However, Paul should be advised that people are given a reasonable time to vacate premises after having their permission withdrawn (**Cornish v Stubbs** (1870) LR 5 CP 334). As this was a fire alarm, Noel should have left straight away, but depending on exactly how long he took, if the timeframe was deemed reasonable, a duty under the 1957 Act will be owed. Further, the facts suggest that Paul breached his duty by leaving obstacles on the corridor floor which then clearly caused the injury.[6]

[5] While you should always give your authority for statements of law, it is particularly important in a statute-based tort that you constantly refer to which part of the Act deals with the point in question in order to demonstrate your knowledge and give strength to your answer.

[6] Remember that while the main focus of the question is whether a duty is owed under the Act, to be liable all of the other aspects of negligence need to be satisfied. Therefore, briefly highlight their presence on the facts by using the language of the elements to complete your account of what has happened.

The fact that the alarm was going off may negate any argument that Noel was negligent himself when leaving in not having seen any hazards. We are not told of any warning signs either, other than the notice saying children were not permitted due to the renovation work. Paul should be advised that, under the 1957 Act, to discharge a duty a notice must specify the danger and be sufficient to keep the visitor reasonably safe (s. 2(5)). It is unlikely that any sign would be so worded as to keep a visitor reasonably safe from trip hazards of the kind which Noel suffered, especially as this is the main walkway. Further, Paul should be advised that the notice is to be judged in all circumstances. As there was a fire alarm going off, this may count against the sufficiency of any notice, as naturally Noel was looking to just vacate the premises as soon as possible.[7] Arguably, the duty would be heightened as it was incumbent upon Paul to ensure that people could leave safely. It would also probably rule out any other defence from the Act, such as voluntary assumption of risk, applying against Noel as he was naturally trying to leave the building as requested.

Regarding Liam, it is clear that as children were not permitted due to the renovation work his situation can only fall within the 1984 Act, so he will be assessed as a non-visitor. Although nothing was said when Liam entered, any argument based on an implied licence will fail as Paul had not noticed him enter.[8] Paul should note that the 1984 Act provides that a duty will be owed to non-visitors for the risk of injury by way of the dangerous state of the premises or by things done on them or omitted to be done (s. 1(1)). The danger here was the broken floorboards by the fire exit.

Paul should be advised that, for him to owe a duty under section 1(3) of the 1984 Act, he would need to be aware[9] of the state of the floorboards, which as the owner he must be, as the area by a fire exit is open and therefore noticeable. Paul would also be the person responsible for checking that the premises, including fire exits, are secure. Further, their location also means it is a danger from which it is reasonable to expect Paul to offer protection as it will be how people try to leave in an emergency.[10] However, the duty is determined by the reference to the likely presence of the actual non-visitor in the vicinity of the danger at the time and place of the danger to him (***Ratcliffe v McConnell*** [1999] 1 WLR 670). Therefore it will be difficult for Liam to establish that Paul had reasonable grounds to know that Liam was in the vicinity at that time. As children were not permitted and he did not see Liam enter the pub with Noel, who he would know would be in the vicinity of the danger, it is hard to see how Paul would have known that a child would be in the vicinity at the time Liam was injured. As such, it is unlikely that Liam satisfies the requirements to be owed a duty in this case.

[7] As this indicates you are not dealing with a normal situation, use this to evaluate the factual situation in a bit more depth rather than just quickly reaching a conclusion on the issue.

[8] From the facts we are told that Paul did not see Liam, so use this to support how there is no chance of Liam being able to argue that he was a visitor.

[9] Although paragraph (a) and paragraph (b) within the subsection discuss reasonable belief as an alternative to actually knowing, as the latter is actually the case in the scenario, do not feel the need to explain the full extent of the paragraph.

[10] While this is paragraph (c) of section 1(3) state it first as it is more likely to be satisfied than paragraph (b). This will give your answer a more logical structure as you will not be discussing an uncertain element which is more likely to be unsatisfied, and then going on to the next requirement and saying how that one is satisfied.

In conclusion, Paul should be advised that Noel is likely to have a successful claim under the 1957 Act as he left hazards in the main walkway from the hall to the exit and knew that Noel would be using that route. Paul may have more success against any claim by Liam, as he would not have had grounds to believe Liam was on the premises, and so not owed him a duty of care.

 Make your answer stand out

- Highlight how, even if unsuccessful under the occupiers' liability legislation, the pair may still have a claim against Paul in common law negligence, especially Liam.
- Consider the 1984 Act in relation to Noel if you conclude that his claim under the 1957 Act may be unsuccessful.
- Provide some context to the 1984 Act and some depth as to how it differs from the 1957 Act.
- Explore the extent of the duty that would be owed by Paul if Liam does satisfy section 1(3) of the 1984 Act, and use *Donoghue* v *Folkestone Properties Ltd* [2003] EWCA Civ 231 to explain the relationship between section 1(3) and (4) of the 1984 Act.

! Don't be tempted to . . .

- Go into depth on the common law definitions of the terms, as they are not really issues in the question.
- Show your full range of knowledge by being too descriptive about both Acts and outlining provisions which are not relevant to the issues.

Question 3

'The law with regard to occupiers' liability to persons coming on to their land was then so unsatisfactory that Parliament found it necessary to pass for England and Wales the Occupiers' Liability Act 1957.' (*Per* Lord Reid in *British Railways Board* v *Herrington* [1972] AC 877, 897)

Critically evaluate the need for, and extent of, statutory law reform in this area of law in order to adequately protect people entering premises occupied by another.

Diagram plan

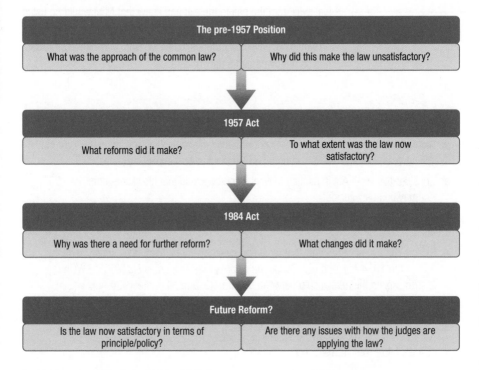

The pre-1957 Position

| What was the approach of the common law? | Why did this make the law unsatisfactory? |

1957 Act

| What reforms did it make? | To what extent was the law now satisfactory? |

1984 Act

| Why was there a need for further reform? | What changes did it make? |

Future Reform?

| Is the law now satisfactory in terms of principle/policy? | Are there any issues with how the judges are applying the law? |

A printable version of this diagram plan is available from **www.pearsoned.co.uk/lawexpressqa**

Answer plan

→ Outline the state of the law prior to the enactment of the Occupiers' Liability Act 1957.

→ Discuss the purpose and scope of that legislation, evaluating its provisions and how they are applied by the courts.

→ Analyse what gaps were left by the 1957 Act and therefore why further legislation was needed in 1984.

→ Evaluate the provision of the 1984 Act and the extent that it solved any remaining issues left by the 1957 Act.

→ Conclude with an assessment of the level of protection provided and whether further reform is needed.

Answer

[1] It is important that you mention this in your introduction as the question does not expressly mention it, but if you properly understand the question and the law you will see how this discussion is inherently connected to the express wording of the question. Demonstrating this will get your marker onside early on and let them know that you know what is expected.

[2] The point which you should be trying to convey here is the need for the legislative reform and why the common law was, therefore, unsatisfactory. This will set up your discussion of the 1957 Act.

[3] For the purposes of fully answering the question, it is important that you highlight what the Act was trying to do. This is because this will influence your concluding arguments on the state of the law, namely that both Acts sought, on policy grounds, to build in a distinction between the levels of protection offered. Therefore, there is no need for further legislation on that basis.

[4] Naturally, building from the previous comments, you then need to explain what the policy reason is for the distinction which the 1957 Act left.

The issue here is the extent to which the common law was unsatisfactory and warranted parliamentary intervention in the form of the 1957 Act. This will also require exploring the need for the second intervention in 1984[1] as arguably while the 1957 Act did resolve some issues it also created others. It will be argued that reform was required both times; however, while there is unequal protection between visitors and non-visitors, no further reform is needed as the discrepancy is justifiable.

While the common law imposed a duty of care, the protection provided varied depending on the classification given to the injured individual, based on their reason for being on the premises. The classifications ranged from those present under a contract with the occupier through to trespassers. In between were invitees and licensees, namely those to whom the occupier gave an invitation or permission to enter the premises. Although very similar, the law made a distinction between them based on the invitee's common interest with the occupier for being on the premises, which resulted in more protection for invitees. This was overly, and unnecessarily, complex with litigation focusing on determining the relevant status. The artificial nature of the distinction led to calls for its abolition by the Law Commission in their 1954 Report.[2] This report led to the 1957 Act which has the primary purpose of simplifying the law and creating certainty as to when a duty would arise and its extent.[3] Section 1(2) defined 'occupier' like the common law, namely the person who has sufficient control over the premises so that they ought to realise that a failure of care on their part may lead to injury to another (***Wheat v E. Lacon Co. Ltd*** [1966] AC 552). While defined the same, it applied differently. Protection was afforded to all lawful visitors, i.e. anyone not a trespasser at common law. Therefore, this change generally removed the difficulties of ascertaining the category of visitor and the uncertainty as to what level of duty would be imposed. However, consequently, trespassers at common law still lacked protection unless the injury was caused from deliberate intentional acts of the occupier or acts which were done with reckless disregard for the trespassers' presence (***Addie v Dumbreck*** [1929] AC 358). No protection was given from negligent acts, as the view was taken that trespassers came onto the premises at their own risk.[4]

[5] It is important that you evaluate the merits of the Act and its consequences; otherwise, you risk just having a description of it and you will lose the thread of the argument which would otherwise run through your answer.

[6] This is why *Jolley* is a good case to give as an example here; as opposed to other famous cases such as *Phipps v Rochester Corp* [1955] 1 QB 450 and *Glasgow Corp v Muir* [1943] AC 448. It allows you to evaluate whether this was just a pre-1984 issue.

[7] A concluding remark such as this is needed if you are building to a conclusion that no further reform is needed. Without it, you have left an unanswered question mark over the adequacy of the law.

[8] This links the discussion back to the previous discussion of this aspect of the issue and so gives it more strength. Of more importance though is that commenting on this here allows your answer to flow nicely and directly into why the 1984 Act came about. To maintain a good structure, you need to ensure that you do not just simply move on to describing what the 1984 Act does.

[9] This fact was important to the decision as it warranted some fault being placed on the defendant, so it is equally important that you highlight it.

While the 1957 Act successfully resolved difficulties over whether someone was an invitee or licensee, it simply created a new problem over who was a visitor, especially regarding children.[5] Even in the absence of express permission for a child to enter the premises, a duty may arise if the premises contain an allurement which is deemed to provide implied permission. *Jolley v Sutton LBC* [2000] 1 WLR 1082 illustrates the point: a rotting boat on the defendant's land was held to be an attractive plaything for children and, in light of its accessibility, there was thus implied permission to enter. The relative recentness suggests that the 1984 Act has not completely removed the need for the courts to undertake such an exercise[6] with the issue perhaps complicated by the fact that the term 'trespasser' covers such a wide range of people, from children who had wandered onto the land to those with criminal intent. However, the case also shows that the courts can deal with the issue adequately.[7]

The duty is to take such care as is reasonable in the circumstances to ensure that the visitor is reasonably safe using the premises for the purpose for which they are permitted to be there (s. 2(2)). Therefore, if the visitor is acting inconsistently with their permission for being there, they lose the Act's protection; and the occupier is also permitted to alter their duty through contract, albeit now subject to the Unfair Contract Terms Act 1977. The Act does still make some allowance for the type of visitor. Under section 2(3)(b) the occupier can expect those on the premises exercising their trade to guard against the risks associated with that calling. Conversely, they must expect children to exercise less care than adults (s. 2(3)(a)). Although seeming justifiable, in light of the readiness to find implied licences for children, a greater burden is created towards people who arguably should not be on their premises, particularly unsupervised.[8]

This matter came to a head in *British Railway Board v Herrington* [1972] AC 877 where a duty was found towards a boy injured trespassing over a railway line between two dilapidated fences.[9] While decided unanimously, the judicial opinions lacked clarity as to when this duty would arise and its extent. This naturally caused significant uncertainty and detriment for landowners who now faced liability for people not allowed on their land. As a result, the Law Commission produced another report in 1976 which formed the basis of the 1984 Act.

[10] By explaining the point of the Act, you highlight your understanding of both Acts as the intention was never to offer the same protection as the 1957 Act due to policy considerations.

This sought to achieve a better balance between not burdening occupiers too much in respect of trespassers, while offering protection when injury occurs through the fault of the occupier.[10]

Section 1(1) imposes a duty to non-visitors in respect of injuries suffered while on the premises by reason of a danger arising from things done or omitted to be done on the premises. Therefore, the 1984 Act can immediately be seen to afford less protection, as visitors are owed a duty including when the premises are non-dangerous. Even then, the non-visitor must still satisfy the requirements of section 1(3).

[11] Put these in a separate paragraph so that the analysis and evaluation that you offer previously does not get lost in the detail.

The requirements are[11] that the occupier is aware of the danger or has reasonable grounds to believe it exists; he knows or has reasonable grounds to believe the other, regardless of lawful authority, is in the vicinity of the danger, or may come within it; and the risk is one which, in the circumstances, it is reasonable to expect him to protect the other from. If satisfied, the duty is to take such care as is reasonable in the circumstances to see that injury from that danger does not occur. There is no duty for injury by other means reflecting Parliament's intention to distinguish the protection given to non-visitors in contrast to visitors.

[12] Start your conclusion with a definitive statement as to the overall merit of the sentiment expressed within the statement of the question, and then proceed to summarise why you have reached that view.

Therefore, the common law was unsatisfactory and needed parliamentary reform[12] as it was too complex and full of unnecessary distinctions. However, by failing to deal with all categories of individuals, the 1957 Act merely created new problems which led to the necessity for further reform. This was arguably foreseeable and the law would have been better served by reforming the whole area in the first place. That said, the matter is now settled and while the statutory reforms retain unequal protection between visitors and non-visitors, no further reform is needed as policy justifies the different treatment. Further, the lack of reported appeal cases suggests that the judiciary have also reached a clear and settled understanding as to the purpose and application of each statute.[13]

[13] There are arguably two reasons for possible reform, one that the different treatment is unwarranted; or, secondly, that the law remains unclear and ambiguous. This shows that you are aware and have considered both. Also by referring to the lack of appeal cases, which would generally deal with the second issue, you demonstrate your knowledge of the current state of the law and judicial thinking.

Make your answer stand out

■ Consider what form any future reform could take if you conclude more is needed.

■ Read the Law Reform Committee (1954) *Third Report: Occupiers' Liability to Invitees, Licensees and Trespassers* and the Law Commission Report (1976) *Report on Liability for Damage or Injury to Trespassers and Related Questions of Occupiers' Liability* to gain a full insight of the primary reasons for each statute.

■ Read *Herrington* and formulate your own views as to the extent, if any, it created problems in the law in relation to trespassers.

■ Include judicial comments surrounding the application of the legislation; especially *Tomlinson* v *Congleton Borough Council* [2004] 1 AC 46.

■ Supplement your arguments on the different issues with academic opinion from journals and books.

 Don't be tempted to . . .

■ Ignore the 1984 Act even though it is not expressly mentioned in the question. An omission in this regard would create the impression that you are not even aware of it.

■ Dwell too long on the common law position; simply use it to highlight why the initial statutory reform was needed and as a lead into your discussion of the 1957 Act.

■ Extensively discuss the different provisions of each statute. The question is focused on you evaluating the need for each Act and the extent that, overall, they provide adequate protection. Focus on a comparative evaluation of each rather than a description of each.

www.pearsoned.co.uk/lawexpressqa

Go online to access more revision support including additional essay and problem questions with diagram plans, You be the marker questions, and download all diagrams from the book.

10

Trespass to land

How this topic may come up in exams

Trespass to land is a rather small and uncomplicated area and, as such, means that essay questions are rare. However, you could be asked about the need for the tort and the role it plays in the wider context of protecting interests in land. As for problem questions, it is common to find an element of trespass to land combined with other torts such as trespass to the person, occupiers' liability or nuisance. Always check your question to see whether there is an aspect of someone entering another's land without permission or acting in a manner which is inconsistent with their permission.

■ Before you begin

It's a good idea to consider the following key themes of trespass to land before tackling a question on this topic.

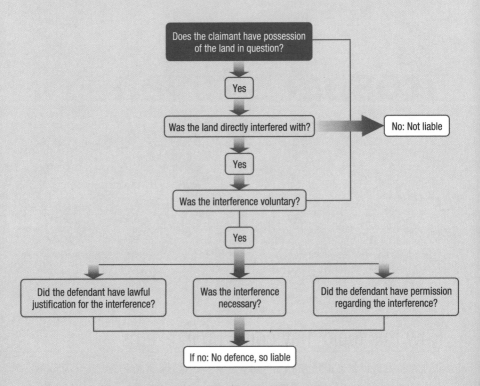

A printable version of this diagram plan is available from **www.pearsoned.co.uk/lawexpressqa**

❓ Question 1

Harry recently purchased an old mansion in the village of Snapeton, which has significant history and interest to the local community. Feeling philanthropic, Harry opened parts of the mansion and grounds up to the public and turns some of the rooms into a museum. The rest forms Harry's private residence. Entry is free, but visitors must have a valid ticket, which lists the conditions of entry. These are also repeated on various signs.

To help advertise the new museum, Harry placed a large sign at the end of the driveway; however, this protruded slightly onto the land owned by Tom. Tom has repeatedly asked for this to be moved, but Harry dismisses him saying the sign must be protruding 'by a matter of inches' and to 'get over it, boy'. Furious, one night Tom threw a large rock at the sign, but missed, smashing a window in an outhouse of Harry's.

Besides the incidents with Tom, Harry has also suffered additional difficulties.

Some of the conditions are that the grounds are no smoking, food is prohibited and no photography is allowed. During a tour of the grounds Harry caught Brian eating by the ornamental pond and saw cigarettes on the ground. Harry demanded that he leave, but Brian shouted that he 'would be back as you can't stop me coming'.

Molly was leaving the grounds after a visit. Despite a sign saying that she could exit through the east road, Molly wanted to leave by the north road and thought as it was not blocked off it must still be OK. Missing a sign saying 'No Exit, Road Under Repair' Molly proceeded up the north road, hit a divot in the road, lost control of her car and crashed. This resulted in Molly damaging some fencing.

Advise Harry of these events and what action may result.

Diagram plan

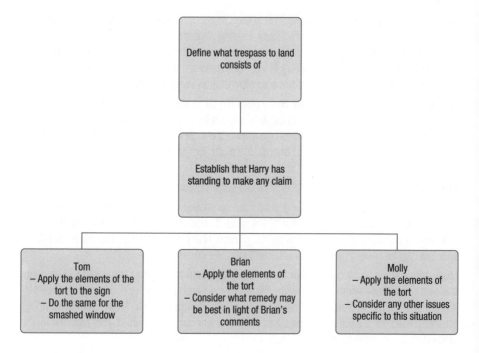

A printable version of this diagram plan is available from **www.pearsoned.co.uk/lawexpressqa**

Answer plan

→ Define what is meant by trespass to land.

→ Establish that Harry and Tom have possession of their respective land so that each may bring a claim.

→ Examine each incident of trespass complained of in turn as to whether it was voluntarily directed at the land.

→ Consider any possible justification for each interference.

→ Advise Harry as to what remedy he should seek in relation to the different actions directed at his land.

Answer

The question requires advising Harry predominantly on several aspects of trespass to land and the suitability of the potential remedies he may seek under that tort. Trespass to land is defined by *Winfield*

[1] You will not be expected to put a full reference in your answer but you should try to put some information down, such as the year if it is a book or the journal abbreviation if it is a journal.

[2] Clearly, it would not be much of a question if Harry did not have standing to bring a claim, but for completeness you should demonstrate your knowledge of the point.

[3] As the question does not have any element of trespass to the person, you can shorten the name of the tort, as there is no need to distinguish it from trespass to the person.

[4] Use the facts of the question to support why he will have possession and thus standing.

[5] Obviously, you are not expressly told this, so this makes it all the more important to draw on the facts of the question to support the proposition.

[6] As Harry was quite dismissive of Tom's complaint, and felt it was doing no harm due to the small nature of the infringement, it is important that you offer some explanation as to why he faces liability.

and Jolowicz on Tort (Rogers, 2010)[1] as the unjustifiable interference with the possession of land, and Harry should be advised that it is actionable without any proof of damage. This is important in this scenario, as not all of the incidents have led to any physical damage; rather, they have resulted in mere disturbance. It will be argued that Harry is likely to have an actionable claim against Tom, Brian and Molly, but could also face claims from Tom and Molly.

The first issue to determine is that Harry can actually bring a claim[2] for trespass.[3] Although a lawful estate is not required, physical presence on the land is insufficient to bring a claim; there must be actual possession. As Harry owns and lives in the property,[4] he has the necessary possession. Similarly, Tom also has standing to make a claim against Harry in relation to the sign.

In dealing with the dispute with Tom first, Harry should be advised that the fact that Tom does not enter Harry's land will not prevent an action for trespass, as the authority of **Smith v Stone** (1647) Style 65 states throwing a stone onto another's land will suffice; this clearly mirrors the facts here. Further, as we are told that Tom did this due to being 'furious' with Harry's comments, this suggests it was clearly an intentional act directed against Harry's land, which cannot be justified.[5] As Tom has no defence, Harry would be successful in obtaining damages. There seems to be no reason for an injunction at this time unless repeated instances were likely. However, Harry should be advised that he is similarly liable to a claim of trespass by Tom even though he may not have entered Tom's land. The case of **Kelsen v Imperial Tobacco Co.** [1957] 2 QB 334 involved a sign overhanging on the claimant's land by a small amount, and the tort was held to be made out as one's land extends skywards. Harry should be advised that even though there is no damage caused by the sign, liability reflects the premise that one's land should be inviolate, especially from intentional acts of interference.[6]

In relation to Brian, Harry should be advised that, as required, there is clearly an immediate, direct and intentional interference with his land as he has voluntarily entered the grounds. As he is in an area where he has permission to be, at first glance it appears this is a justifiable interference, as Brian has a contractual licence to be there. However, Harry should be advised that, where a licence is given to someone, conditions can be attached. This has occurred here as conditions of entry and, therefore,

[7] Although clearly not an issue of the question, you should show your wider knowledge of the related areas to trespass as you are advising an individual, and in real life this may be an issue.

[8] While this latter point seemingly makes the previous point regarding *Cornish* irrelevant, it is still worth mentioning that authority as it shows not only that you know that aspect of the law, but also understand it within the context of the question by not applying it.

[9] Use the facts to lead you into a discussion of the appropriateness of the tort's remedies, which will allow you to show the full range of your knowledge and understanding.

[10] A line such as this just reinforces the extent of your knowledge and shows your awareness of the differences in the types of remedies available.

[11] Although the question is clearly focused on trespass, the rubric gives you scope to explore other torts, so take the opportunity to show your wider knowledge of tort and how different torts may feature on similar facts.

conditions for obtaining a licence to be on his grounds, are that visitors must not smoke, take photography or eat whilst on the grounds. The presence of these conditions also indicate that, even though Brian has a contractual licence, it can be revoked without Harry being in breach of contract.[7] As Brian has broken these conditions, his presence, even in a permitted area, is inconsistent with his permission to be there and so this will be a trespass. Harry should, however, be advised that normally where a licence is revoked, the licensee must be given a reasonable time to collect their goods and leave (***Cornish v Stubbs*** (1870) LR 5 CP 334). Thus, there would be no action against Brian unless he took an unreasonably long time to leave. However, as Brian's entry was in breach of the entry conditions, this will be deemed to be a trespass from the moment that he entered Harry's property.[8] Additionally, as we are told that this has happened repeatedly, Harry should be advised that he may want to seek a permanent injunction as a remedy rather than just merely damages as this will, despite what Brian claims, prevent him from entering the grounds.[9]

The situation with Molly is slightly different to Brian, and the question is whether her presence on the road was justifiable, i.e. did she have permission to be on that part of the grounds. We are not told whether there was an entry condition regarding how to leave the grounds. However, the signs stating that people were not to exit via the north road can be said to signify that entrants did not have permission to be on that road. If there is no permission to use that exit, then it could be argued that there was no permission to use the road leading to the exit. Harry should be advised that this lack of permission could have been made clearer but, if Molly were to argue that she did not intend to trespass by using the road as she did not know the exit was not in use, this would be irrelevant as it must be the act of entry which is intended, which it clearly was as Molly intended to take that exit. Even a mistaken entry amounts to trespass (***Conway v George Wimpey & Co. Ltd*** [1951] 2 KB 266), therefore, as Molly directly, immediately and intentionally drove along the north road without permission, this would constitute a trespass. As Harry has suffered injury to his property from the incident, the most appropriate remedy would be damages and there would seem little point in an injunction in this instance.[10] Further, the existence of actual property damage means Harry could alternatively claim damages under negligence against Molly if there were concerns as to whether permission for being on the north road had been withheld.[11] Harry should be advised though that, if Molly suffered an injury in the crash, she might have a possible claim against him under the occupiers' liability legislation, even if she was trespassing on the road. He would have a strong chance in defeating such a claim though, or having a partial defence of contributory negligence, at least.

To conclude, it would appear that Harry has an actionable claim for trespass against all of the parties, but he faces a claim for trespass by Tom; however, he should succeed in defeating any claim by Molly.

✓ Make your answer stand out

- Discuss the theoretical basis of trespass to illustrate to Harry why he would still be liable even if the sign is only protruding by a couple of inches.
- Explain in detail how Harry might get an injunction if he wanted one.
- Consider in more detail the possible claim in negligence against Molly.
- Show your awareness of the other areas of the law of torts which the situation may give rise to, such as a claim for damages by Molly under the occupiers' liability legislation, if she suffered any injuries in the crash.

! Don't be tempted to . . .

- Just assume that Harry is eligible to bring an action or gloss over this requirement that needs to be satisfied.
- Ignore the potential claims by Tom and just concentrate on what claims Harry can make, as the question does not restrict you in that way.
- Overlook the subsidiary claims Harry could make as, again, while the question is predominantly on trespass to land; it does not completely restrict you to that tort.

 Question 2

'It is clear from *Home Brewery Co.* v *William Davis & Co. (Loughborough) Ltd* [1987] QB 339 that if an infringement of one's land causes damage then it does not matter whether an action is brought in trespass or nuisance.'

In light of this statement, evaluate what, if anything, makes the tort of trespass to land distinct and worthy of ongoing retention as a standalone tort.

Diagram plan

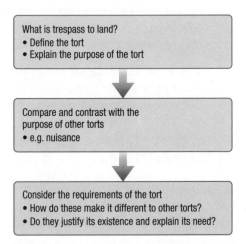

What is trespass to land?
• Define the tort
• Explain the purpose of the tort

Compare and contrast with the purpose of other torts
• e.g. nuisance

Consider the requirements of the tort
• How do these make it different to other torts?
• Do they justify its existence and explain its need?

A printable version of this diagram plan is available from **www.pearsoned.co.uk/lawexpressqa**

Answer plan

→ Define what is meant by trespass to land and explain the purpose of the tort.

→ Draw a comparison with similar torts such as nuisance while identifying where the actions have differences.

→ Analyse the requirements of the tort in order to further distinguish it from others and show how its different mode of operation further justifies its existence.

→ Conclude by considering whether the tort is distinct and whether it is needed to perform the role it does.

Answer

The issue to determine is whether the tort of trespass is distinct enough to warrant remaining a tort in its own right or whether the role that it performs could be played by another tort. If liability for infringing one's land could arise without basing the action in trespass then it is questionable whether it is needed. Abolishing the tort would be significant though as trespass is the only tort protecting land interests which is actionable *per se.* It will be argued that while other torts do offer similar protection, it is the fact that trespass is actionable *per se* which makes it distinct and justifies its retention; as this reflects the fundamental importance of a person's rights in land.

[1] Although you would not necessarily have to go in to detail here as to what is protected, this gives an early indicator that you are aware of the scope of the tort.

[2] At each stage of your answer, and especially where you have highlighted similarities with other torts, try to differentiate trespass to show why it can justifiably be said to be distinct. This will also makes sure your answer is not purely descriptive.

[3] Although the question does not ask specifically for a comparison to nuisance, it does require you to look at whether trespass is sufficiently distinct from other torts so a comparison is needed to at least one. Focusing on nuisance has merit as there are similarities and as it is referred to in the statement, by using it you are clearly relating your discussion back to the question.

[4] The aim here is to conclude the point that you raised at the start of the paragraph while again providing some context to the evaluative discussion that you are having by relating it back to the proposition in the question. Nuisance in its current form could not perform the same role as trespass. You can then also build on the point made by flowing straight into the requirements that trespass's purpose requires.

Clerk & Lindsell on Torts (Jones *et al.*, 2014) define trespass to land as consisting of any unjustifiable intrusion by one person upon land in the possession of another. Therefore, the tort has much broader scope than the layperson's traditional idea of someone wandering on to their land.[1] The tort exists to protect a person's interest in property arising through possession as opposed to stemming from ownership. Therefore, the purpose, protecting land from interference, is indeed similar to that of the tort of nuisance. Further, to bring an action in trespass the claimant must first demonstrate a proprietary interest in the land and exclusive possession of it (***Mason v Clarke*** [1955] AC 778). As such, more is needed than mere licence rights such as simple occupation or control of the land; although, if coupled with exclusive possession this may suffice (***National Provincial Bank Ltd v Ainsworth*** [1965] AC 1175). This requirement also applies to nuisance and may face a challenge on human rights grounds in that tort. However, as trespass aims to protect against interferences with the possession of the land the requirement is more strongly justified in trespass in light of the different aims of the torts.[2]

The statement is premised on the notion that other torts do the same job as trespass and so it could be said to serve no distinct purpose. However, while the statement may have merit in circumstances where actual damage is caused by the interference, this also highlights the limitation to the quote's sentiment. Where there is seemingly no physical damage, the basis of the action would matter. In potentially comparable torts some form of damage is necessary for liability to result. While nuisance[3] is again seemingly similar to trespass by protecting against interferences with the use or enjoyment of the land, an important difference is that the interference in nuisance must be substantial, reflecting the need for some give and take between neighbours (***Sedleigh-Denfield v O'Callaghan*** [1940] AC 880). Therefore, claimants in cases such as ***Kelsen v Imperial Tobacco*** [1957] 2 QB 334 where a sign marginally hung over the boundary line would be left without redress, as the interference was not sufficient to lead to a nuisance. In nuisance, this can be justified as the tort is concerned with protecting the land from consequential interference. This is not the case in trespass, which deals with direct and intended acts of interference. Therefore, the purpose of each tort is in fact fulfilled in different ways to nuisance through the need to prove specific requirements which means that how the interference comes may also influence which tort the action needs to be brought in.[4]

As noted, trespass requires direct interference with the land which must also be the result of an intended act. This interference can take many forms and can relate to the land's surface, subsoil or airspace. Examples include simple entering of the land, remaining there after one should leave, and even just placing a stone against a wall (**Gregory v Piper** (1829) 109 ER 220).[5] This means that there is an extremely low threshold for liability. In **Gregory**, arguably, no harm was actually done. However, this clearly illustrates the distinctiveness of the tort and its value: no actual damage to the land is required. Trespass's role is to protect the proprietary interest and possession of the clamant. If a person voluntarily and intentionally performs an act which directly interferes with another's land, then surely the law is justified in holding that person liable, even without actual damage resulting.[6] The problem of the low threshold is exacerbated by the fact that it is simply the act of interference which needs be intended not the actual interference. Clearly, some harshness flows from this, e.g. in **Conway v George Wimpey & Co. Ltd** [1951] 2 KB 266[7] liability resulted where the entry followed a completely innocent mistake because the entry onto the land was still intended. However, there could be said to be damage present in both cases in that the protection of a person's interest in property is a fundamental right, as seen in Article 1 of the First Protocol of the European Convention on Human Rights. Therefore, the mere fact that it has been interfered with, warrants the imposition of liability. The right owner should be able to determine who enters the land.

Therefore, it is clear from the requirements of trespass that its operation and, therefore, applicability to a given situation is unique. It has a different scope to other torts which allow it to fill a void in the level of protection afforded by tort which would otherwise exist if the issue was left to just nuisance or negligence which are more indirect in nature.[8] Further, only one act is required for a claim to arise and, therefore, other torts such as harassment, based on a course of conduct, offer no relief in such a situation.

To conclude, while there are similarities with other torts, the underlying function of trespass to land shows that it is ultimately aimed at providing a different form of redress to torts such as nuisance and negligence. The purpose and operation of the protection is unique and other torts can only satisfactorily replace trespass in circumstances

[5] Such examples are arguably not needed as you have explained what is required. However, using examples show that you more fully understand the requirement and the broader range of situations that it applies to which leads into the point you are about to make.

[6] What you are doing here is evaluating the role of trespass and justifying its existence in theoretical terms and principle rather than just because it is different to other torts. By doing so, you are not just describing the requirements, but also providing a critique of them.

[7] As the example you are going on to explain here is a different issue from that which you highlighted earlier in the paragraph, it is fine to draw on another case as you are not simply listing cases on the same point.

[8] A sentence along these lines is important in order to tie your answer back to the question and reinforce the impression that you are aware of the full scope of the question. It also naturally leads you into a discussion of the requirements of the tort in your next paragraph.

where there is something more akin to actual damage, and so what they are in effect protecting is something different. Therefore a distinct tort embodied by trespass to land is needed to protect rights in land when the injury is to the right of possession and ownership of the land itself. This differentiation is seen in the requirements which must be satisfied for liability under the action. The simple act of direct interference with that interest is sufficient damage even if the land is not physically affected. If this is not recognised, then all forms of trespass to the person would also need abolishing.[9]

[9] The purpose of this sentence is to indicate that you are aware how this tort sits with the other forms of trespass and that you are aware of the wider repercussions of simply abolishing the tort.

✓ Make your answer stand out

- Evaluate the justification for trespass as a distinct tort constantly as you progress through your answer rather than just including a passage at the end of an account of the requirements.
- Make clear what function is performed by the tort and compare whether that function is in fact performed by any other torts.
- Consider the broader role that the tort plays in terms of settling disputes as to rights over land.
- Explore in detail what other consequences may arise from not retaining the tort.

! Don't be tempted to . . .

- Simply describe the requirements of the tort; you need to evaluate each as you deal with them.
- Provide a detailed account of the requirements of any other torts that you discuss. Instead, just ensure that you highlight the role that those torts play, their purpose and whether they could perform the same function as trespass in a more justifiable manner.
- Just agree with the proposition in the question; feel free to disagree with it if that is what you feel.

---

www.pearsoned.co.uk/lawexpressqa

Go online to access more revision support including additional essay and problem questions with diagram plans, You be the marker questions, and download all diagrams from the book.

11
Nuisance

How this topic may come up in exams

Nuisance problem questions require several different factors to be considered to determine whether a claim has been made out. You will also have to determine whether the nuisance is private or public and whether the nuisance is covered by statute such as environmental protection legislation. In addition, there is the possibility of a question having the potential to explore issues of negligence and the rule in *Rylands* v *Fletcher* as well. There is also a significant human rights impact in this tort, particularly Article 8 of the European Convention on Human Rights and the implications this has for *Hunter* v *Canary Wharf* and the necessity for a proprietary interest to bring an action, which can form the basis of essay questions.

Before you begin

It's a good idea to consider the following key themes of nuisance before tackling a question on this topic.

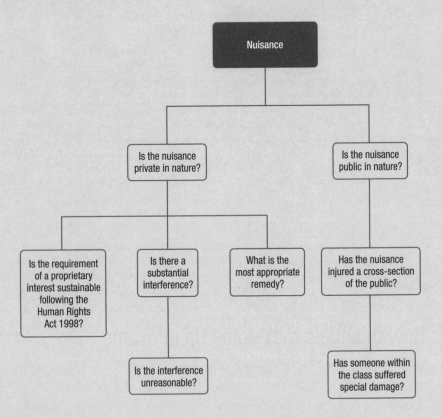

A printable version of this diagram plan is available from **www.pearsoned.co.uk/lawexpressqa**

❓ Question 1

Declan purchased a large country estate last year called McDonnell House. The estate consists of a large detached mansion at its centre, surrounded by idyllic grounds, including a golf course. In order to diversify his revenue streams Declan also decided to use part of the grounds to host weddings. McDonnell House neighbours land adjacent to that owned by Anthony. Anthony is a British civil war enthusiast who uses his farmland to re-enact the War of the Roses for the public to attend. The events are also combined with lectures on the war to inform people about the history of the war. The re-enactments are staged Thursday through to Sunday and last for eight hours each day. These events have always been extremely popular, especially with schools from across the country. Anthony has won several tourist and educational awards for the events and has significantly increased the number of employees he employs as a result.

However, the staging of the re-enactments clash with the main days for golf players and weddings on Declan's land. The noise from the battles soon started to cause problems for Declan and many customers complained that they could not concentrate on their golf play. Declan also had to give full refunds to two wedding parties who claimed that their wedding was ruined by the interference from the re-enactments, and several weddings have been cancelled. Declan has now reached the stage where he feels his own personal enjoyment of the estate is being diminished and so he has reluctantly moved out to live in another property that he owns. As such, he has sought to put an end to Anthony's use of his land. Declan was aware of the re-enactments when he first purchased McDonell House.

Advise Anthony:

(a) whether he could successfully contest an action by Declan in nuisance; and

(b) whether, if not, he could at least stop an injunction being granted.

Diagram plan

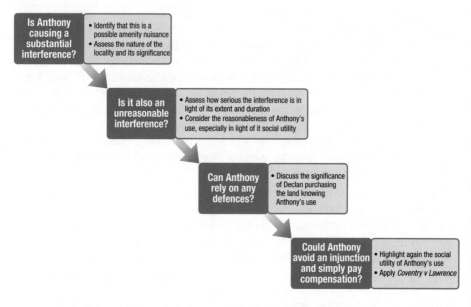

A printable version of this diagram plan is available from **www.pearsoned.co.uk/lawexpressqa**

Answer plan

→ Confirm that Declan is eligible to a claim against Anthony.

→ Consider whether there is a substantial interference with Declan's use and enjoyment of his land.

→ Evaluate whether this interference is unreasonable.

→ Determine separately whether the social utility of the use of the land by Anthony could justify any interference being suffered.

→ Assess what remedies are available to Declan and which one Anthony is most likely to face if he cannot defend the claim.

[1] Show at the start that you have correctly identified the nature of the nuisance.

[2] As you are advising Declan, explain to him what the tort consists of. Again, this will also give an early indicator to your marker that you know how the tort works.

Answer

The issue is whether Declan has an action for private nuisance as it appears his use and enjoyment of his land is being interfered with by Anthony.[1] Resolving this is important as it could potentially result in Anthony being prevented from carrying on his activities.[2] It will be argued that the requirements of the tort may be satisfied, but that

[3] While this may seem obvious, this requirement has been strictly applied and so for completeness you should briefly state it.

[4] Briefly show that you understand what process the law is going through with this aspect of the tort as this conflict lies at the heart of the tort, before going into your application. This will allow you to demonstrate that you appreciate what the tort is about rather than just what its requirements are.

[5] By adding this you also show how the tension behind the tort impacts on the application of the requirements for the tort.

[6] By phrasing in this way you can show that you know both factors but more importantly that you understand their application by not going into detail on sensitivity as it does not seem on the facts that it is an issue. You can then use the time saved to explain the additional importance of locality to the type of injury allegedly suffered.

[7] It is still worth considering this fact though in order to give some balance to your discussion and further the level of evaluation that your answer contains.

due to the social utility of Anthony's use of his land, he may be able to resist Declan obtaining an injunction.

As Declan owns McDonnell House he will have a sufficient enough proprietary interest to enable him to have standing to bring an action against Anthony[3] (**Hunter v Canary Wharf Ltd** [1997] AC 655). There is clearly an interference with Declan's land, but to be actionable Declan will need to show that the noise amounts to a substantial interference with the use and enjoyment of his land. The tort strikes a balance between the competing interests of one person's interest in using their land as they wish with that of another's interest to be free from interference,[4] and the matter is determined on a case-by-case basis depending on the individual facts (**Sturgess v Bridgman** (1879) 11 Ch D 852).[5]

As the interference claimed by Declan does not appear to result from any particular sensitivity of his land, the focus will be on the nature of the locality of the area.[6] Consideration of the locality is also important as we are just dealing with personal discomfort rather than material damage. Furthering the idea that there should be some give and take between neighbours in such a situation, the law looks at the locality of the land in order to determine whether the interference is substantial. Therefore, what could constitute a nuisance in one type of area may not be in another (**Sturgess**). As this is the countryside it is naturally quieter than an urban setting and so the increased noise of the re-enactments would be more noticeable; yet the countryside is also the natural location for Anthony's activity. However, Anthony should be advised that conducting an activity in an appropriate location does not prevent it being a nuisance.[7] The fact that it appears to travel some distance and affect the house in the centre of the estate would suggest it is significantly loud.

Before this amounts to a nuisance though the substantial interference must also be unreasonable. Anthony should be advised that this involves assessing the seriousness of his interference and then whether his use of his land is reasonable. In determining the seriousness of the interference its duration and extent must be considered. While we do not know the exact level of the noise, we do know that it goes on for eight hours a day four days a week. We also know that the noise is so great that two weddings have had to be refunded and others have cancelled in light of the noise.

⁸ While there are no precise facts given you cannot avoid a discussion. At the same time you must not assume facts or make them up. Draw on what you can to advance an argument on the issue, but make sure you write it in a way that reflects the inherent vagueness of the question.

⁹ Following from the previous point, it is important that you introduce the next issue in this way to continue with the caveat to your advice that you have highlighted and maintain a consistent approach.

¹⁰ The actual quote by Lord Goff is not necessarily needed, instead you just need to refer to the case as the authority for the point that you are advancing.

¹¹ As this appears to be the main factor and therefore your main area of discussion make sure that you separate it out so that your argument stands out.

¹² You do not know for sure and it may be that they are, so you should place this qualification to your statement for completeness.

¹³ As this is not a defence, but something which is considered more as part of the reasonableness of the defendant's use, deal with this before the actual defences.

Further Declan has moved out of the mansion in the centre of the property.⁸ This would suggest that not only are the noise levels substantial, but also serious.

On the basis that there is sufficient seriousness,⁹ the next issue to determine is whether Anthony is a reasonable user of his land. Although liability in nuisance centres on the interference with the claimant's interest in the land being unreasonable there is, as Lord Goff noted in **Cambridge Water Co. Ltd v Eastern Counties Leather plc** [1994] 2 AC 264,¹⁰ an inter-relationship with whether the defendant's conduct is reasonable. Again, there are several factors to consider for determining this. It does not appear that Anthony is acting maliciously and it seems unlikely that the interference could be easily prevented, both of which would lend support the interference not being unreasonable. However, this must be weighed against the fact that while liability for nuisance is strict, and thus not based on the need to take reasonable care not to cause the interference, liability may still arise where the harm caused is reasonably foreseeable liability (**Cambridge Water**). The harm here is interference with Declan's use and enjoyment of his land from the noise of the battles and although this may depend upon some unknown factors it was arguably foreseeable as the lands are adjacent.

Another factor in relation to the reasonableness of Anthony's use of his land is the fact that it seems to generate a lot of public benefit.¹¹ On the basis that the re-enactments are not illegal¹² there is nothing unreasonable *per se* about his use. In fact, his use of his land may actually be deemed reasonable due to its social utility in that it acts as a learning environment by educating people about the war, generates employment and is a popular family attraction. However, benefiting the public cannot provide an immunity¹³ and the courts are reluctant to let private rights, such as those enjoyed by Declan, be extinguished in favour of the general public without some form of statutory authority. Therefore, Anthony should be advised that the court may still find this an actionable nuisance, but the social utility of his actions could be taken into account when dealing with what remedy to award if Anthony is not found

[14] While it may seem natural to flow straight into the discussion of *Coventry* and what remedy may be obtained, especially as you will have spotted that there is no valid defence on the facts. However you do need to advise Anthony of the fact that he will have no defence and in doing so show the marker that you do know and understand that aspect of the tort. Therefore, briefly move into defences from this point as structurally it will not make sense logically and structurally to deal with defences either before this paragraph or at the end.

[15] As mentioned earlier in relation to sensitivity, by referring to prescription in this manner you show that you know that there is such a defence but that you understand that it is not applicable.

to have any defence[14] (***Dennis v Ministry of Defence*** [2003] Env LR 34).

As Declan has not had his proprietary interest interfered with for 20 years Anthony could not claim a defence of prescription.[15] A more obvious factor for Anthony to seek to rely on is the fact that Declan purchased his land knowing of Anthony's activities, and therefore, he came to the nuisance. However, this has consistently been held to not be a defence since ***Bliss v Hall*** (1838) 4 Bing NC183. Therefore, Anthony does face being liable.

In terms of possible remedy, following ***Coventry v Lawrence*** [2014] UKSC 14 this issue should be approached with more flexibility and not slavishly follow the previous criteria from ***Shelfer v City of London Electric Lighting Co.*** [1895] 1 Ch. 287. Lord Neuberger expressly mentioned the prospect of the defendant's business closing, and the resultant consequences if an injunction is granted should be considered. The decision means damages in lieu of an injunction may be more freely awarded. This should assist Anthony by allowing him to compensate Declan for the difference in monetary value between what his interest was worth before and after the nuisance (***Moss v Christchurch RDC*** [1925] 2 KB750). This would still allow Anthony to pursue his activities.

In conclusion, Anthony's use of his land is likely to be considered a substantial and unreasonable interference with Declan's use and enjoyment of his land. However, while Declan may seek an injunction, in light of the potential social utility of the use to which Anthony is using his land, an award of damages is more likely.

 Make your answer stand out

- Consider the comments in *Coventry* v *Lawrence* regarding the 'defence' of coming to the nuisance and how it could apply where the claimant subsequently alters the use of their land in the knowledge of how the defendant uses their land.

- Explore in more detail, and draw on, the opinions in *Coventry* in relation to when damages should be granted in place of an injunction.

- Explain in more detail the theoretical basis of the tort and provide a bit more insight as to the balance which lies at the heart of it.

Make your answer stand out

■ Read Murphy, J. (2010) *The Law of Nuisance.* Oxford: Oxford University Press, during your revision, and try to incorporate some academic views as to how the courts look at the various factors which need to be considered in deciding the matter.

! Don't be tempted to . . .

■ Try to explain every factor which could be assessed as part of establishing whether the tort is made out; just focus on those which seem most applicable on the facts. Otherwise, you will lose the structure of your answer and could in fact show a lack of understanding, as they are not all relevant to the question.

■ Go too deep into analysing the nature of the tort. While some discussion will push your answer on, and provide context, you need to bear in mind this is a problem question not an essay.

Question 2

'Once it is understood that nuisances "productive of sensible personal discomfort" do not constitute a separate tort of causing discomfort to people but are merely part of a single tort of causing injury to land, the rule that the plaintiff must have an interest in the lands falls into place as logical and, indeed, inevitable.' (*Per* Lord Hoffman in *Hunter* v *Canary Wharf Ltd* [1997] AC 655 at 707)

In light of this statement, evaluate the function of the tort of nuisance and assess, with regard to human rights considerations, the merits of this restriction as to who may have an action.

Diagram plan

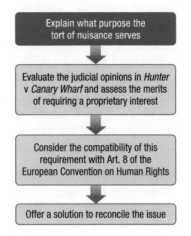

A printable version of this diagram plan is available from **www.pearsoned.co.uk/lawexpressqa**

Answer plan

→ Explain the tort's function and what it seeks to protect.

→ Evaluate *Hunter* and explain why the restriction on standing was insisted upon.

→ Consider the viability of this requirement following the incorporation of the ECHR into English law.

→ Assess whether there is a satisfactory way of retaining the essence of the tort with human rights considerations.

Answer

The tort of nuisance offers redress for those who suffer injury to their land; however, because of the firm statements by the Law Lords in **Hunter v Canary Wharf Ltd** [1997] AC 655 that very purpose means that those who may seek the protection of the tort are restricted and so some individuals succeed while others miss out on redress, even though they have suffered the same interference. It will be argued that, while the reasoning in **Hunter** has merit, it cannot be sustained in the longer term owing to human rights considerations, and standing should be given to those in residential occupation of the land, perhaps under a new and analogous tort.[1]

[1] As you have just indicated that you are going to disagree with the position adopted by the House of Lords, you should offer an insight into what you propose that the law should be.

Nuisance offers protection to interests in land and can take two forms (***St. Helen's Smelting Co. v Tipping*** (1865) HL Cas 642). First, there is protection from material damage to the land. Claims for such damage are relatively straightforward and involve the defendant's act causing a form of physical damage to the claimant's land. The land itself is damaged and thus it is logical that any claim should be brought by the owner of that land. The second one is nuisance producing sensible personal discomfort. The act interferes with the enjoyment of the land, for example producing noise and smells. Therefore, it interferes with the enjoyment of all those present on the land, creating an issue as to who will have an action.

This issue came to the fore in ***Hunter*** where a group of residents claimed nuisance from local construction work. Notably, not all of the residents were householders and included spouses, partners, children and other relations. Their claim initially failed but succeeded in the Court of Appeal where Pill LJ held that, where the claimant occupied the land as a home, there would be a sufficient link to the land to provide standing.[2]

[2] Obviously, this reasoning was rejected by the majority of the House of Lords, but it is worth stating as a point of reference for your answer later on.

Lord Goff rejected the test applied by Pill LJ. He noted that parties may seek negotiations over the matter in order to reach an agreement, but the usefulness of such negotiations require the creator of the nuisance to know who he needs to negotiate with. The usefulness of such arrangements could be diminished if one was needed with everyone who lived in the property. This concern seems fair but, as Lord Cooke highlighted, it could be dealt with by imposing implied authorisation on the homeowner to represent non-owning residents.[3] More persuasively, Lord Goff noted definitional problems with 'substantial link'. While Pill LJ intended his phrase to include the owner's immediate family, he questioned whether it should include lodgers and au pairs who also live there. He then questioned why it would not extend to cover the workplace. A reference point is needed to determine standing; otherwise any individual could bring an action, such as a regular visitor to the house. However, this was overcome by Lord Cooke, dissenting,[4] who argued it was 'weak' to not lay down a rule which was justifiable in relation to spouses and children just because of a grey area as to where the line is ultimately drawn. While the issue may be one of creating legal certainty as well as giving justice to the claimants, this opinion has force in that it could, as Lord Goff observed, be limited quite easily to the immediate family of the homeowner.

[3] Although, here, you are advancing the reasons of the majority and why the case was ultimately decided the way it was, you need to subject this reasoning to analysis, and so try to assess the merit of each point you state. You need to look at the flaws directly related to this reasoning before you get on to advancing the specific arguments *for* the alternate view. If you wait until later, your structure will not be as strong.

[4] This needs to be made clear so that the contradictory views make sense.

Other residents could be dealt with on the facts of their case. Lord Cooke further observed that, as employees are the concern of their employers, there was no policy basis for allowing the law to extend to non-resident employees.

[5] Tie this part of your discussion back to the quote in the question.

As the quote illustrates,[5] Lord Hoffman also felt the requirement was needed. However, his view was based on the purpose of the tort being to protect land. He argued it was vital to appreciate that in *Tipping*, while the two forms of nuisance were mentioned, they still amounted to one tort concerned with the protection of land from injury. As such, the basis for an action under the second type was not the nuisance causing personal discomfort; it was because the utility of the land is diminished and, therefore, the land has suffered injury. The tort exists to protect land from injury, and as such it must be the landowner who sues for its injury. He felt that to develop the common law in the manner suggested by Pill LJ would mean distorting the very principles of the tort[6] to fill the gap by moving it away from a land-based tort.

[6] This is why it is really important that you know the purpose of the tort and can explain it, as this was used to justify the majority's decision. If you do not know the theory behind the tort, then you are less able to fully assess the implications and merit of that decision. The tort's purpose is the bar from which you judge the arguments.

In principle, Lord Hoffman's reasoning has considerable merit; however, the consequence is that a non-owning occupier who has their utility of the land diminished is left without a remedy. While such an occupier suffering personal injury as a result of the nuisance may claim in negligence, one suffering distress, discomfort and inconvenience from the act of nuisance has no remedy in that tort. As Lord Hoffman notes, the land's utility is reflected in the amenity value of the land, and the decision denies the existence of any enjoyment of such amenity by anyone bar the owner. However, their individual right remains negated.

[7] As *Hunter* was decided before the incorporation of the Act, it is important that you then move on to consider, regardless of the merits of Lord Cooke's opinion, whether this now acts as a driver for reforming the position adopted by the majority.

The long-term viability of the requirement from *Hunter* is questionable in that, subsequent to the decision, the Human Rights Act[7] was passed and came into force. Importantly, this incorporates the Article 8 right to respect for privacy and family life. The significance of this is that the Article uses the term 'home', and in *Khatun v UK* 26 EHRR CD 212 this was held to be 'autonomous' and did not require defining domestically. As such, the case arising from the same facts as *Hunter* stated that a proprietary interest was not needed under Article 8. Therefore, anyone whose home is subjected to an actionable nuisance would have a claim. The law's development must give effect to this right (*Douglas v Hello Ltd* [2001] 2 WLR 992), and an insight as to how this was done was given in *McKenna v British*

[8] As the case was not a full trial and may appear as a lower court at odds with *Hunter,* you need to provide this context.

Aluminium Ltd [2002] Env LR 30. Here a striking-out application[8] was rejected on the basis that the claimants, similar in make-up to those in *Hunter*, were said to have an actionable case in light of Article 8. Neuberger J, while not offering any further view of the need for a proprietary interest, was mindful that the claim included a tort analogous to nuisance.

It is submitted, in conclusion, that developing an analogous tort based on the interference with the home, actionable by all residents, would give effect to Article 8 while overcoming the principle objections of Lord Hoffman to adapting nuisance, and providing redress to non-owning occupiers whose enjoyment of the land is diminished.[9] Either this, or *Hunter* will need to be revisited as there is now a clear divergence with human rights jurisprudence.

[9] Explain the merit of your position to demonstrate that you have thought out the consequences of such an approach.

✓ Make your answer stand out

- Highlight some of the requirements of the tort to illustrate how they relate to the tort's function.

- Expand on the appropriateness of a negligence claim for people in the position of the residents in *Hunter,* considering whether they fall into a void.

- Give some more insight as to how the analogous tort could look; consider whether it would be an exact replica but with different standing requirements.

- Read Geach, N. (2012) The nuisance of the proprietary interest: Lord Cooke's dissent in *Hunter* v *Canary Wharf Ltd* [1997] AC 655, in Geach and Monaghan (eds) *Dissenting Judgments in the Law.* London: Wildy, Simmonds & Hill, to garner academic opinion on the issue.

! Don't be tempted to . . .

- Go on into great detail as to the requirements of the tort, as the focus is on the eligibility criteria to make a claim, not what is required for a successful claim.

- Dismiss the opinion of Lord Cooke in *Hunter* simply because it was dissenting, as it provides material from which to evaluate the merits of the majority's view. He also gives an insight as to how the law could be developed while being kept within reasonable bounds.

❓ Question 3

Gidsville is an estate which is predominantly residential in nature although there are some businesses. However, to regenerate an area on the edge of the estate, the council recently gave planning permission to Prento Petroleum to build a factory there. The company is a large manufacturer of parts for the oil industry. Having recently won another large contract, Prento Petroleum has had to extend the working day to include shifts up to midnight rather than have the staff work weekends. As a result, the company has employed large numbers of local residents, but the work has generated a large amount of smoke and particularly noise which can be heard over the estate. One of the businesses on the estate, Di Rossi's, an Italian restaurant, has witnessed a drop in trade.

Additionally, Spencer, who works the late shift at the factory, bought a flat opposite Di Rossi's three years ago. However, since he started working the late shift six months ago he has had problems himself with Di Rossi's deliveries arriving at 10 a.m. and waking him up. When he complained, the owner of Di Rossi's, Morgan, pointed out that the deliveries have been turning up at that time for over 20 years and no one has ever complained.

Advise Morgan about any claim he may have for the loss in trade, and also regarding Spencer's complaints.

Diagram plan

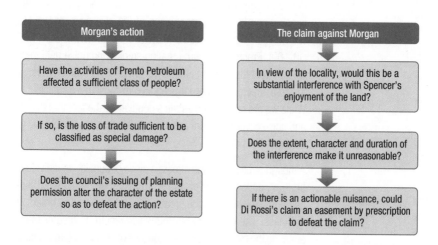

A printable version of this diagram plan is available from **www.pearsoned.co.uk/lawexpressqa**

Answer plan

→ Identify whether the estate constitutes a sufficient class of people affected by the activities of Prento Petroleum.

→ Establish whether Morgan has suffered special damage so as to make an action applicable.

→ Discuss whether Prento Petroleum can rely on the council's planning permission to defeat any action.

→ Advise Morgan of the claim he faces by Spencer.

→ Evaluate whether the interference is substantial.

→ Consider whether the use of the land by Morgan is reasonable.

→ Advise as to the merits of a defence, if required, based on prescription.

Answer

Morgan requires advice as to the tort of nuisance, owing to the threat to his business from Prento Petroleum and also claims he may face from Spencer. It will be argued that Morgan is likely to be successful in an action for public nuisance against the factory, while his actions are unlikely to be sufficient for any private nuisance claim against him.[1]

[1] Demonstrate at the start that you understand that both forms of nuisance are applicable to the question and which type relates to each claim.

Public nuisance requires an act which 'materially affects the reasonable comfort and convenience of life of a class of Her Majesty's subjects' (*per* Romer LJ in *AG v PYA Quarries Ltd* [1957] 2 QB 169). Prento Petroleum creating smoke and noise until midnight would affect the comfort and convenience of the residents. However, the area affected must be large enough to constitute a sufficient class. While we are not told the estate's population, the fact that the smoke and noise cover the entire estate suggests that this community would be a sufficient class.

Although public nuisance affects a class of people, an individual can bring an action. However, Morgan must show he suffered 'special damage', which is damage greater than that suffered by others within the class. The damage suffered which would be greater than that affecting the rest of the estate is the loss of custom. Morgan should be advised that while negligence looks less favourably on pure economic losses[2] such as this, a loss of business is sufficient for nuisance (*Benjamin v Storr* (1874) LR 9 CP 400). This particular loss must also be direct and substantial. By analogy with *Benjamin*, the facts here suggest that Morgan satisfies the requirements for an action.

[2] This may not appear totally relevant but it is an anomaly with the law which has attracted judicial criticism, and so by mentioning it briefly, and in the context shown, you maintain relevance while also showing your knowledge of this point.

[3] As you are giving advice
to Morgan and the facts are
silent, you must ensure that
you explain the situation if
this was the unknown factual
situation.

[4] As you have ended the
previous paragraph with an
element of doubt as to the
claim, you should start the
next part of your discussion
in this manner so that it
follows on from the previous
paragraph.

[5] Make sure that you use
the facts of the question to
support your argument on
this point, as they give a good
indication as to what the
position will be.

[6] Start with the remedy of an
injunction, as this is more
likely to be the most desired
as well as the least likely
to succeed. Therefore, you
can finish on the stronger,
consolation point that he
would at least receive
damages.

[7] Start this section of your
answer by identifying exactly
the issue that Morgan is faced
with.

[8] Show that you know how the
tort operates.

However, if any of the other businesses have suffered a loss in trade, Morgan's claim would fail as he has suffered no greater loss than others within the class.[3]

The loss suffered is also foreseeable and so no issue of remoteness exists. Therefore, on the basis that Morgan has suffered special damage,[4] Prento Petroleum will argue that the granting of planning permission authorised any resultant nuisance. While statutory authority provides immunity against nuisance, the position is different with regard to mere planning permission (*Wheeler* v *J.J. Saunders Ltd* [1996] Ch 19). *Wheeler* held that planning authorities have no general power to authorise a nuisance; although they possibly could to the extent that they may alter the character of a neighbourhood through their decisions. Therefore, the question is whether, by granting permission for the factory, the council has altered the estate's character. Regeneration was a factor behind the decision, so this may be the case; however, we are told that this was just for an area on the edge of the estate, not the whole estate. As Gidsville is predominantly a residential area,[5] it is unlikely that the planning permission has sufficiently altered the overall area's character and so the defence will fail.

If Morgan is successful, it is unlikely that an injunction[6] would be awarded to prevent the company's actions completely as this would create unemployment. However, in view of the noise affecting the entire estate, one may be granted to restrict the working times so that work stops earlier. In any event, Morgan would be able to claim damages for his lost trade.

In relation now to the claim against Morgan, the nuisance being claimed is interference with Spencer's use and enjoyment of his land caused by the delivery trucks.[7] The merits of this claim will be weighed, on the facts, against Morgan's right to use his land in a way that he wishes (*Sturgess* v *Bridgman* (1879) 11 Ch D 852).[8] As this only affects Spencer, the action would be for private nuisance and so it must be confirmed that, as the owner of the flat, Spencer would have the necessary standing to bring a claim (*Hunter* v *Canary Wharf Ltd* [1997] AC 655).

The interference must be substantial in nature. Spencer is not using his land in a particularly sensitive way and so the factor to consider is that of locality. While the whole estate is predominantly residential, we would need to know about this particular part of the estate, as what may be a nuisance in one part may not be in another. Noise from

[9] Even if you have concluded the previous discussion with a view that it is not substantial, the absence of concrete facts means it could be. However, to maintain consistency in your answer, you will need to phrase the introduction of the next point of discussion in a more tentative manner.

[10] Use your common sense to make informed argument in order to overcome the absence of concrete facts. It is important that you do not just ignore the issue.

[11] While being an issue of land law, it is a significant point in relation to the defence against the tort succeeding, and so you should discuss it, drawing on your knowledge of land law.

delivery vans in a general residential area would probably be substantial; however, a restaurant is unlikely to exist on a general residential road. Further, the fact that Spencer's property is a flat suggests that this could also be above one of the other shops. If so, then noise from the vans is unlikely to be substantial.

On the basis that this is deemed to be a substantial interference,[9] the next issue is whether the substantial interference is unreasonable. There are several factors to advise Morgan but of most relevance are the duration of the interference, its extent and its character. The character of the interference is obviously noise, although it appears it is only an issue because it wakes Spencer up, which suggests that the interference is not an issue otherwise. From the facts, we are told the vans arrive at 10 a.m., although we are not told whether this is daily or how long they stay. Arguably, this is a reasonable time to deliver when most people would already be awake. Further, as delivery vans usually have several stops the noise is unlikely to go on for long.[10] The suggestion that Morgan is a reasonable user is supported by the fact that no one else has complained over a long period and even Spencer has not complained until now. Therefore, even if the noise is deemed substantial, it is unlikely to be unreasonable unless perhaps the noise is excessively loud and goes on for an excessive period. If overall the nuisance is deemed negligible, it will not be actionable against Morgan.

However, Morgan should be advised that, if the noise is deemed actionable, any claim will probably succeed as he does not appear to have a defence. The only possibility is an easement by prescription. This means that a proprietary interest has been created by long usage (over 20 years). This would be unsuccessful because it is unlikely that noise from delivery vans would constitute an easement, as there is no benefit to the land.[11] Additionally, while the noise has been going on for over 20 years, there was no actionable nuisance during that time as there was no interference with Spencer's land. There would need to be a 20-year period from the time the interference began (*Sturgess v Bridgman*). The interference has only started since Spencer started working the shifts six months ago.

In conclusion, Morgan should be advised that he should be able to recuperate his losses caused by Prento Petroleum; in relation to Spencer, it is unlikely that the interference from the vans will be sufficient to warrant a successful action.

Make your answer stand out

■ Provide more of an outline as to the differences between the two forms of nuisance action.

■ If there is deemed to be no special damage, advise Morgan of the possibility of petitioning the Attorney General to bring a relator action on behalf of the whole estate.

■ Consider whether the factory may in fact have breached the statutory nuisance provision within section 79 of the Environmental Protection Act 1990.

■ Expand your discussion of Morgan's remedies and consider *Andrae* v *Selfridge & Co. Ltd* [1938] Ch 1. Although foreseeable, would it be unreasonable in the circumstances to allow the full extent of his losses?

! Don't be tempted to . . .

■ Litter the second part of the answer with case examples of the factors which are assessed. The important thing is to apply the standard factors to the facts of the scenario. If a case is similar, or if it is a specific authority for a point, then refer to it but otherwise use your time to concentrate on your application.

■ Turn your discussion of Morgan's possible defence into a land law answer with regard to whether this is capable of constituting an easement.

■ Get too bogged down discussing the theoretical differences between the two types of nuisance action at the expense of actually applying the requirements of each to the facts of the question.

www.pearsoned.co.uk/lawexpressqa

 Go online to access more revision support including additional essay and problem questions with diagram plans, You be the marker questions, and download all diagrams from the book.

The rule in *Rylands* v *Fletcher*

How this topic may come up in exams

While it is a long-standing tort in its own right providing strict liability, the rule is now seen as a sub-species of nuisance dealing with incidents of a one-off escape. As such, while a problem question could consist solely of the tort on its own, you should be aware of the possibility of a nuisance action being present as well, particularly if there is some form of material damage to the land. The development of the tort also means that you could have scope to discuss issues of negligence. As such, make sure you are also able to deal with an essay question concerning the future of the tort and its relevance today.

■ Before you begin

It's a good idea to consider the following key themes of the rule in *Rylands* v *Fletcher* before tackling a question on this topic.

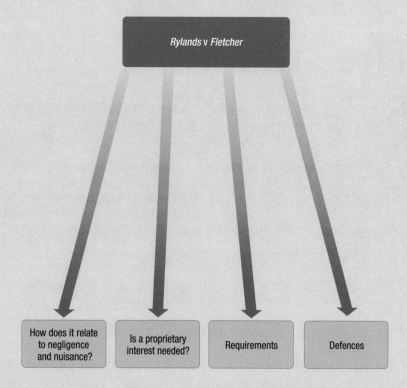

A printable version of this diagram plan is available from **www.pearsoned.co.uk/lawexpressqa**

❓ Question 1

Hydrotricity Ltd is a provider of renewable energy using hydropower. To help meet the consumer demand for green energy the company sought permission to build two artificial dams on the outskirts of Chemersham as part of a large pumped-storage power generation plant. Permission was given for the proposal under the provisions of the (fictitious) Green Energy Act 2013. This was despite some environmental objections by certain groups on the grounds that it would harm local wildlife, especially migratory fish and the surrounding countryside. The construction of the facility generated significant high-skilled jobs for the area and provided a much needed boost to the local economy. As part of the efforts to win approval for the plan, the local residents of Chemersham would receive discounted energy prices.

However, despite its successful construction, protests about the plant have continued. As part of these protests, Owen, a well-known opponent of the plant, devised a plan to discredit the safety of the plant by engineering a leak from one of the dams. Owen believed that he could control the direction of the resulting flooding, and limit its extent, so as not to cause damage to neighbouring properties. Following several attempts, Owen successfully entered the plant as a maintenance entrance had not been properly secured, and he managed to cause a leak. However, he did so as water was being released back to the lower dam so it escaped with far more force than he anticipated, and more water subsequently escaped.

As a result, Eric who runs a farm on the neighbouring property, suffered severe flooding to his fields and the loss of the whole of that season's crops.

Advise the company on their chances of successfully defending a claim for the damage suffered by Eric.

Diagram plan

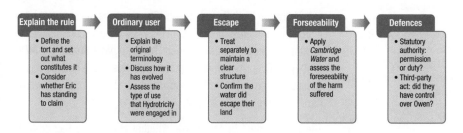

A printable version of this diagram plan is available from **www.pearsoned.co.uk/lawexpressqa**

Answer plan

→ Explain the scope of the rule.

→ Consider whether Eric would be eligible to claim damages under the rule.

→ Identify the water as the 'thing' which Hydrotricity has brought on to their land and consider whether this is an extraordinary use of the land.

→ State briefly how there has clearly been an escape of the water.

→ Evaluate the foreseeability of the harm which would be caused by such an escape.

→ Discuss the potential defences Hydrotricity may have under statute and due to the escape being caused by a third-party act.

Answer

[1] Show that you know exactly how the tort operates and how it is distinguishable from other torts which concern proprietary interests.

[2] By highlighting this here, you show the person marking your work that you have fully identified all of the relevant issues which need to be discussed.

[3] Before you start to apply the different requirements to the problem, it is worth outlining what the rule consists of. However, paraphrase the rule as stated by Blackburn J to emphasise that you understand the individual parts.

[4] So as to not make it look like you are assuming facts, you either need to spell out exactly why you think this to be the case (he runs the farm and his crops were damaged) or use a phrase like this to illustrate you are relying on the facts.

The circumstances surrounding the damage suffered by Eric requires advising him on the rule in *Rylands* v *Fletcher* (1866) LR 1 Ex 265. This tort, while similar to other land torts, offers protection for interests in property which are injured by a one-off occurrence.[1] As such, Eric will be advised as to the elements of the rule and whether the actions of Owen and the statutory permission mean that Hydrotricity has a valid defence.[2]

Hydrotricity should be advised that the applicable tort covers where someone brings something on to their land in furtherance of a non-natural use of their land, which if it escaped would be liable to cause harm. If the 'thing' does escape, then the person is liable for all of the damage which is a consequence of the escape, regardless of their fault in the 'thing' escaping.[3] To bring a claim, Eric must have a proprietary interest in the land affected by the escape of the waste and that his property was damaged (*Transco plc* v *Stockport MBC* [2004] 2 AC 1). We are not expressly told this, but it is likely this is satisfied based on the information we have.[4] On that basis, he would have standing to make a claim.

The first element to consider is whether Hydrotricity has brought something on to their land which amounts to a non-natural use of the land. Underpinning the rule is the idea that if the person has voluntarily brought a 'thing' on to their land and kept it there at their peril – here, the water – liability will arise where the 'thing' is not naturally there or its use is unordinary. Originally, this was held to mean a special use which brought increased danger and not some use which is proper

⁵ Although part of this has now been doubted, and so will not be applicable, including it in this way allows you to get across some analytical and evaluative comment in your answer, and illustrate your knowledge of the debate.

⁶ Be specific here as, for example, Lord Hoffmann did not think that ordinary use was any better than non-natural use. You, therefore, show more in-depth knowledge.

⁷ While it may seem as though this has obviously been satisfied, it still needs to be shown, albeit briefly.

⁸ Explaining the rationale for this element allows you to build up the level of evaluation in your answer, especially as it has been seen as being a relatively new requirement.

⁹ At the end of applying the elements, you should give a mini-conclusion as to whether the tort is likely to be made out in order to explain why there is a need to discuss defences.

for the general benefit of the community (***Rickards v Lothian*** [1913] AC 263). Therefore, ***Rickards*** is significant as Hydrotricity's use of the land for power generation has brought a significant upturn to the local economy and financial benefits to local consumers. This could be said, therefore, to benefit the community notwithstanding what has happened to Eric's farm.⁵ However, doubt was cast on the latter part of the ***Rickards*** interpretation in ***Cambridge Water Co. Ltd v Eastern Counties Leather plc*** [1994] 2 AC 264 where the creation of employment, in itself, was held not sufficient. This was affirmed in ***Transco*** where Lord Bingham⁶ said the focus should be on the increased danger to others from the use, with the question being simply whether the use is extraordinary in light of the time and place that it is done. Ordinary uses, bringing little risk, will be outside the rule. There may be scope to argue that this was an ordinary use in the circumstances, but storing large quantities of water, such as this, does bring increased danger to the neighbouring land if there were an escape. Ultimately, the number of cases which have held that storing water in large quantities on land is an extraordinary/non-natural use, including ***Rylands*** itself, means that this requirement will be satisfied by Eric.

The next aspect of the rule is that of escape.⁷ For a claim to succeed, the 'thing' must cross Hydrotricity's boundary and enter land not within their control (***Read v Lyons*** [1947] AC 156). This is clearly seen here as we are told that the water leaked out and flooded Eric's farm.

However, the harm caused by the escape must have been a type which was foreseeable. As the rule requires the person to keep the thing at their peril in case it escapes, then, in view of liability being strict, it is just to require that it is foreseeable that damage will be caused.⁸ Hydrotricity should be advised that in ***Cambridge Water*** it was stressed that the tort is not based on negligence and, therefore, even if the company demonstrates that it took all reasonable precautions to prevent the escape, this would not affect the issue of foreseeability of damage if the escape did happen. As the farm is next to the plant, it must have been foreseeable that the farm would suffer flooding if there was an escape of the accumulated water and, therefore, the harm which has occurred — damage to the field and the destruction of the crops must also be foreseeable. Therefore, it appears that, provided the use of the land is deemed an unusual use, the tort has been made out.⁹

[10] Even if you have determined straightaway that the defence will not help, it is worth including it as the facts raise it. Sometimes defences may be applicable for discussion even if they will not be successful. The key is to keep it brief and ensure that you include a line demonstrating you know why it does not apply, and therefore, understand its operation.

[11] Ultimately this defence will also be likely to fail so you could discuss the defences in either order. However, where one has more chance of success it is better to end with that as if it does succeed there is no need to consider the others. In this case, it is probably better to deal with this second as there is at least more of a debate to be had.

[12] These facts are important in determining whether there is any chance that Eric's claim may still succeed and so you need to use them to illustrate why, when it appears the defence is valid, he may still have a chance of success.

[13] Before you end, this is a final opportunity to show your understanding of the relationship between negligence and the rule and whether there is scope for the former to apply in the latter.

Hydrotricity should be advised that, while liability under the rule is strict, there are various defences to a claim. As the construction and operation of the plant was authorised by statute, they would seemingly be able to rely on the defence of statutory authority. However, the defence is only applicable if they were acting under a duty to accumulate the water on their land, and not simply where they have permission to accumulate the water (***Smeaton v Ilford Corporation*** [1954] Ch 45). Therefore, this will not aid them.[10]

The defence which Hydrotricity may have more success with[11] is that the escape was due to an act of a third-party, whom they had no control over (***Box v Jubb*** (1879) 4 Ex D 76). To defeat the claim on the basis that Hydrotricity is not at fault for the escape may seem at odds with the overall purpose of the tort, but there is some justification where it is a completely independent act of a stranger. This appears to be the case here as Owen is completely independent of Hydrotricity and intentionally caused the leak, and thus the flood, and so there should be no liability (***Rickards***). However, Hydrotricity should be advised that the defence, in fact, only applies if the third-party act could not have reasonably been contemplated and guarded against (***Perry v Kendricks Transport Ltd*** [1956] 1 WLR 85). Owen was a 'well-known' protestor and had made several efforts to gain entry to the plant[12] which suggests that the incident should have been in Hydrotricity's mind and efforts should have been made to prevent him gaining entry. Yet what happened was that a door was not properly secured which allowed him access. This suggests negligence on their part and so the defence would be defeated. Hydrotricity should be advised that, in view of the comments in ***Cambridge Water*** about the irrelevance to liability of taking reasonable care, and that in ***Transco*** negligence was again held not to play a part, even if they had not been negligent, they would still probably face liability notwithstanding ***Perry***.[13]

In conclusion, Hydrotricity face liability as the facts suggest that this is a non-ordinary use of such land, regardless of what benefits it has brought, and therefore the rule will apply to their activities, which they were not obliged to do. While the escape was caused by Owen, his act was arguably something which Hydrotricity had control over and so any defence on that basis will probably fail.

Make your answer stand out

- Highlight the background to the rule and the reason for its creation.
- Discuss in more depth the problem with the interpretation in *Rickards* and the significance of the move away from 'non-natural use' made by *Transco*, assessing its merit as you do.
- Consider the validity of distinguishing statutory authority on the grounds of acting with permission as opposed under a duty.
- Explore the extent that fault, or negligence, has become a part of what is a strict liability tort and whether this is a justifiable development.
- Even though it is a problem question, look to include some of the academic opinion relied on by the judges in their judgments.

! Don't be tempted to . . .

- Briefly apply the elements and finish the answer quickly. Make sure that you consider potential practical aspects of the question which may impact on the application of the elements.
- Discuss defences such as act of God or consent, which have no relevance and are not alluded to by the facts, in order to show that you know them and fill your answer out. Use any time and space you have to include more evaluation of the other issues.
- Over emphasise the relationship with torts such as nuisance.
- Get into a debate as to the future of the tort.

Question 2

'It has often been said, and continues to be said, that the rule in *Rylands* v *Fletcher* is but a sub-species of private nuisance. This claim represents the consumption of the former by the latter; but the claim rests on the flimsiest of foundations.' (Murphy (2010) *The Law of Nuisance*. Oxford: Oxford University Press)

Evaluate the requirements of the rule in *Rylands* v *Fletcher*, and, in light of the above, assess the merits of its ongoing retention as an independent tort or as an ancillary part of nuisance.

Diagram plan

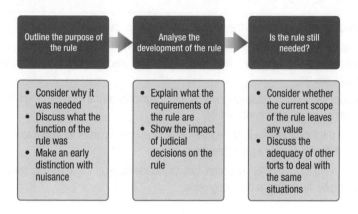

Outline the purpose of the rule	Analyse the development of the rule	Is the rule still needed?
• Consider why it was needed • Discuss what the function of the rule was • Make an early distinction with nuisance	• Explain what the requirements of the rule are • Show the impact of judicial decisions on the rule	• Consider whether the current scope of the rule leaves any value • Discuss the adequacy of other torts to deal with the same situations

A printable version of this diagram plan is available from **www.pearsoned.co.uk/lawexpressqa**

Answer plan

→ Outline the rule explaining the purpose it traditionally serves.

→ Discuss the differences between the rule and the tort of nuisance.

→ Evaluate the different elements of the rule, explaining why that aspect is needed.

→ Consider whether the function of the tort should resort to being an independent tort, a subsidiary of nuisance or abolished in favour of a tort such as negligence.

Answer

[1] It is important that you show the marker early that you understand the premise of the question and how the quote relates to what you have to do. Highlight briefly at the start the perceived link between the rule's development and its loss of distinctiveness, and therefore, its purpose.

The rule in **Rylands v Fletcher** has provided long-standing liability for a person who damages his neighbour's land through the escape of something which is not naturally present there. However, judicial thinking now treats the rule as part of nuisance, and this in turn has caused academics to question the ongoing merit of retaining the rule, indeed it has already been abolished in Australia.[1] It is argued that the tort, properly understood, is distinct and so still has a purpose to serve which warrants its retention.

The rule in **Rylands v Fletcher** is that, where a person brings on to land which he controls something which is not there naturally and is something which will foreseeably cause harm to neighbouring land if it escapes, liability will result where that eventuality occurs.

[2] As the English position is
that the rule is an extension
of nuisance, you should early
in your answer clearly set out
the rule's purpose and how
it differs. However, if you are
of the view that the rule is
justifiably part of nuisance,
then do the reverse. Make the
case early as to why it is, and
provide a platform from which
you can discuss whether there
is a role for the rule or not.
[3] The full citation is below
but, as explained elsewhere,
in an exam you are unlikely
to have time to write the full
citation but naturally you must
reference your influences.
Therefore, give a clear and
concise indication of your
source. It is also important to
distinguish this reference from
the quote by Murphy in the
question and make the reader
aware that you are referring to
a different text.

[4] Show that you know what
the wider reasoning was
for Lord Goff's opinion,
particularly as it goes to the
heart of the question: namely,
whether the tort is needed if it
is just a part of another tort.
[5] After your analysis of the
purpose of the tort, for clarity
and to aid the flow into the
elements of the tort, you
should restate briefly what
role the tort serves.

[6] As you discuss each
requirement you should try
to show how this supports or
otherwise the rule's retention
so that you are fully dealing
with the question at all times.

While it is one of a number of torts which protect land, the elements of the rule indicate its uniqueness. The rule targets the defendant's activities, imposing strict liability when they risk bringing something on to their land which may harm another's property. This could be seen as a response to industrialisation and the changing nature of land use to encompass more hazardous activities. Therefore, the rule differs from nuisance, which focuses on injury inflicted on the claimant's land.[2] The rule only refers to land which the defendant controls and the focus is on material damage from that land. While nuisance has led to recovery for material damage to the land, the orthodox position is that it concerns amenity interference. Therefore, traditionally there is a clear divide between the purposes of the torts. Historically, owing to the purpose of the rule, no proprietary interest was needed for standing; however, it was stated *obiter* in ***Transco plc v Stockport Metropolitan Borough Council*** [2004] 2 AC 1 that this is required. Murphy (2004)[3] has previously argued that nuisance developed to protect interests in land because of the link between land and social status, but this was not the reason behind the development of the rule and so it is questionable whether this requirement for standing is warranted which, if correct, confirms a distinct position for the rule. In ***Cambridge Water Co. v Eastern Counties Leather plc*** [1994] 2 AC 264, adopting the analysis of Newark,[4] Lord Goff held that the rule was a sub-species of nuisance, a position endorsed in ***Transco***. Today, the rule exists to deal with one-off escapes of substances from the defendant's land which cause harm,[5] but the acceptance of Newark's (1949) analysis has brought into question aspects of the tort.

For liability under the rule, the defendant must first bring something on to his land. This in itself does not need to be inherently dangerous, as seen in ***Rylands*** where the 'thing' was water. The 'thing' must then escape to an area not controlled by the defendant (***Read v Lyons*** (1947) AC 156). As the 'thing' must be likely to do harm upon escape, one escape is sufficient, and so there is a further distinction from nuisance. Nuisance involves looking at factors such as the sensitivity of the claimant and the duration of the interference. Therefore, certain acts may not equate to nuisance, but they would fall within the rule. Further, historically, personal injury was actionable under the rule; although the view of the rule as an extension of nuisance means this is no longer the case. Therefore, a return to its origins would increase the merit in retaining the rule as it would be serving a wider function.[6]

The rule was originally stated by Blackburn J in **Rylands** as requiring the 'thing' to not naturally be on the land; however, this was amended in the House of Lords to 'non-natural use'. This was interpreted in **Rickards v Lothian** [1913] AC 263 as a use which brings increased danger and is not merely the ordinary use of it. This additional requirement has been doubted in **Cambridge Water**, but the essence of the statement was retained in **Transco**; although, it was held preferable to apply a test of extraordinary and unusual use.[7] Lord Bingham emphasised that this may vary in different times and places; again, while having echoes of the assessed factors in nuisance, it must be remembered that what is being assessed is different. In nuisance it is the interference, whereas under the rule it is the use of the land by the defendant. Further, a use may be extraordinary but reasonable in nuisance, but unreasonableness would not matter under the rule.

[7] What you should be trying to do here is show that you appreciate how the phrase has developed through the case law but without getting too bogged down and losing some of the thrust of your structure which is the level of distinctiveness between the two torts.

The final requirement under the rule is that it is foreseeable that harm would occur upon the thing's escape. This was added in **Cambridge Water** for the purposes of determining remoteness of damage. Lord Goff felt it important to affirm this point because of the similarity he saw between the rule and nuisance, where it is required.[8] The basis for this requirement, however, is within the original rule itself where it talks about the 'thing' being 'likely' to cause mischief. Clearly, while the word was not used to determine this, it must be based upon foreseeability as this then justifies the strictness of liability.[9]

[8] By stating this you are trying to balance your argument by showing support for the view that the two torts are the same, particularly when the relationship with nuisance was not necessarily needed to decide the point in the case.

[9] Then go on to test the merit of the previously advanced view by seeing if the link to nuisance was needed.

While the English judiciary have increasingly merged the rule within nuisance, Australia has completely abolished the rule, using negligence to cover the same situations instead.[10] In **Burnie Port Authority v General Jones Pty** (1994) 120 ALR 42 the idea of a non-delegable duty to be owed by those in control of premises was adopted. As the scope of negligence had, over time, been greatly expanded while the rule's operation had been restricted, the difference between the two actions was now negligible and incidents covered by the rule were also captured within negligence, in fact more so in light of the current restrictions on personal injury claims under the rule. Countering this, Murphy (2004) suggests relying on negligence instead of the rule may be detrimental in industrial use cases as it will be harder for claimants to prove the necessary standard was breached; additionally, safety compliance certificates may deter people from even trying. Further, Nolan (2005) argues that fusion with negligence is misplaced as the rule is one of strict liability and,

[10] What you are about to do here is to engage with the final aspect of the question – whether liability under the rule should be abolished regardless of whether it is an independent tort or not. You should already have considered whether it serves a different function to nuisance, so now you are demonstrating your extended knowledge by evaluating the alternative argument that the rule can be covered by negligence, and so is not needed.

therefore, fault does not play a part, unlike in negligence. Additionally, the reasonableness of the use of land by the defendant, as confirmed by **Transco**, is irrelevant. Therefore, the rule is best not placed within negligence as its function is clearly distinct, and injustice or hardship for claimants could ensue.

In conclusion, there is nothing necessarily wrong in the rule being an aspect of nuisance, provided that the rule is not developed restrictively in a manner at odds from its original, and historical, rationale. However, to ensure this, and in light of the differences between the two, it would be best to revert to two distinct torts with different functions.

✓ Make your answer stand out

- To give your answer more academic depth read the following articles Nolan, D. (2005) The distinctiveness of *Rylands* v *Fletcher. Law Quarterly Review*, 121: 421–51; and Murphy, J. (2004) The merits of *Rylands* v *Fletcher. Oxford Journal of Legal Studies*, 24: 643.
- Discuss the justification of strict liability; is it right to have liability without fault?
- Write a fuller comparative evaluation of the rule and negligence in order to assess whether the Australian position may be advantageous.
- Draw on what was said by Lord Bingham in *Transco* as to what role the rule could serve in the future and, therefore, why it should be retained.

! Don't be tempted to . . .

- Go into detail on the torts of nuisance and negligence. The question allows you to judge whether the function of the rule could be performed by these but it is primarily a question on *Rylands* v *Fletcher*.
- Give just an overview of the rule and its elements; the second part of the question as to the need for the tort must be addressed.
- Just follow the premise in the quote; the actual question leaves it open for you to adopt whatever view you wish as to the worth of the rule.

❓ Question 3

LIS Ltd makes insulation products in its factory in Winfieldshire. Roger is employed to work the hot wire machine which is used to cut polystyrene into suitable size blocks. One day while working on the machine, which gets up to extremely high temperatures, Roger received a phone call from his girlfriend whom he had fallen out with that morning. Wanting to patch things up, Roger decided to take the call and got so involved with the conversation that he forgot to turn the machine off while he was on the phone, which lasted about 45 minutes.

Upset by how the conversation had gone, Roger went outside for a cigarette. When he returned inside, to his horror he saw that the polystyrene which he had been feeding into the machine had overheated. This had caught fire and, combined with sparks from the machine, had ignited some chemical gas which was stored in the factory. Upon seeing the fire, Roger panicked and ran out without trying to put the fire out but did set the alarm off. The fire destroyed not only the factory but also the neighbouring unit which was occupied by a furniture maker, Weir & Co. Ltd.

Advise LIS Ltd as to its potential liability to Weir & Co. Ltd.

Diagram plan

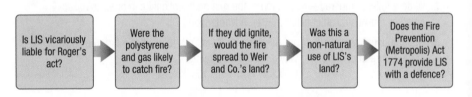

A printable version of this diagram plan is available from **www.pearsoned.co.uk/lawexpressqa**

Answer plan

→ Outline the background to the rule and its application to cases involving fire.

→ Consider the application of the requirements from the fire cases which seem to apply a variant of the rule.

→ Discuss *Gore* v *Stannard (t/a Wyvern Tyres)* [2012] EWCA Civ 1248 and assess the impact of applying the rule as stated in *Transco* to the situation.

→ Consider the application of the Fire Prevention (Metropolis) Act 1774 and any other possible defence.

Answer

The issue to advise LIS on is its potential liability under the rule in **Rylands v Fletcher** (1866) LR 1 Ex 265 for the damage caused by the fire spreading to the neighbouring property. This is important as liability, if found, is strict and will be imposed for all of the damage caused by the fire spreading.[1] It will be argued that there may be liability under the rule in light of some authorities as to how the rule applies to incidents of fire.[2] If not, there may still be liability for negligence.

The first issue to advise LIS on is that, while the fire was caused by Roger's inattention, as he is LIS's employee and the act occurred during the course of his employment, he was employed to operate the machine safely and did not do so during work time, LIS will be vicariously liable[3] for his actions. It also needs establishing that Weir & Co. Ltd have standing to bring an action against them. LIS should be advised that, while they would have suffered property damage as their unit was destroyed, they also need a proprietary interest in their unit (**Transco plc v Stockport MBC** [2004] 2 AC 1). As they operate a business from the unit and are a limited company, it is likely that the occupation would be on a formal footing such as a lease, so satisfying the requirement.

The rule itself provides that where a person brings something on to their land which is a non-natural use of that land, and which is likely to do mischief should it escape, liability will be imposed for the damage caused as a consequence of the 'thing' escaping. If fire itself had been brought on to LIS's land and escaped into neighbouring land, the application would be relatively straightforward as fire would be something likely to cause mischief upon escaping. The issue here is that no fire was brought on to the land; one was merely caused and then spread: thus what was brought on to the land did not escape.[4] However, LIS should be advised that the rule has been applied in such instances (**Musgrove v Pandelis** [1919] 2 KB 43).

The apparently applicable principles to apply[5] were stated in **LMS International Ltd v Styrene Packaging and Insulation Ltd** [2006] Build LR 50. The first requirement is that LIS brought on to its land things which were likely to catch fire and kept them in conditions which meant that if they did ignite they would spread to the claimant's land.

[1] As you are required to advise as to LIS's liability, you should state what the consequences would be if they are deemed liable.

[2] Give an early indication that you are aware that this situation is not necessarily a direct application of the rule.

[3] While the question is not specifically on vicarious liability, as with issues of standing, it should always be briefly addressed as the company does not appear to have done anything wrong here.

[4] This builds on from what was said in the introduction and shows that you understand the difference between the application of the rule proper and its varied form for fires.

[5] As will be explained later, there is some doubt as to the application of these principles; however, the old cases on which they are based have not expressly been overruled, so introduce them in this way.

Here LIS brought the hot wire machine, polystyrene and the gas chemicals which, particularly in the case of the latter, are two 'things' likely to catch fire. Although we are not told of the conditions under which these items were kept, the fact that this was a production factory suggests that significant quantities would be kept there. Additionally, the gas must have been kept reasonably close to the machine for the spark to have ignited the gas. Therefore, the conditions are likely to have been such that, if an item did ignite, there was sufficient other flammable material in the factory to generate a fire which would spread to the neighbouring unit. Obviously, more information would be needed here, and if the converse was established on the facts, there would be no liability.[6]

[6] As you are advising LIS as to its liability, explain with as much certainty as you can what the situation is, including whether LIS would have cause for optimism. Do not just make a definitive statement when the facts are silent.

However, on the basis that such conditions are deemed to exist,[7] the next factor to determine is whether this was done in the course of an extraordinary use of the land, considering the place and time that it is done. This relates back to whether the things were kept in conditions which were likely to spread, with the words 'non-natural use' referring to whether the 'thing' is naturally there. In *Mason v Levy Auto Parts* [1967] 2 QB 530, a range of flammable materials kept in a store was deemed such a use of the land. This was based on the quantity of materials, how they were stored and the character of the neighbourhood. As discussed above, the first two of these factors are likely to be equally present, and arguably so is the third. The fact that there is a neighbouring property adjacent to the factory does raise questions as to the holding of flammable material in the factory, particularly if the quantities are high.[8] In view of the similarities to *Mason*, this aspect may be satisfied.

[7] As doubt has just been raised whether the preceding requirement has been satisfied, you need to phrase the introduction to the next requirement in a way that follows on.

[8] Use the facts of the case to support your application of the requirement to the problem and whether it is satisfied by highlighting the similarities.

[9] Demonstrate that you have a wider appreciation of the issues and the debate which surrounds the area, and incorporate it into your answer by assessing whether it strictly matters whether it is a pure application of the rule or not.

Lastly, the 'thing' must actually ignite and a fire spread to the neighbouring property. Clearly, this has happened here and whereas under the traditional rule, the harm which occurs needs to be foreseeable, this was stated in *Mason* not to be sensible in fire cases as the 'thing' brought on to the land does not escape. While this furthers the debate as to whether this is indeed liability under the rule owing to the differing circumstances between the two situations,[9] LIS should be advised that it is generally accepted that liability is the same under both (Rogers, 2010).[10]

[10] Show that you have undertaken some wider reading, as well as adding depth to your evaluation, by including reference to some academic opinion on the matter.

However, recently in *Gore v Stannard (t/a Wyvern Tyres)* [2012] EWCA Civ 1248 it was strongly held that the traditional form of the rule, as stated in **Transco**, applies to fire, and questioned previous authorities such as **Musgrove** which suggested otherwise. While factually this is slightly different to **Gore**, in its traditional form the rule may not apply as the gas is unlikely to have escaped, just the fire.

[11] By covering the defences like this, you show that you know that they exist but also understand that they are clearly not applicable here, and so you do not waste time giving a fuller account of them.

LIS should be advised that, if the rule applies, the defences that the fire was caused by an act of God or by a stranger over whom they had no control would not be applicable.[11] Further, whilst section 86 of the Fire Prevention (Metropolis) Act 1774 provides a defence for accidental fires, which LIS may feel this is, 'accidentally' in the section has been construed restrictively to not include where the fire began through negligence (**Filliter v Phippard** (1847) 11 QB 347). The facts surrounding Roger's actions suggest negligence in operating the machine by leaving it unattended for so long with material in the machine. Further, the Act has been held not applicable where there was negligence in letting the fire spread (**Goldman v Hargrave** [1967] 1 AC 645). As we are told Roger did not attempt to prevent the fire spreading, this would appear to be the case.

In conclusion, LIS should be advised that it is vicariously liable for the acts of its employees in the course of their employment. That said, LIS may well be unlikely to be liable for the damage under the rule in **Rylands v Fletcher**, but, as Roger appears negligent, may be found liable under the tort of negligence itself.

✓ Make your answer stand out

■ Develop the point as to whether the rule should even apply to cases involving fire and, if so, whether it should be in its traditional form or the adapted form of cases such as *Musgrove* and *Mason*. Refer to *Gore* v *Stannard (t/a Wyvern Tyres)* in furtherance of this.

■ Consider whether there could be liability under another tort such as negligence or nuisance.

■ Provide more depth as to the application of vicarious liability.

■ Look at Ogus, A. I. (1969) Vagaries in liability for the escape of fire. *Cambridge Law Journal,* 27: 104, and use the views expressed in the article to support your arguments.

! Don't be tempted to . . .

- Make up facts, such as the conditions under which the gas was stored, to aid your argument. Advise LIS as to the position based on what you are told and what it could be in the event of further information.

- Fail to explain what the rule is in its original form, as you need to explain how the requirements for fire have developed from that.

- Treat the question simply as one of negligence. You could consider negligence as a possible alternative action if you have time, but where a question involves damage to land and a substance leaving one person's land and entering another's, the question will primarily be on the rule in *Rylands* v *Fletcher*.

www.pearsoned.co.uk/lawexpressqa

Go online to access more revision support including additional essay and problem questions with diagram plans, You be the marker questions, and download all diagrams from the book.

13

Trespass
to the person

How this topic may come up in exams

Trespass to the person consists of assault, battery and false imprisonment but each is relatively small in size and straightforward to apply to the facts so it is common for all of them to appear in the same problem question. You need to take the time to check the scope of how you are taught this tort to check whether you can expect other torts alongside it, such as the rule from *Wilkinson* v *Downton* or other forms of trespass. Essays will be rarer, but when they do arise will look at the effectiveness of the tort and its purpose.

Before you begin

It's a good idea to consider the following key themes of trespass to the person before tackling a question on this topic.

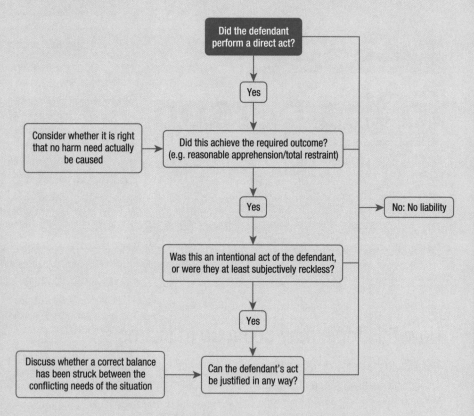

A printable version of this diagram plan is available from **www.pearsoned.co.uk/lawexpressqa**

❓ Question 1

Following a government announcement of changes to student funding a student demonstration was organised which was to include a rally in Academic Square. To try to ensure the peacefulness of the rally, the police allowed some protesters to enter the Square but, as intelligence had shown the rally might turn violent as the day went on, the police formed a line across all entrances to the Square and refused to allow anyone to enter or leave.

In anger at what he felt was the denial of his right to join the protest, Roy threw a dustbin at the police; although it missed the officers, it did smash a police car window. PC Barnes, having seen where the bin was thrown from, ran over and, believing Sandra had thrown the bin, pushed her to the floor yelling, 'That was utter madness; you'll pay the consequences for that.' Sandra was taken to a nearby police station. However, it was later proven that it had not been her who had thrown the bin and she was released. An administrative error meant though that the information was not passed to the custody officer, and Sandra had been detained for 26 hours by the time of her release.

Harriet had arrived at the Square to join the rally. However, she was informed by PC Arthur that she was too late and would have to protest elsewhere. Furious, Harriet yelled at PC Arthur, 'I know my rights! You need to let me past now!' PC Arthur just laughed at her, and informed Harriet that if she carried on he would arrest her. Harriet disconsolately threw a banner that she was carrying at PC Arthur's face and walked away.

Shocked, PC Arthur shouted back, 'You wouldn't be walking away if the Sergeant wasn't over there, you would be heading off in the ambulance. Remember, though, I can find out where you live.'

Advise the parties as to what actions they may take as a result of these instances.

Diagram plan

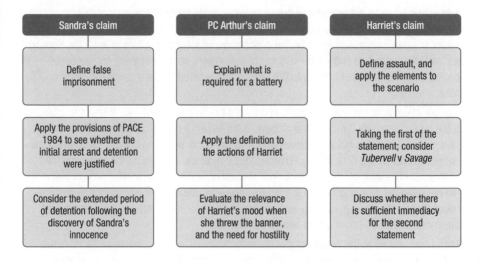

A printable version of this diagram plan is available from **www.pearsoned.co.uk/lawexpressqa**

Answer plan

→ Assess whether the initial arrest and detention of Sandra can be justified as lawful under PACE 1984 or whether it would amount to a false imprisonment.

→ Consider the significance and implication of the overall length of Sandra's detention.

→ Explain the requirements for a battery and apply these to Harriet's throwing of the banner at PC Arthur.

→ Evaluate the elements of assault and determine whether Harriet will have a claim.

[1] Including this here does make the introduction to this answer longer than usual. While you could deal with this in a second paragraph before you get into each incident, it can legitimately be outlined here. This allows you to show early on your understanding of the nature of these torts and keep a specific structure to your answer, dealing with each tort in turn.

Answer

The instances which have occurred during the demonstration potentially give rise to several claims under the tort of trespass to the person. This tort comprises assault, battery and false imprisonment with all three requiring discussion on the facts. The fact that it is these torts in question is significant because each is actionable *per se* without any need to show that the respective claimants have suffered any harm. This is because the interests that the tort protects are bodily integrity and liberty, and thus they are deemed to warrant heightened protection from even the slightest interference.[1] Each incident shall

[2] Where you have a multitude of instances in a scenario such as this one it is important that you provide an indication of how you will be dealing with them so your marker can follow your answer.

be taken in turn[2] with advice being given to those who have allegedly been the victim of the torts. It will be argued that, while PC Arthur has a claim for battery, Sandra for false imprisonment and possibly battery, Harriet will be unsuccessful in any claim.

The first incident involves Sandra, who should be advised as to false imprisonment where 'false' effectively means unlawful. False imprisonment requires intentionally and directly causing the total restraint of the claimant within an area set by the defendant, without lawful authority for doing so (**Bird v Jones** (1845) 7 QB 742). It is clear that PC Barnes did completely restrain Sandra as she was pushed to the ground and then taken to a police station, and this was all clearly intentional, particularly in light of his comments.[3] Obviously the police have the lawful authority to make arrests, but to be lawfully justified they must follow the procedures of the Police and Criminal Evidence Act (PACE) 1984. First, under section 24, PC Barnes needs to have had reasonable grounds for suspecting that Sandra had committed an offence. An offence has clearly been committed by throwing the bin, and it came from the vicinity where Sandra was. We are not told why Sandra was picked out as opposed to anyone else, but so long as he had reasonable grounds, this would be justified thus far. The issue comes, however, with how the arrest was conducted. Under section 28, Sandra would need to be informed that she was under arrest and the basis for doing so. We are not told that this was not complied with, but from what we are told was said it appears unlikely.[4] The section specifies that it must be complied with even where it is obvious. Here it would not be, especially if Sandra had seen Roy throw the bin. If not done at the time, it must be done as soon as is reasonably practicable afterwards. There does not appear any reason on the facts why it could not have been done at the time. If it was not done, the arrest and detention are unlawful, and Sandra would have an action for false imprisonment, and also battery[5] from when she was pushed to the ground.

[3] Use the facts as often as you can to support why you are making the assertion that you are. You need to make sure that the reader knows what you are thinking and why you are thinking it.

[4] It is common for students to think that because the facts are silent on a point it did not occur. Make sure you avoid making assumptions on this, but do give a view as to what is likely to be the case.

[5] Don't overlook the fact that, in order to arrest somebody, you need to touch them. If the arrest is unlawful, so is the touching, and therefore there is another action that Sandra can bring.

[6] Phrase this in this way to distinguish what you have just discussed, and what therefore may be lawful, with what you are about to discuss, which is the extended period of detention.

Even if the initial arrest and detention[6] are deemed to be lawful, it appears that Sandra would still have a claim based on the amount of time that she spent is custody. Once the reasons for detention are known to no longer apply a person should be released (s. 34, PACE). In any event, the maximum time spent in custody without charge can only be 24 hours. Even though this was 'an administrative error', Sandra should be advised that acting in good faith is no justification for restraining a person's liberty (**Evans v Governor of Brockhill Prison** [2001] 2 AC 19). Therefore, even if the initial arrest and period of detention was justified, once it became known that she did not commit the offence and she was not released, she has an action for false imprisonment.

[7] At this stage you have not established on the facts that the tort has been made out so, regardless of the apparent clear-cut nature of the incident, do not refer to the incident just yet as a definite tort, although you can be a bit more assertive than usual in your language.

The next incident concerns PC Arthur, who appears to have a clear claim against Harriet for battery.[7] A battery is an intentional, immediate and direct act which causes unlawful physical contact with the claimant. In relation to the first factor, even if Harriet asserts that she did not intend to hit PC Arthur when she threw the banner, subjective recklessness will suffice (**Bici v Ministry of Defence** [2004] EWHC 786). While it could be argued that the contact was made by the banner and not Harriet, this is irrelevant and there is long-standing authority that an intervening object may be used such as **Pursell v Horn** 112 ER 966. Strengthening PC Arthur's claim is the fact that, although Harriet threw the banner disconsolately as she walked away, a lack of hostility on her part will not defeat a claim. One of the earliest definitions of battery was said by Lord Holt CJ in **Cole v Turner** (1704) 87 ER 907 to be 'the least touching of another in anger' which suggests a hostility requirement in order to make the touching unjustifiable,[8] and this was certainly the view taken in **Wilson v Pringle** [1987] QB 237. In **F v West Berkshire Health Authority** [1990] 2 AC 1, however, Lord Goff explained that using hostility as the qualification for whether touching becomes unlawful ignores the fact that actions such as a slap on the back and non-consensual surgery are both battery yet both lack hostility. Instead what would take Harriet's actions outside of the remit of battery[9] is if it could be said to be within the bounds of generally accepted standards of everyday life. It would be very hard for her to successfully argue that throwing an object, especially the object in question, at someone performing their job simply because she could not get her way would not be acceptable, and thus this is a battery.[10]

[8] Explain why there is a debate as to hostility. This allows you to show your knowledge and analytical skills.

[9] Make sure that you use a phrase such as this to emphasise why the hostility is taking place.

[10] Now that you have fully gone through the tort and evaluated its applicability you should fully assert that it is a battery.

Finally, Harriet may claim for an assault by PC Arthur. Clearly the words used by PC Arthur indicate a willingness to inflict a battery on Harriet by having her require an ambulance. However, assault is causing the claimant to reasonably apprehend the immediate infliction of a battery (**Thomas v NUM** [1986] Ch 20). It is the requirement of reasonable apprehension which will see any claim defeated, as PC Arthur's words signify that he has no intention of actually injuring

[11] Don't forget about this additional comment by PC Arthur as it could be said to be an assault, but it has a different focus as to why the claim may not succeed. Therefore, your answer would not be complete without mentioning it.

Harriet because his sergeant is nearby. His words, as in **Tubervell v Savage** (1669) 86 ER 684, in fact negate any assault. The second comment as to knowing where she lives would also arguably lack any sufficient immediacy so as to be actionable either, even if the comment was deemed to lead to the reasonable apprehension of a battery.[11]

To conclude, Harriet will not have any claim following the incidents, but may find herself sued for battery by PC Arthur. The Chief Constable of the police force will possibly face an action for false imprisonment and battery by Sandra if it is established PC Barnes failed to comply with PACE.

✓ Make your answer stand out

- Highlight how, for actions against the police, the Chief Constable of the force in question will be deemed vicariously liable under the Police Act 1996, section 88.
- Using authorities such as *Harnett* v *Bond* [1925] AC 669 and *Warner* v *Riddiford* (1858) 4 CNBS 180, discuss also the possibility of a claim for false imprisonment against the Chief Constable for preventing people from leaving Academic Square.
- Highlight how, if Roy can be located, there could be a claim for trespass to goods against him by the police.
- From your general academic reading include some material so as to explain in a bit more depth some of the theoretical basis which underpins trespass and why it has strict liability and is actionable per se. You can also draw further on the views of Lord Goff in cases such as *Collins* and *F* for this purpose.

! Don't be tempted to . . .

- Go into aspects of false imprisonment which are not relevant such as whether the claimant knew they were restrained.
- View the question as quite straightforward and just race through an application of the law to the facts. Make sure you still try to evaluate the law, such as with regard to the need for hostility in battery, and use this to develop your argument. Otherwise you will miss out on marks for the depth of your analysis and evaluation.

❓ Question 2

Francesco and Edoardo were walking home from university one day, taking the path which runs alongside a very wide, deep and fast flowing river. As they were walking they saw Bubba and Dustin approaching on the other side of the river on their way to the local golf course. The four had recently had an argument after Edoardo had reported Bubba and Dustin for cheating in an exam which saw Bubba get expelled while Dustin was found innocent.

When Bubba saw Edoardo he yelled, 'You are dead for reporting me; I am going to put you in hospital for that!' Edoardo, feeling scared, decided to run so he could get home quickly. Feeling aggrieved by being reported when he was innocent, Dustin decided to chip a golf ball across the river at Edoardo as he ran off. However, he misjudged the shot and instead struck Francesco – who had decided to carry on walking home – in the back of the head.

When Edoardo got home, he decided to get his own back by ringing Bubba's house and playing a prank on Bubba's elderly grandfather, Zach, whom Bubba lived with, by informing him that Bubba had been run over and killed on his way to the golf course and that the police would probably be with Zach shortly. Upon hearing this Zach went into shock.

Advise Bubba, Dustin and Edoardo as to any liability they may face.

Diagram plan

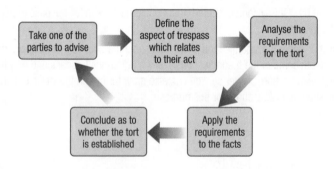

A printable version of this diagram plan is available from **www.pearsoned.co.uk/lawexpressqa**

Answer plan

➜ Define assault and consider whether there is sufficient reasonableness and immediacy to Bubba's threat.

➜ Outline the requirements for battery and consider the issue of transferred intent in relation to Dustin's act.

➜ Advise Edoardo as to the rule in *Wilkinson* v *Downton* and apply it to his call to Zach.

Answer

[1] By briefly demonstrating here your understanding of tort, you can get into the main premise of the question quickly so that you have enough time to fully evaluate the issues arising from the facts. You can then refer back to the tort's nature as required.

[2] Keep this brief as it is only the introduction. Set out in depth what the tort is about when you come to discuss Edoardo's liability. Simply show that you have appreciated that the rule is distinct and requires discussion.

[3] The reason for only including the name of the case in here is that you are seeking to draw a parallel with the facts of the case in order to use this as the authority for the argument which you will go on to advance. There will be no need to then state the facts as the marker will know from how you have structured the sentence that the two aspects of the definition which you are discussing were at issue in *Thomas*.

[4] This is why, although 'reasonable' comes first in the definition, you should address it second in your answer.

Bubba and Dustin will need to be advised respectively as to the torts of assault and battery, actions which overall constitute the tort of trespass to the person. These protect a person's bodily integrity and are actionable without proof of actual harm. This reflects the importance that tort places on this interest.[1] Edoardo's advice differs slightly in that he faces liability under the rule in ***Wilkinson* v *Downton*** [1897] 2 QB 57 which, while related to trespass owing to it having an element of intention, is a separate tort.[2] Each will be advised in turn.

The tort which Bubba may be liable for is assault. This is intentionally causing a person to reasonably apprehend the immediate infliction of a battery. The fact that Edoardo ran off scared after hearing Bubba's threat would suggest that he felt he was going to attack him. However, Bubba should be advised that this is not sufficient to establish liability and, as in ***Thomas* v *NUM*** [1986] Ch 20, there are two aspects of the definition which should mean that Bubba will escape liability.[3] The first is that the carrying out of the threat, the infliction of the battery, must be immediate. We are told that they were on different sides of a river which, from the description given, would appear impassable. This would mean that it was not possible for Bubba to actually perform the unlawful touching necessary for battery immediately. Even though some delay is permissible (***R* v *Ireland*** [1998] AC 147), Edoardo would still need to reasonably believe that the battery is imminent, which, on the facts seems unlikely. This leads into the second aspect of the definition which is an issue here,[4] namely the reasonableness of the apprehension. It is not sufficient that Edoardo subjectively felt that he was about to be hit, it must, objectively on the facts, be reasonable for him to apprehend this event. As it seems there was no possibility of Bubba crossing the river, and therefore no immediate danger, any apprehension he felt was not reasonable as Bubba was not going to be able to carry out the threat.

Dustin faces liability under the tort of battery. This is defined as an intentional, immediate and direct act which causes unjustifiable physical contact with the claimant. From the facts, there is clearly no issue around the requirement for an immediate act. Additionally, although it is a golf ball which makes contact rather than Dustin physically touching Francesco, this will also not matter; it is clear from case law that direct does not mean instantaneous and an intervening object can be used (e.g. in **Hopper v Reeve** (1817) 129 ER 278, where throwing water over someone was a battery). Dustin should be advised that even though his intention was to hit Edoardo rather than Francesco, this will not enable him to avoid liability. What must be intended is the act and not the result (**Bici v Ministry of Defence** [2004] EWHC 786), so Dustin's intention to hit Edoardo will simply be transferred to hitting Franceso. The application of the concept of transferred malice was first acknowledged in English law in **Bici** and one of the reasons for its application is by analogy with the criminal law. However, its application has been firmly rejected by Beever's (2009) article in the *Legal Studies* journal.[5] He argues that, unlike criminal law, in tort the identity of the claimant has significant importance and is essential to the cause of action and therefore the analogy does not work and the doctrine should not apply. If this were the case then Dustin, by not intending to strike Francesco, would not be liable to him for battery.[6] Therefore as **Bici** is only a High Court judgment, it is open for Dustin to defend any claim by Francesco on the basis that the doctrine should not apply in tort, but he should be advised that as the law currently stands he will be liable for battery. However, Dustin should be advised that even if successful on this point, it may instead lead to him being liable in negligence.[7]

In relation to Edoardo, the harm which his actions have led to did not flow directly from what he did: it was more indirect harm. As such, he could not face any claim under trespass.[8] However, where someone intentionally conducts themselves in a way which causes indirect harm, the rule in **Wilkinson v Downton** [1897] 2 QB 57 may be used to impose liability. In **Wilkinson** a prank call caused the recipient to suffer psychiatric injury, which was not recoverable at the time in negligence. The judge found the defendant liable on the basis that he had wilfully done an unjustified act calculated to cause harm; therefore, the intention to cause the harm which occurred was imputed by the judge. This appears very similar to what has happened with Edoardo. The rule was subjected, though, to extensive analysis in **Wainwright v Home Office** [2004] 2 AC 406 where it was held that imputed intention should not be used and that there must be an actual intention to cause harm, or the defendant would need to have acted without caring whether he caused harm. We are not told that Edoardo had an intention to cause harm, but it would seem that he was at the very least not caring whether he caused harm. The question is what

[5] You will not need to write the full article title and citation, but provide your marker with enough indication as to what work you are referring to.

[6] This is why it is worth commenting on the academic discussion around this issue, as it could form the basis of Dustin avoiding liability, which is what your task essentially is. More importantly, this also allows you to add to the analytical depth of your answer.

[7] Although the question is not on negligence, show your wider knowledge of tort by highlighting that you have seen further potential liability from Dustin's actions.

[8] By highlighting why Edoardo could not be sued in trespass, you not only show more depth to your understanding of that tort, you also create a platform from which to introduce the rule in *Wilkinson v Downton*.

sort of harm Edoardo's phone call has caused. We are told that Zach went into shock but no more. If this is a fully recognised psychiatric injury, then Edoardo is very likely to face liability either under the rule or in negligence. In *Wainwright*, Lord Hoffmann felt negligence was the better cause of action but subsequently the rule was used for this type of injury in *C v D* [2006] EWHC 166.[9] However, if the 'shock' was in fact merely a case of distress, then it would appear that Edoardo will not face any liability. Lord Hoffmann stated the rule does not provide a remedy in such instances and, while he was cautious about creating a tort of intentionally causing distress to deal with such a scenario, Lord Scott was strongly opposed to the idea, a view adopted in *Mbasogo v Logo Ltd* [2007] QB 846.

In conclusion, Bubba is unlikely to face any liability for assault, but Dustin is likely to be liable for battery; even if Dustin can avoid this, he may instead be liable in negligence. Determining the position of Edoardo requires more evidence as to the nature of Zach's injury. If it was simply distress that was suffered, he will not be liable, but if he suffered a medically recognised psychiatric injury, then Edoardo will face liability under the rule in *Wilkinson v Downton* or alternatively in negligence.

[9] Your aim is to pass comment on the rule, not to argue whether there is negligence. As the rule has been subjected to significant criticism, you should reproduce this and assess whether it is a suitable basis of liability for Edoardo.

✓ Make your answer stand out

■ Read Beever, A. (2009) Tranferred malice in tort law? *Legal Studies,* 29(3): 400–20 in full, to be able to add further points to your argument regarding Dustin and whether he should be liable for battery.

■ Discuss in more depth the future role of the rule in *Wilkinson v Downton* and whether there should be a tort covering the intentional infliction of distress.

■ Expand your comment as to Dustin being alternatively potentially liable in negligence to illustrate just how this may be the case.

■ When dealing with Edoardo not being able to be sued in trespass, consider the issue of negligent trespass arising out of the decision in *Letang v Cooper* [1965] QB 232.

! Don't be tempted to . . .

- Get too sidetracked regarding the merits of applying transferred malice in tort. Make sure you stay focused structurally on applying the law to the issue.
- Go through and apply all of the requirements of negligence, if you do discuss it. This could lead to your marker thinking that you have misidentified the main essence of the question, which is trespass, and you will also risk running out of time. By highlighting it, you will have shown an appreciation of that tort by way of the fact that you have seen its potential application.

? Question 3

Yvette (22) and Ed (21), two university students, had been sitting at a table on the patio of a coffee shop owned by Chuka, a small, elderly man in his sixties. A sign states that the patio area is only to be used by paying customers. As the pair had not purchased anything for about two hours and the shop was getting busy, Chuka approached them and asked that if they were finished could they leave so other customers could use the table. After a further 30 minutes, with the pair still there, Chuka return and shouted, 'If you lazy spongers don't clear off now, I will have to throw you off my property myself you know!' Chuka then went to shoo them away with a wet tea towel. Yvette was hit, however, and in trying to avoid it she rocked back on her chair. This was done too fast and she fell backwards falling on metal railing which pierced her body. Chuka rushed forward to help, but fearing that Chuka was about to attack him next, Ed picked up a glass ashtray and struck Chuka in the face with it causing a broken jaw.

Yvette was taken to hospital where she was seen to by Dr Burnham who rushed her into emergency surgery. Due to the level of blood loss, Dr Burnham conducted a blood transfusion. Naturally, Yvette was unconscious at the time and gave no consent for the procedure. Due to her religious beliefs, Yvette would not have consented even if she was conscious. Dr Burnham insisted that she would have died without it.

Advise the parties as to their liability.

Diagram plan

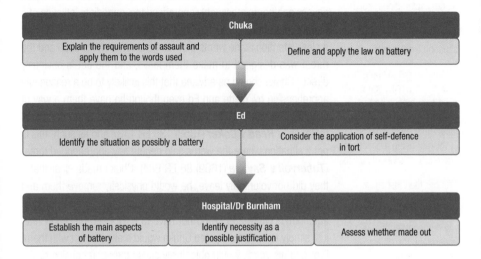

Chuka	
Explain the requirements of assault and apply them to the words used	Define and apply the law on battery

Ed	
Identify the situation as possibly a battery	Consider the application of self-defence in tort

Hospital/Dr Burnham		
Establish the main aspects of battery	Identify necessity as a possible justification	Assess whether made out

A printable version of this diagram plan is available from **www.pearsoned.co.uk/lawexpressqa**

Answer plan

→ Explain what assault is and discuss the relevance of the condition which Chuka had attached to his words.

→ Outline the requirements for battery in full and apply them to Chuka hitting Yvette with the tea towel.

→ Consider whether Ed can argue he was acting in self-defence when he struck Chuka with the ashtray.

→ Advise Dr Burnham as to battery, explaining whether he could claim that he was justified due to the necessity for carrying out the procedure.

Answer

[1] By highlighting these factors here, you show that you have identified all the topics in the question and where the complications may lie.

The potential liabilities of the parties all relate to trespass to the person and specifically the torts of assault and battery. While these torts are actionable without proof of damage, clearly some damage has occurred here. However, the issue, particularly for the latter two acts, is whether the actions were justifiable in the circumstances due to self-defence and necessity.[1]

[2] Obviously, you have not defined battery yet, so provide a brief explanation here. This will enable you to apply the requirements of assault to this situation more easily.

[3] Do not forget to apply this aspect. Generally, you would need to substantiate this statement but here, on the facts there really is no issue of this not being a direct act. Therefore, this would suffice.

[4] Rather than just show your knowledge of both of these cases, make sure you demonstrate that you understand the difference between them by explaining why one is considered unacceptable.

[5] Use the absence of clear factual evidence to support why you are not being more decisive.

[6] Again this is self-evident so you should simply state this fact and move on to the main discussion point of whether the touching was justified as an act of self-defence. As you have defined battery above, there is no need to do so again.

[7] Although a tort answer, you are still making an assertion of legal principle to set out your argument, so you should cite the criminal law authority for it. Your aim is to compare the two approaches and show that you have a real grasp of the basis of tort law and the principles underpinning it.

The first issue is whether Chuka is liable for assaulting Yvette and Ed. For an assault, there must be an intentional and direct act which causes another to reasonably apprehend the immediate infliction of a battery, the unlawful touching of that person.[2] Arguably, Chuka had a clear intention as he wants them to go away from his shop and the threat was designed to make them leave, and the act is obviously direct.[3] Chuka should be advised that this is likely to be a reasonable apprehension by Yvette and Ed even though he gave them a way of avoiding any battery. His words simply amounted to a conditional threat as in **Read v Coker** (1853) 138 ER 1437 and as such, this is not a situation where the words said negate any apprehended threat (**Tubervell v Savage** (1669) 86 ER 684). Chuka made clear that if they did not voluntarily leave, he would physically remove them and thereby sought to exert control over their movement and personal autonomy.[4] Yvette and Ed do not have to have been placed in fear, just simply to have anticipated Chuka would make contact with them. Provided his words would objectively cause the apprehension of the battery, which is supported by the movement towards them having previously hit Yvette with the tea towel, Chuka will be liable for the assault.

Chuka faces a more clear-cut case of liability for battery against Yvette. Battery is the intentional, direct touching of another without lawful justification. Intention must relate to intending to make contact with the person, and contact may be direct even if an intervening object has been used to achieve it (**Hopper v Reeve** (1817) 7 Taunt 698). We are told that Chuka simply intended to shoo them away which is not enough information to determine the matter;[5] however, under **Bici v Ministry of Defence** [2004] EWHC 786 (QB) subjective recklessness will suffice. Therefore, this is likely to amount to battery.

Ed also faces liability for battery. It is clear that by striking Chuka with the ashtray Ed has satisfied all of the elements of the tort.[6] Ed could avoid liability by proving he acted in self-defence and, therefore, the touching was, in fact, justified and so not a battery. Ed's issue is that while he felt Chuka was going to attack him imminently, he was mistaken. Under the criminal law, acting under an honest, but mistaken, belief is sufficient for self-defence irrespective of how unreasonable the mistaken belief was (**R v Williams (Gladstone)** [1987] 3 All ER 411).[7] However, self-defence is different in tort, and the mistaken belief must have been reasonable to hold (**Ashley v Chief Constable**

[8] All of the judges stated an opinion on this so remember to be specific as to who you are referring to, as this shows that you have a greater level of knowledge of the case.

[9] Raise this as a prospect in order to show that you appreciate the connection between the two torts.

[10] The point of writing your answer in this way rather than talking about the 'defence' of necessity is that it indicates you have a deeper understanding of the tort by recognising that, if the touching is not unlawful, there is no tort from the start – not that there was a tort but a defence applies to negate liability.

[11] It is important on this point to make sure to draw on the specific factual wording of the question to support the conclusion you are drawing.

[12] You have just created some doubt, so make sure you clearly explain that you are proceeding with your advice on the basis that it will be proven. Otherwise your answer could lack coherence.

of Sussex [2008] UKHL 25). Lord Scott[8] noted the different purposes of tort and crime. Therefore, if tort adopted the same approach to self-defence, the wrong balance would be struck between a person's right not to be subjected to physical harm and another's right to prevent an imminent attack with reasonable force. As a person's liberty would be at stake, not imposing a criminal sanction on a person in such circumstances is justifiable. However, setting aside one's right to physical integrity based on an unreasonably held belief would not be justifiable. Therefore, Ed's liability rests on the reasonableness of his belief that he was going to be imminently attacked. Arguably, Chuka's demeanour could suggest an imminent physical attack. However, much depends on how the words were said and his demeanor. Further the proximity of Ed to Yvette would be a factor. If there was distance between them it is hard to maintain a belief that Ed reasonably thought Chuka was coming for him. Overall, while perhaps honest, the reasonableness of the belief is questionable which might, in turn, raise questions over whether there was an assault by Chuka.[9]

However, even if Ed satisfies the reasonableness requirement, he must also have acted proportionately to the threat posed by Chuka (*Lane v Holloway* [1968] 1 QB 379). Here Chuka was, at the time in question, unarmed and significantly older that Ed, yet Ed struck him in the face with a glass ashtray. This could be said to be disproportionate and so Ed would be liable for the battery.

The remaining issue is whether Dr Burnham is liable in battery for operating on Yvette without her consent. By performing the transfusion, the initial elements of a battery are clearly present. The issue is whether this was a justifiable intrusion of Yvette's physical integrity due to the situation. Liability will, therefore, rest on whether the intrusion was justified on the grounds of necessity. If so justified, the fundamental essence of the tort, unlawfulness, is missing.[10] This issue is governed by *F v West Berkshire HA* [1990] 2 AC 1 and the touching must be shown to be necessary in the circumstances, and that it was not practicable to communicate with Yvette. As she was unconscious, it was clearly not possible to ask for her consent. Therefore, it must be considered whether it was practicable to wait until she regained consciousness. We are told that Dr Burnham felt it was an emergency and Yvette would have died from the blood loss without the transfusion.[11] While this needs to be proven, on that basis though[12] it was not practicable to wait to seek Yvette's consent.

13 In terms of advising
Dr Burnham of his liability,
this would be an important
piece of information for him
and impacts ultimately on
whether he would be held
liable or not. Although no
specific mention is made
of advising the hospital,
or of vicarious liability, by
mentioning this you will gain
marks for having recognised
that the doctrine will
operate here.

The action taken must also have been reasonable in the circumstances in which it occurred. This requires evidence from a reasonable body of medical opinion demonstrating support for Dr Burnham's action. We are not told whether this is the case, but if it was a life and death matter it would be likely. If it was reasonable, there would be no liability under *F.* However, in any event, Dr Burnham should be advised that any claim would probably be brought against the hospital under the doctrine of vicarious liability. Therefore, even if the transfusion was an unjustified intrusion, and thus there was a battery, he should avoid personal liability for his performance of the operation[13] (***Cassidy v Ministry of Health*** [1951] 2 KB 343).

In conclusion, Chuka is likely to be found liable for assault and battery; Ed is also likely to be liable for battery as, even if deemed reasonable, it was potentially disproportionate. Dr Burnham and/or the hospital will, however, not be liable due to him acting out of necessity.

✓ Make your answer stand out

- Consider including a short discussion on trespass to land. The question does not limit you to trespass to the person, and the facts would support the view that Yvette and Ed had become trespassers. This would demonstrate the breadth of your knowledge.

- Include a discussion of the need for hostility in relation to battery.

- Ensure that you explain why the hospital is vicariously liable for Dr Burnham. It is something which should be considered, but it can easily be forgotten in the exam room, especially when the question is not specifically on vicarious liability.

- Discuss the merits of adopting the solution proposed by Lord Scott in *Ashley.* This would require you to think of the consequences of such a change and its merits. To aid this, you may want to look at the Court of Appeal judgment from the case and particularly paragraphs 63 to 78 where Lord Clarke MR discusses this.

- Read *Re A, (Children) (Conjoined Twins: Surgical Separation)* [2001] Fam 147 for a detailed overview of the law on necessity which you could then draw on in your answer.

! Don't be tempted to . . .

■ Repeatedly define each tort and state what is required. Structure your answer in a way which avoids this.

■ Avoid the debate over self-defence, or deal with it too briefly, as this is arguably the key point in the question where you can gain extra marks for the level of evaluation within your answer.

■ Turn your answer into an essay on the nature of self-defence. It may seem tricky but you have to strike an appropriate balance between demonstrating a deeper level of knowledge and understanding and adding analytical depth with the fundamental need to employ a good structure and answer the question that has been set.

■ Discuss other defences which have no application on the facts just to show that you know them. This will just show that you have not understood the question properly and is indicative of a descriptive, narrative type answer.

www.pearsoned.co.uk/lawexpressqa

Go online to access more revision support including additional essay and problem questions with diagram plans, You be the marker questions, and download all diagrams from the book.

Interests in reputation and private information

How this topic may come up in exams

The scope and media prominence of these issues make them a popular exam area. You should check your module to see the extent you cover the misuse of private information in conjunction with defamation, as while separate torts, they are linked. The structure of defamation and its defences lends itself well to problem questions. Whereas the wide-ranging arguments as to whether there should be a general tort protecting privacy, and the development of a tort of misuse of private information, means that this lends itself extremely well to essay questions, the opposite of both is also common. Overall, it is important to know the influence of human rights on both torts as both consist of a balance between Articles 8 and 10.

■ Before you begin

It's a good idea to consider the following key themes of interests in reputation and private information before tackling a question on this topic.

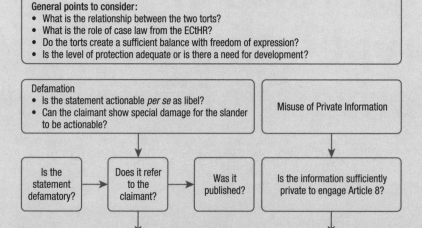

A printable version of this diagram plan is available from **www.pearsoned.co.uk/lawexpressqa**

❓ Question 1

Michael Paxman is an investigative reporter for the *Westminster Echo,* a weekly political magazine. He has been looking into a local MP, Peter Seldon. Peter Seldon is also currently the housing minister with responsibility for planning applications, and before entering Parliament was a director of a national house-building company. Michael's investigations have uncovered that Peter's previous company has received preferential treatment in planning decisions. Additionally, he has established that Seldon had retained shares in the company which he has just sold for a sizeable profit after the company had obtained planning permission for a new town development. Michael has now published his investigation in the latest edition of the *Westminster Echo;* an extract on the front page reads:

'Today we reveal how housing minister, Peter Seldon, joins the list of corrupt MPs who shame Parliament. Evidence indicates he is favouring former business associates in deciding planning applications. Not content with doing favours for those associates, he has also pocketed thousands of pounds from a shareholding in the company.'

Inside the magazine, however, the story states that Peter had registered the shares in the register of members' interests, and stresses that there is no evidence of him receiving financial payments from the company for the decision.

During a televised debate in the House of Commons on housing policy, Peter responds:

'Michael Paxman, a two-bob journalist with a history of fabricating and plagiarising stories: it is he who brings shame on his profession.'

Advise both parties as to whether they have a claim for the respective comments in defamation.

Diagram plan

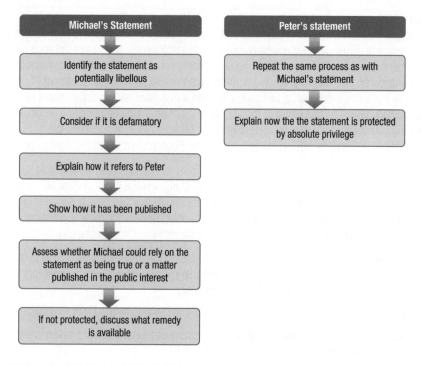

A printable version of this diagram plan is available from **www.pearsoned.co.uk/lawexpressqa**

Answer plan

→ Define what defamation is and establish that we are concerned with libel.

→ Apply the three requirements of defamation, in turn, to the newspaper story and ensure that you identify the key allegation against Peter.

→ Consider the possible defences which could apply to the paper, namely truth and publication on a matter of public interest. If not applicable, advise of the remedy available.

→ Repeat the application of the requirements of defamation to the comments by Peter.

→ Discuss the defence of absolute privilege for Peter.

Answer

The issue to consider is the validity of claims by both parties for defamation. Such claims bring into focus the tension between protecting one's reputation while recognising free speech and the need for a free press. This is significant here as the matter involves investigative journalism into

[1] In a defamation action it is important to note who the claim is against as it is an expensive process. A media organisation is well equipped to fight such claims, as opposed to an individual journalist, and this may have a bearing on whether Peter will want to bring a claim, especially if you advise him that the claim may not succeed.

parliamentary corruption. It will be argued that while both statements appear defamatory, the defence of privilege will protect Peter, but his own claim may be defeated due to the statement being in the public interest.

Advising Peter first, it should be noted that while the comment was by Michael any action should be brought against *The Westminster Echo*[1] as ultimately being responsible for the story. He should also be advised that defamation can take two forms: libel or slander. The former is where the comment is made in a permanent format and thus is actionable *per se*. As the comment has been printed, it would be libel and significantly means Peter will not need to show damage from the statement. Defamation is the publication of a statement about a person which lowers their reputation in the eyes of society. However, under section 1 of the Defamation Act 2013, the harm caused, or likely to be caused, to Peter's reputation must be serious. This would appear to be the case in light of the allegation and his position. As such, three elements need satisfying.

[2] Not only is it important that you clarify for the purposes of this element which statement may be actionable, but it is also important when you discuss defences, so make sure you spell out what exactly it is that was said which was defamatory.

The first requirement is whether the statement is defamatory meaning Peter's reputation is lowered in the estimation of right-thinking members of society (**Sim v Stretch** [1936] 2 All ER 1237). This is determined with reference to the fair-minded and not unduly suspicious reasonable man (**Lewis v Daily Telegraph** [1964] AC 234). There appears to be no issue here: looking at the front page extract, the allegation is that Peter is corrupt, making ministerial decisions for profit. However, under **Charleston v News Group Newspapers** [1995] 2 All ER 313, a passage cannot be taken in isolation where other parts negate the effect of the libel. From the overall story, it is clear that no financial wrongdoing is alleged. Therefore, Peter could not base a claim on such suggestions, but the story does not negate the allegation of corruption by favouring associates,[2] which would lower the reputation of a politician in the public's eyes. The second and third elements, that the statement refers to the claimant and is then published to a third party, respectively, are clearly satisfied as the article is about the housing minister, Peter Seldon, and has been printed in a national magazine.[3]

[3] As there are no contentious issues in the facts on these points, keep them brief to save you time to discuss the more relevant aspects.

[4] Although the old law referred to the 'sting' and you may still see it used, this is the word in the section so demonstrate your knowledge by using it.

While Peter may have a claim for defamation, reflecting the need to create a balance with freedom of expression, several defences are recognised which may assist *The Westminster Echo*. These have recently been placed on a statutory footing by the Defamation Act 2013. The first defence is whether the story is true (s. 2). The key imputation[4] is that Peter is corrupt by favouring former associates in determining planning

[5] This is why you should discuss this defence second. It comes into play if the statement cannot be shown to be true so you can show your knowledge of both. Whereas it would not make sense to talk about trying to show the statement is true if you have satisfied the other defence.

[6] Set out some background to the new defence to provide some context and show your wider knowledge, but don't get too diverted into a tangential discussion.

[7] This allows you to show your knowledge of how the new and old defence relate to each other. Further, as the defence is still new it has not been developed through case law as yet; therefore, some of the old law will still be relevant for now to help explain some aspects.

[8] Include something like this to indicate that you have picked up on the subtlety and nuance of the section in that something may be a matter of public interest, but would not be reasonable in the public interest to publish, e.g. claims of police incompetence not being reasonable to publish due to the impact on national security.

decisions and *The Westminster Echo* will need to show it is substantially true (s. 2(1)). The extract suggests Michael has evidence that Peter's former company has received preferential treatment so this may be the case.

In the event of not being able to prove it is substantially true *The Westminster Echo* could rely on the section 4 defence[5] of publication on a matter of public interest which has replaced the old defence from ***Reynolds* v *Times Newspapers Ltd*** [2001] 2 AC 127. Although it will apply in similar circumstances to the *Reynolds* defence it aims to be clearer and simpler in its application, particularly by breaking the link with privilege. It is broader in that it applies to statements of fact and opinions.[6] The defence has two limbs: first the statement must be one of a matter of public interest (s. 4(1 (a)) and must be determined in light of all of the circumstances of the case (s. 4(2)). In light of the nature of the allegation this would clearly seem to be satisfied as it relates to a government minister abusing his position. Further, the public would want to know all aspects of the story as it involves how the government is operating and making important decisions notwithstanding any suggestions of corruption.

The second aspect of the defence is that *The Westminster Echo* reasonably believed that publishing the statement was in the public interest (s. 4(1)(b)). Peter must be advised that this is again determined in light of all of the circumstances of the case, and allowance must be given for editorial judgement (s. 4(4)). Under the old law, focus was given to how responsible the journalist had been in gathering the story and the statement could not be motivated out of malice. However, while these concepts are not expressly covered by the new defence similar considerations do apply.[7] If *The Westminster Echo* has acted irresponsibly or maliciously it would affect the reasonableness of their belief in the story being in the public interest. Indeed, it would also raise questions as to whether the statement was even in the public interest to publish in the first place. Ultimately, the statement in issue – preferential treatment – is sufficiently integral to the overall story to warrant inclusion: it is the story itself so the excercise of such editorial judgement can be justified. As we are informed that *The Westminster Echo* has evidence to support its claims, on the basis that it is credible and sourced responsibly, it would be reasonable to believe the public should know the allegation, especially as there is no apparent countervailing public interest in not publishing the story.[8] Therefore, *The Westminster Echo* would most likely have a defence to a claim by Peter.

In switching to advise Michael now, the matter would again be libel as, although it involved spoken words, the debate was televised (Broadcasting Act 1996, s. 166). The words spoken are therefore published and by naming Michael directly it would be considered as referring to him.

Even though it is a common name, the context clearly refers to Michael (*Jameel* v *Wall Street Journal Europe* [2006] UKHL 44). There is also no apparent issue with the statement being defamatory as it clearly suggests that Michael makes up his stories and copies the work of others.[9] However, Peter will have the defence of absolute privilege. MPs, under Article 9 of the Bill of Rights 1689, cannot be questioned in court on statements from parliamentary proceedings. As the statement was made during a parliamentary debate, the defence will apply unless Peter waives his right to the defence under the Defamation Act 1996, s. 13. Otherwise, Michael cannot seek redress.

In conclusion, it appears that *The Westminster Echo* may well have a defence to any claim by Peter; however, Michael would certainly be unsuccessful in any claim against Peter.[10]

[9] As before, you just need to simply apply the elements to the statement and show how they are made out.

[10] Although you have effectively concluded each party's claim and this may seem like repetition, you should round off the answer with a summary of the position.

✓ Make your answer stand out

- Consider the position for the parties of any re-publications which may occur.
- Highlight the human rights considerations regarding freedom of expression which are inherent in the tort.
- Read Mullis, A. and Scott, A. (2014) Tilting at Windmills: the Defamation Act 2013. *Modern Law Review*, 77(1): 87–109 to supplement your discussion regarding the application of the new defences with academic opinion and commentary.

! Don't be tempted to . . .

- Discuss aspects of the tort, such as whether the statement was published, which are not issues in dispute; similarly don't consider defences just to show you are up-to-date with the changes brought about by the new Act.
- Go into great detail as to the *Reynolds* defence and the factors to consider whether something is responsible journalism.
- Make definitive statements as to the liability of the parties, as the facts do not support such findings.
- Give detail as to slander, as it is not the form of defamation within the question.

❓ Question 2

Kyle Springer is a famous Christian TV presenter who during his shows regularly advocates a life of purity for his viewers. The gambling industry is often a target for his tirades against immoral living and he calls those involved in organising gambling events 'parasites on the poor and vulnerable'. His strong moral convictions have led to his TV show attracting millions of viewers and resulted in his receiving a vast income through endorsing various products.

However, investigative reporter, Morgan Douglas, found out that Kyle hosted a weekly poker night at his mansion. To protect his reputation, the poker nights are strictly private and by invitation only; the guests only ever include Kyle's closest circle of friends. On the night of the March event, using long-range photography, Morgan managed to secretly take a photo of Kyle standing in his doorway with a pack of cards and some poker chips in his hand.

A fortnight later, Morgan's newspaper, the *Daily Reflection,* ran a story with the headline: 'Springer's gambling shame! "Moral" star in regular gambling sessions'. The photos were also published alongside the story. Prior to the publication, Kyle had checked himself into rehab, acknowledging that he had a gambling addiction which he cited as the reason for his anti-gambling tirades. This fact was also published within the body of the story.

Traumatised by the publication of the poker nights and details of his rehabilitation, Kyle now seeks your advice over the matter.

Diagram plan

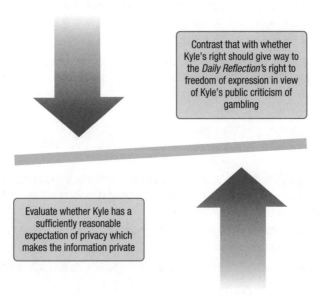

Contrast that with whether Kyle's right should give way to the *Daily Reflection's* right to freedom of expression in view of Kyle's public criticism of gambling

Evaluate whether Kyle has a sufficiently reasonable expectation of privacy which makes the information private

A printable version of this diagram plan is available from **www.pearsoned.co.uk/lawexpressqa**

Answer plan

→ Outline what the cause of action would be.

→ Explain why there is no general tort regarding the invasion of privacy.

→ Set out the requirements for the tort of misuse of private information.

→ Balance Kyle's right to privacy against the *Daily Reflection's* right to freedom of expression.

→ Consider whether the details of the story and the inclusion of the photos were a necessary and proportionate response to any public interest in publishing.

→ Assess what remedy Kyle could expect, if successful.

Answer

[1] Indicate your awareness of the extent of privacy protection in tort and what Kyle's action could be.

[2] By mentioning *Campbell*, you show the parallels between Kyle's situation and *Campbell*, and how that authority will form the basis of your answer.

[3] Use this wording to show your awareness of the context around the debate on privacy protection and the workings of the Act. This allows you to develop this point later to show how Kyle's action may come about.

[4] Demonstrate your knowledge of the background to the action and how it arose to make existing laws compatible with the Convention.

The issue to determine here is the extent to which Kyle may have redress in tort for the publication of his hosting of poker nights and his subsequent rehabilitation. This will involve assessing the extent to which the law recognises rights to privacy and protects them under the tort of misuse of private information.[1] It will be argued that Kyle may be entitled to damages because of the parallels with **Campbell v MGN Ltd** [2004] UKHL 22,[2] depending on the level of detail published in relation to his treatment.

Notwithstanding that privacy is a fundamental human right under Article 8 of the ECHR, which has been incorporated into English law by the Human Rights Act 1998, the absence of any horizontal effect between private citizens[3] means there is no general tort protecting invasions of privacy as has happened here. This was clearly stated in **Wainwright v Home Office** [2003] UKHL 53 which saw no need for its creation, particularly by the judiciary. However, Kyle should be advised that this does not mean he automatically has no redress. As Hunt (1998) has argued, while the courts do not have the power to create new rights to achieve compatibility with the ECHR, as public bodies they must develop and interpret existing laws in a manner which is compatible with Convention rights. Therefore, Kyle may have an action under the tort of misuse of private information which has developed out of the equitable doctrine of breach of confidence. In developing this in light of the HRA, the requirement for a prior confidential relationship has gone[4] (**Campbell**).

To bring an action, Kyle will have to demonstrate that the information published was private and thus protected by Article 8, and then demonstrate that his interest in this information remaining private outweighs the paper's right of freedom of expression under Article 10 (*McKennit* v *Ash* [2008] QB 73).

[5] While there appears to be some agreement on this point by the majority, they all gave separate opinions and the minority only dissented on the application of the balance to be struck in the instant case. Therefore, you should be specific as to whom you are referring when referencing aspects of *Campbell*.

In proving the first requirement, the courts, following *Campbell*, employ a 'reasonable expectation of privacy' test. In *Campbell*, Lord Hope[5] explained that where the information published is obviously identifiable as being private, a reasonable expectation of privacy would result. The fact that the poker games occurred in Kyle's own home, and by strictly private invitation only, suggests that this information can objectively be identified as private. Objectively looking at the situation, as *Campbell* said we should, it would appear that people should have an expectation of privacy in relation to what they legally[6] do with their friends at home, particularly as it has been held to attach to routine daily acts (*Murray* v *Express Newspapers plc* [2008] EMLR 12).[7] The information of his gambling addiction and rehabilitation is clearly private and thus would warrant protection under Article 8. Therefore, it seems that Kyle had a reasonable expectation of privacy in relation to the matter.

[6] Including this avoids questions as to your logic; if this were an illegal drug-taking party, it might be harder to say that it should carry an expectation of privacy. You prevent the marker having issues with the proposition.

[7] Mentioning this reinforces that acts within the home are capable of having a reasonable expectation of privacy.

However, Kyle should be aware that, just because he has an expectation to privacy, it does not mean he has an automatic right to keep the information private. Under the breach of confidence action a public interest defence always existed which has now been developed to balance Articles 8 and 10, which both Articles themselves make clear should happen where it is necessary for a democratic society. Therefore, Kyle will have to show that his interest in keeping the information private outweighs any public interest in the story. Kyle may have problems here as the thrust of the information is that he is a habitual gambler when he has made a career out of denouncing such activities. This obviously leaves him open to charges of hypocrisy and as he is a public figure creates a public interest in highlighting this. The same issue was the basis for the claim in *Campbell* except that it concerned drug-taking. In *Campbell* it was accepted by all, including the claimant, that a public interest in publicising her drug-taking existed in light of her previous denials. That marks an important distinction between these situations, as *Campbell* involved not only hypocrisy but also illegal activity, whereas Kyle's gambling is legal. However, it must be considered that Kyle has made substantial sums of money from criticising those who organise gambling activities. Therefore, while legal, his actions do carry a sufficient public interest and thus there is sufficient reason for the paper to interfere with his privacy right.

Notwithstanding this potential public interest, Kyle should be advised that the information published must be proportionate to the legitimate aim that is being pursued by the paper through the exercise of their freedom of expression: otherwise, a claim will succeed. This was explained in **Campbell,** as again involving a balancing exercise between the two conflicting rights. In **Campbell** the publication of the information of the claimant's condition and the fact that treatment was being sought was deemed to be a proportionate response. However, the reason why **Campbell** succeeded in her claim was because the newspaper published details as to the nature of her treatment as well as photos of her leaving the treatment centre. This information was held to be disproportionate to the legitimate aim of highlighting her illegal drug-taking. To advise Kyle further we would need to know whether the paper merely stated that he was attending rehabilitation or went further.[8] If it was just the former, then under the authority of **Campbell** any action would not succeed, but if further information as to his treatment was published, he could have a successful claim under the tort. While we do know that they have published photos of Kyle, these are distinguishable from **Campbell**[9] in that they were simply of him at his house with the cards and poker chips. Although taken covertly, of him and of his house, these could be said to simply provide credibility to the claims in the story which the public has an interest in knowing, as a form of factual evidence unlike the **Campbell** photos.

In conclusion, Kyle should be advised that it is unlikely he would have a successful claim merely for the revelation that he is a gambling addict receiving treatment, with the publication of the photo unlikely to change this. However, a claim may succeed if the story featured specific details as to his treatment. If this is the case, Kyle would be entitled to damages, although these tend to be low.[10] He could also seek an order for delivery of any remaining photos and copies of the information which the paper still holds. He should also be advised that if the paper is seeking to publish a further story, he could then seek an injunction in order to prevent that additional publication.[11]

[8] Remember we are not told this definitively and so you should not frame any statement more assertively than this.

[9] Owing to the factual similarity to *Campbell,* a lot of your answer will require demonstration of your factual knowledge of *Campbell* and understanding of the law in order to compare and contrast it to Kyle's situation and what Kyle may do.

[10] This highlights your awareness that, unlike with libel, any action is not likely to bring much compensation. Further, it is good to include as it is the sort of information a client may want to know before deciding whether to bring a claim.

[11] While we are not told if this is the case, it is often how newspapers work in order to prolong stories over time; therefore, by referencing it in this way you show your knowledge of the other remedies available but in a context relevant to the question.

Make your answer stand out

- Read the article by Hunt, M. (1998) The 'horizontal effect' of the Human Rights Act 1998. *Public Law*, Autumn, 423–43.
- Make sure you fully understand the case of *Campbell* and use your knowledge to substantiate your answer by drawing parallels and/or distinctions.
- Discuss what options Kyle may have if the paper were to have further stories which they want to publish.
- Highlight the seemingly different approach that the courts take between claims based around misuse of private information and those based on defamation.

! Don't be tempted to . . .

- Spend too long discussing why there is no general tort and whether this is justified. Remember there is a recognised action which he could use, and it is your knowledge and understanding of that action which the question is seeking to assess you on.
- Give a long factual account of *Campbell;* while you need to compare the two situations, this does not necessarily mean you have to provide a detailed factual account of *Campbell.* Concentrate on applying the legal principles to Kyle and using *Campbell* to simply support your reasoning.
- Include numerous references to other cases just to show you know them. If citing them adds substance to your argument, then do so, if not then leave them out.

? Question 3

Dermott is an ageing but still famous singer who has just released a new album containing a series of love songs, which is a radical departure from his usual rock tracks. This followed his recent secret wedding to a young fan, Tulisa, and was recorded as a sign of his everlasting love to her; although only a handful of people in the record industry knew this. The album was exclusively reviewed in the influential music magazine, *Top Hits!*. However, the review was quite negative with the writer, Louis Barlow ending by saying:

> 'While it may seem out of place on the album musically in light of the reason for this change of music direction, it is surprising not to see a cover version of *Money, Money, Money* by Abba on there.'

Additionally, the online version of the review had a comment section where readers could leave their views. One blogger, 'Singing Simon' posted the following:

'This album is so cheesy it should come with a sideboard of crackers and grapes. It may not be that bad if he could sing, but the way he tries to hit the high notes on track 6 is laughable! This is the voice of an angel ..... being throttled! I feel so let down.'

To leave a comment, people must register their personal details with the magazine. To gauge the response to the album, Dermott went online to read the comments. Dermott was furious, claiming Louis Barlow's comment was a clear criticism of Tulisa. He was also furious with the comment by 'Singing Simon' and, as it was one of the first, thought it may put people off the album and complained. However, several days later the comment was still there, and *Top Hits!* have refused to reveal the identity of 'Singing Simon'.

Advise Dermott as to his options in relation to the makers of each statement.

Diagram plan

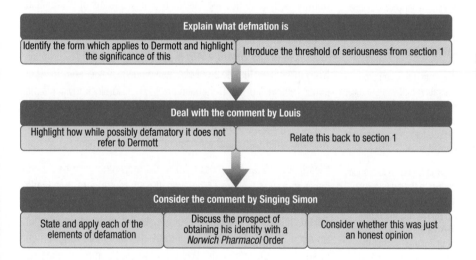

A printable version of this diagram plan is available from **www.pearsoned.co.uk/lawexpressqa**

Answer plan

➜ Define defamation and identify what form we are dealing with.

➜ Apply the criteria for the tort in turn to the blogger's comments.

➜ Explain the steps that Dermott will need to undertake in order to obtain the registration details of the blogger from *Top Hits!*

➜ Touch on any defences 'Singing Simon' may have if he is identified.

[1] This provides some context to your answer which you can draw on later. It also demonstrates that you are aware of the human rights issues which influence the area and the difficulties faced by the law.

[2] You should already have determined when reading the question that the comment does not refer to Dermott personally, but the question simply says advise Dermott. Therefore, allude to the fact that you have seen this now and advise him more broadly later that Tulisa could bring an action for that comment.

[3] By stating this you are illustrating that you are aware of the difference between libel and slander without using up time fully explaining what slander is.

[4] Normally you should apply the law to the facts as you state it. However, when you do not it is important to explain that you will be doing so later so that the marker does not think you have forgotten to do it. In this question, it may make sense to show how the requirement is not satisfied in the context of the other elements of the tort. This is because the facts will mean that your reasoning applies twice over. Dealing with the seriousness point later allows you to get into the requirements to demonstrate your knowledge of those while maintaining a structural flow to your answer.

Answer

Dermott requires advice as to the tort of defamation and its application to the Internet. This is an important issue as it involves balancing the competing interests of protecting one's reputation with free speech and press freedom. The issue is further complicated by the Internet itself which emboldens people through perceived anonymity to express their views with reduced inhibition.[1] It will be argued that Louis' comment will not be actionable by Dermott personally;[2] and Dermott may struggle to mount a claim against 'Singing Simon' who, even then, may have a defence. The possibility of a claim against the magazine is considered if the claim can be established.

Dermott should be advised that there are two forms of defamation: libel and slander. Although blogging can be seen to be analogous to slander in that it is similar to an oral conversation, it has been held to be libel (*Nigel Smith* v *ADFN plc* [2008] EWHC 1797). Importantly this means that no proof of actual damage is needed.[3] However, under section 1 of the Defamation Act 2013, to block trivial claims, the statement must cause, or be likely to cause, serious harm to Dermott's reputation. As will be discussed below,[4] it is questionable whether either statement will overcome this requirement.

Clearly any statement must refer to Dermott otherwise he has no basis to make a claim.[5] However, the facts suggest that Louis' comment is an innuendo inferring that Tulisa is a gold-digger.[6] This is potentially actionable, but only by Tulisa as it refers to her. As such, it also unlikely to overcome the threshold requirement in section 1 on this basis. While the second comment does not directly refer to Dermott,[7] as it is a comment on a review about his album then it is reasonable that people would believe Dermott is being referred to (*Morgan* v *Odhams Press Ltd* [1971] 2 All ER 1156).

The next requirement is that the statement is defamatory. The statement must lower the regard with which right-thinking members of society hold the claimant (*Sim* v *Stretch* [1936] 2 All ER 1237). Applying this to 'Singing Simon's' comment, the natural meaning which Dermott will seek to apply is that he cannot sing; especially high notes. It is unlikely that people will shun Dermott personally, but they may avoid his album. Similarly, it could cause people to

[5] While it is more common to deal with the requirement that the statement is defamatory first, taking this element first allows you to draw a line under the comment by Louis, as Dermott clearly does not satisfy this requirement in relation to that comment. This leaves you to then concentrate on the action he has more chance of succeeding in.

[6] Include this here, even though it relates to a different requirement, as it allows you to show the marker that you picked up on the innuendo and allude to your knowledge of the law in relation to that. Then simply dismiss the comment as being actionable by Dermott for not referring to him.

[7] Do not just assume that this element is satisfied as the comment does not use his name.

[8] As in relation to the comment with Tulisa, it is important to expressly emphasise that you have dealt with this point now so that the marker knows that you have covered it.

[9] Where you have two contrasting positions, make sure that you take a view on which is best, and use the facts to show why. Otherwise, your answer will not make total sense as to why you are proceeding with your advice.

lower the regard that they have for his singing. However, Dermott should be advised that the comment could instead be viewed as simple abuse which is why it may struggle to satisfy the section 1 threshold.[8] Abuse can amount to defamation in libel (*Berkoff v Burchill* [1996] 4 All ER 1008), but following the *Nigel Smith* case it would need to be shown that the comment was intended to be taken seriously by casual readers; which was held to not often be the case. However, this is a comment on an album review by someone who may be a fan. Looking at the words 'I feel so let down', a casual reader may well take this to be a reflection of Dermott's singing and its impact on his fans, particularly in light of any negative tone in the review.[9]

Finally, the statement must be published to a third party. This was satisfied once the comment was posted on the website (*Godfrey v Demon Internet Ltd* [2001] QB 201). Every download of the page will be another publication; although, only one action will result, and Dermott will have one year from the date the comment was uploaded to bring a claim (s. 8).[10] The amount of any damages will be reflected by the overall scale of publication (*John v MGN Ltd* [1997] QB 586).

However, even if all the elements are satisfied, the tortfeasor needs identifying as only a pseudonym is provided. Dermott will need a *Norwich Pharmacal* order which would require the magazine to reveal the blogger's identity from their registration details. The requirements for this were outlined in *Mitsui Ltd v Nexen Petroleum UK Ltd* [2005] EWHC 625. First, Dermott needs to show that he has suffered a wrong; this will be satisfied if the elements of defamation are met.[11] Secondly, the order must be needed in order to bring an action against the wrongdoer, which is also satisfied, as Dermott only knows the tortfeasor as 'Singing Simon'. Lastly, the magazine will need to be shown to be involved in the wrongdoing so as to have facilitated the wrong, whilst also being able to provide the information needed to bring an action. This latter part is satisfied as the statement appeared on their website and all users register their personal details. On similar facts *Sheffield Wednesday FC v Hargreaves* [2007] EWHC 2375 acknowledged the privacy concerns of bloggers/posters[12] stating that courts have discretion not to grant the order where the statement, while strictly defamatory, is more trivial in nature. This is an issue for Dermott because, as noted previously, the post could be said to

[10] Refer to this so that you show that you are aware of the practicalities of bringing a claim and issues such as the limitation period. This enables you to demonstrate that you have a full range of knowledge as to the subsidiary issues of the tort as well as the fundamental requirements.

[11] It would be important to phrase this along these lines if you have indicated some doubt as to the defamatory nature of the comment previously in your answer.

[12] While this is relevant to the answer, it also shows that you are aware of the context in which decisions are taken, and so it shows that you have a broader understanding of the area.

[13] Although the question says to advise Dermott regarding a claim against the blogger, the facts allude to a possible claim against the magazine, so do not dismiss it, especially as the claim against the blogger may fail.

[14] Until case law builds up on the new defences, make sure you draw on what Parliament said in relation to what the sections mean and require.

[15] There is not much that can be argued here by way of application of the facts, so instead demonstrate that you understand the theory behind the defence by highlighting what it is for and how it compares to that which it replaced.

simply be abusive and not serious. If the court does not grant the order though, it would open up the possibility of suing the magazine instead (Defamation Act 2013, s. 5(3)).[13]

If granted, the next issue is whether the blogger has any possible defence. As the post is a reply to the album review, which invited comments, the defence of honest opinion arises. This requires the statement to be one of opinion which also includes the basis for the opinion (s. 3(2), (3)). The opinion here is that Dermott cannot sing and the performance on track 6, in particular, is cited as the basis. The opinion then needs to be capable of being held by an honest person on the basis of any fact existing at the time it was expressed and is assessed objectively. The explanatory notes to the section explain[14] that provided the fact relied on is capable of supporting the belief, it can be honestly held; we would need to hear the album to say for definite. However, in theory the fact could support the belief, but if the blogger, subjectively, did not honestly hold the belief, the defence would fail (s. 4(5)). This continues the trend of the old common law version of the defence whereby the spite of the statement maker is irrelevant so as to not be inconsistent with the aim of the defence: to protect hard-hitting views.[15]

In conclusion, Dermott may succeed in a claim against 'Singing Simon' provided that he can show the statement was likely to cause serious harm to his reputation. Naturally Dermott would have to obtain 'Singing Simon's' identity first. However, owing to the nature of the comment and where it was published, it is likely that the claim could be successfully defended as honest opinion. If the identity of 'Singing Simon' was not obtained, Dermott could instead successfully claim against the magazine as a website operator who, when notified of the content of the post, took no action (s. 5(3)).

Make your answer stand out

■ Make sure you have read and understood cases such as *Nigel Smith* which are to do with blogging and the Internet rather than applying old, albeit more well-known, cases to a new situation. This will show that you are up to date with developments and the new context within which the law is operating. The application of the tort to the Internet is very important and topical so this knowledge will help you.

■ Explore the merits of the analogy of blog posts and comments to slander and consider the consequences for Dermott.

■ Familiarise yourself with the Explanatory Notes to the 2013 Act, and academic opinions on it, to help develop your discussion as to how the new defences will operate.

■ Explain more fully the basis for bringing a claim against the magazine for not removing the comment. Read the Ministry of Justice's (2014) *Guidance on section 5 of the Defamation Act 2013 and Regulations: Complaints about defamatory material posted on websites* to help with this.

! Don't be tempted to . . .

■ Simply conclude that the comment will not be defamatory due to failing to overcome section 1(1) and not consider any further matters.

■ Also conclude at the end of your discussion of the elements of the tort, that it has not been made out and ignore discussing the consequences of it being found to be defamatory.

■ Get side-tracked by the comment by Louis as it is clear on the facts that the innuendo is not referring to Dermott, but do not completely ignore it though as you can briefly show your knowledge of innuendo before applying the requirement of reference to the claimant to finish the discussion.

■ Dwell on the elements for establishing defamation which are not really in issue, as you may well not get on to the other issues which are more relevant for discussion.

■ Overlook the need to discuss the procedural issue of how Dermott could bring a claim, and how he will need to obtain a *Norwich Pharmacol* order.

Question 4

'The task of designing any libel regime must involve reaching an appropriate accommodation between individual rights and social interests in both freedom of expression and reputation.' (Mullis, A. and Scott, A. (2012) The Swing of the Pendulum: Reputation, Expression and the Re-centring of English Libel Law, in D. Capper (ed.), *Modern Defamation Law: Balancing Reputation and Free Expression.* Belfast: Queens University Belfast Press)

In light of this statement critically evaluate the justifications of the new main defences under the Defamation Act 2013 and whether they have helped reach an appropriate accommodation between the competing interests which lie at the heart of the tort.

Diagram plan

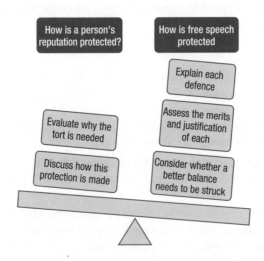

A printable version of this diagram plan is available from **www.pearsoned.co.uk/lawexpressqa**

Answer plan

➜ Overview the two types of defamation, their differences and why the tort is needed.

➜ Explain the elements of defamation.

➜ Balance the need for the tort with an evaluation of the defences, assessing whether they tip the balance too far back in favour of the defendant or do not go far enough.

➜ Consider the need for reform if the balance is still not right.

Answer

Defamation seeks to balance the seemingly irreconcilable issues of protecting one's reputation with the right of others to say what they want. A satisfactory balance is vital so that unfounded claims do not ruin lives while giving effect to the notion of a free society through the promotion of freedom of expression. In assessing the reformed long-standing defences[1], it is argued that while the recent reforms provide a balance, it is the potential cost of litigation which causes the main hurdle to adequately accommodating both interests.

Defamation is where a person is lowered in the estimation of society and takes two forms depending on the permanency of the statement. Slander is transient statements and generally requires proof of financial loss, or loss which is capable of financial assessment. However, libel, which is permanent, is actionable *per se,* thus putting one's reputation on a par with their personal integrity under trespass. It may seem questionable to put reputation on such a level, particularly at the expense of another's free speech. However, reputations are important assets and the justification is that the permanence means more people may see the statement and cause greater damage.[2]

To receive the tort's protection, certain requirements must be met which ensure that a sufficient nexus exists between the statement and the claimant to warrant restricting the maker's free speech.[3] First, the statement must refer to the claimant. Where reference is direct, there will generally be no issue. However, it is sufficient if the reasonable person, having knowledge of the circumstances, would understand the statement as referring to the claimant (***Morgan v Odhams Press Ltd*** [1971] 1 WLR 1239). The statement must then be published, which requires communication to a third party, otherwise, there is no damage to their reputation. Finally, the statement must be defamatory. Fair-minded people within society, as a whole, must think less of the claimant (***Lewis v Daily Telegraph*** [1964] AC 234). Protection extends also to situations where the ordinary words themselves are not defamatory but they contain an innuendo which is damaging. If seemingly weighted in favour of the claimant, some balance has been restored by section 1 which seeks to eliminate trivial actions by providing that the statement will need to be shown to cause, or be likely to cause, serious harm to the reputation if it is to be actionable.

[1] The point here is just to give your marker an indication of what defences you will be covering as in an exam it will be impossible to adequately cover all of them.

[2] After defining defamation, you ought to consider whether such protection is justifiable and judge the merits of the defences against that.

[3] Rather than just explain the elements of the tort, explain the purpose of the elements. You should consider whether insisting on these counters the harshness of not needing to show damage.

[4] Although the defence is not based in the statute, its rationale still lies in the judicial reasoning of old cases so show your understanding by drawing on those to explain why the defence exists.

[5] The fact that the law presumes that one is lying requires you, in light of the statement in the question, to explain the justification for such a position, as it would seem to tilt the balance in favour of the claimant.

[6] After stating why the law adopts the position it does, it is important to evaluate the consequences of that position and where it leaves the balance between the parties.

[7] As with truth, as these are exceptions to when you can injure a reputation, you ought to start with the reason for the defence and then assess its merits against the importance of protecting reputations.

[8] Make sure that you go further in your analysis of the defence by assessing whether the justification of each requirement has merit. If not, it could be argued that the defence is undermined and thus the necessary balance is lost. Alternatively, if the requirements are not rigorous enough the balance is tilted too far from protecting reputations.

The primary defence is that the statement is true (s. 2), as damages should not be awarded for injuring a false reputation (***M'Pherson v Daniels*** (1829) 10 B & C 263).[4] Statements are presumed to be untrue and the defendant must prove otherwise. This is compliant with Article 10 (***Jameel v Wall Street Journal Europe*** [2006] UKHL 44) and justified as one should have to substantiate their claims.[5] However, allegations can be difficult to prove, particularly when they are specific, but provided the statement is proven to be substantially true, the defence will hold. Where a statement has distinct imputations, provided those which cannot be proven are not shown to seriously harm the claimant's reputation, the defence can still be relied upon (s. 2(3)). This is important as the lack of concrete evidence combined with the cost of defending an action may deter people from making statements which are in fact true.[6]

The next substantial defence is honest opinion (s. 3), which embodies the whole idea of free speech as it protects one's right to criticise another.[7] It is a vital defence as the free expression of opinions is essential for good debate, which enhances a democratic society, and allows the truth to come to light. The new defence has sought to retain the essence of the old defence while simplifying and clarifying certain elements. However, so that reputations are protected certain requirements must be met. The statement must be an opinion and the statement containing the opinion must indicate, generally or specifically, what the basis for it is (s. 3(2), (3)). The latter is important in further justifying the defence as readers can make up their own minds as to the validity of the opinion if they can see what it is based on.[8] It supports the idea that misguided opinions do less harm than assertions of facts. The opinion must be capable of being held by an honest person based on a fact existing at the time the opinion was expressed; or anything asserted to be a fact in a privileged statement before the opinion was expressed (s.3(4)). The defence will fail where the maker, subjectively, does not honestly hold the opinion. This replaces the old bar of malice and is better as it reflects the purpose of the defence while recognising that the benefits the defence brings do not materialise if the opinion is not genuine; debate is not legitimately being fuelled.

The next substantial defence is that in section 4, publication on a matter of public interest. The defence replaces the old form of qualified privilege known as the *Reynolds* defence, while retaining the

[9] While developed under the *Reynolds* principles, reportage was arguably a distinct defence with its own operation so it is important you show that you are aware that it has survived and thus understand the full scope of the new defence.

[10] Although no longer the law, it is useful to show your understanding of the old law as you are essentially undertaking a comparison of the two defences.

[11] Allude to your knowledge of the background to the drafting of the Act by referring to how it could have looked. You can then use this knowledge to build up your argument as to the merit of the section's final wording.

[12] While the question refers to the main defences, there are clearly more and you will not be able to cover them all. It is worth at some stage just making your marker aware that you do that you appreciate more exist.

[13] Relate this back to your initial discussion on the elements; if they are meant to act as a hurdle for claims but then are too easy to overcome, does this mean the balance is in the claimant's favour?

[14] You need to bring home to your marker why you think this is the bigger problem and explain how the balance sought by the law could be undermined by this state of affairs.

reportage defence (s. 4(3))[9], and has sought to be simpler by breaking the link with privilege altogether in order to give it a stronger jurisprudential foundation. Whereas the old defence was based on the concept of responsible journalism (even though it applied beyond newspapers)[10] this does not feature in the new defence. The defence requires the statement to, first, be on a matter that is in the public interest; and secondly, that the publisher reasonably believed that publication was in the public interest. The interesting thing about the wording of the requirements is that it suggests that some matters may be in the public interest generally, but it is not reasonable to believe it is in the public interest to publish them, perhaps due to how the story was gathered. When determining the requirements, all of the circumstances of the case should be considered and allowance should be made for editorial judgement. This should mean that the old factors highlighted by Lord Nicholls in *Reynolds* have a role to play still. While denying the defence some certainty as to what is required, it does provide the essential flexibility which is needed to ensure the defence can apply to a wide array of publications which is why certain factors to consider were expressly left out of the final version of the section.[11]

However, while these defences, and the others within the Act,[12] afford suitable theoretical protection of free speech, particularly in their reformed state, the relative ease in satisfying the requirements for defamation still means the threat of litigation restricts speech.[13] Indeed, the cost means that the prospect of financial ruin is detrimental to both parties; damaged reputations may go unchallenged and damning information of public importance left unpublished. In light of the importance of both competing interests, such a state of affairs in unacceptable. Therefore, the cost of the litigation process must now be the focus of further reform.[14]

Make your answer stand out

■ Refer back to the quote in your answer when assessing the importance and justification for each defence.

■ Include aspects of the Act's Explanatory Notes as well as the parliamentary debates leading to its enactment in order to assess what the defences are trying to do and whether a better version was rejected.

■ Draw on some of the wider causes of concern regarding the tort, such as cost and libel tourism.

■ Look out for recent high-profile cases from the news which you can use to show that you are aware of recent developments; notably the libel claim of politician Andrew Mitchell and the 'Plebgate' affair which is reported to have a costs bill of £3 million.

! **Don't be tempted to . . .**

■ Dwell too long on the requirements for a claim. The question is focused on the role of the defences, so you will not leave yourself enough time to address these otherwise.

■ Discuss every defence as you will not have the time to do so in the required depth and provide any worthwhile evaluation. Stick to the substantive defences which provide a full defence to an action.

■ Simply describe the elements of the defences, always aim to consider the justification of each as their existence allows infringements of a fundamental right to go without redress.

Question 5

'*Wainwright* v *Home Office* saw an emphatic repudiation of any notion that English law now recognised a general right to privacy.' (Arden, M. (2010) Human rights and civil wrongs: tort law under the spotlight. *Public Law,* January: 140–59.

Critically evaluate the extent that the tort of misuse of private information has negated the need for a general tort protecting against the invasion of privacy.

Diagram plan

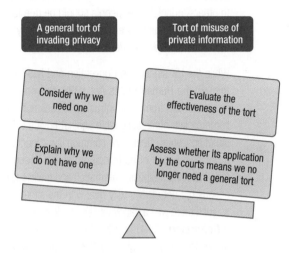

A printable version of this diagram plan is available from **www.pearsoned.co.uk/lawexpressqa**

Answer plan

→ Outline the position stated in *Wainwright* v *Home Office* [2003] UKHL 53.

→ Evaluate the reasoning for this position.

→ Consider how privacy is protected through the existing tort.

→ Determine the effectiveness of the protection.

→ Discuss whether its continued development means that we effectively have a general privacy tort by the back door.

Answer

[1] While this may not seem like it is adding much, you want to get across that you appreciate what privacy is and, therefore, know the context in which you are writing.

The issue to determine is the extent to which the courts have responded to the need to protect privacy by developing the tort of misuse of private information, and whether the presence of this tort means that the lack of a general privacy tort should be a concern. As privacy is a fundamental human right, this is extremely important.[1] However, it is argued that by developing this tort in line with the ECHR an effective privacy regime exists, negating the need for a general tort.

The importance of a citizen's right to a private life has long been recognised, even prior to Article 8 of the ECHR 1950. The rationale

[2] Naturally, you start by introducing the right. However, remembering the sentence in the introduction, you need to go further and explain why it is a right; explain why it is important.

[3] This is something which often gets misunderstood, so it is vital that you show you do know how it operates. Remember that it is because of this fact that there is a need to develop a form of horizontal protection.

[4] You would not need to get into *Kaye* here; your aim is to reinforce what you stated above regarding the need to develop an effective action that would protect a person's privacy against interference by another citizen.

[5] Following your previous discussion and how the Act works, it is important to get across that you are aware of this development: otherwise, your answer may seem contradictory.

[6] By briefly including reference to this case you add some judicial support to Baroness Hale's argument which you are now advancing. This is beneficial because, as you may go on to explain, the other Lords did not discuss this, so questions could be raised as to how authoritative the view is.

is to prevent the state from unjustly intervening in the day-to-day activities of its citizens.[2] The right is the embodiment of Mill's 'harm to others' principle, i.e. people should be free to do what they like in private so long as they are not hurting anybody else. As such, it is a fundamental aspect of democracy.

While the UK signed the Convention and has incorporated it into law through the Human Rights Act 1998, this only means that a citizen has protection from state intrusion. It does not correlate to equivalent common law rights actionable against private citizens; the Act has no direct horizontal effect.[3] The common law, though, has always provided a patchwork quilt of horizontal protection through a diverse range of torts including trespass, defamation and malicious falsehood. Yet these options did not always fully deal with the situation complained of and as such there was a gap when it came to privacy (as illustrated in *Kaye* **v Robertson** [1991] FSR 62).[4] Nevertheless, it was felt in *Kaye* that moves to a general right should come from Parliament. Arguably, the most effective action was the equitable doctrine of breach of confidence, from which the new tort derives. However, that no general tort protecting invasions of privacy exists was emphatically stated in *Wainwright* where Lord Hoffmann stated that it was not a principle of law which could be directly applied to individual claims. His Lordship even noted doubt as to what the concept of 'invasion of privacy' means, while also highlighting the lack of need for a high-level principle for compliance with Article 8. Indeed, he noted that in the USA, where a general right exists, it is broken down into several loosely defined torts. Lord Hoffmann felt that privacy was simply an underlying value which points the way for developing existing law, which has proved to be the case.

Baroness Hale has argued (*Campbell* **v MGN Ltd** [2004] UKHL 22) that, although the ECHR's incorporation does not mean that new rights can be created in a dispute to give effect to Convention rights, existing rights must be interpreted and developed in a manner which is compatible with Convention rights, as the court is a public authority under section 6 and thus expressly obliged to act compatibly[5] (a view previously adopted in *Venables* **v News Group Newspapers Ltd** [2001] Fam 430).[6] While the other Lords in *Campbell* did not opine on the matter, all accepted that the confidence action was the best vehicle to develop, and as such the requirement of a prior confidential relationship was removed. Reflecting this development, Lord Nicholls rechristened the action as the tort of misuse of private information.

This terminology was adopted by the Court of Appeal in *McKennit v Ash* [2008] QB 73 which, in reviewing the opinions in *Campbell*, set out the requirements for the new action.

The first requirement is that the information in question is indeed private, thus protected by Article 8. For this, the courts assess whether the claimant had, in relation to the information, a reasonable expectation of privacy. In *Campbell*, Lord Hope suggested that an expectation exists where the information is obviously private or easily identifiable as such. However, where there was doubt as to whether an expectation should exist, he suggested recourse be had to the 'highly offensive test' from *Australian Broadcasting Corporation v Lenah Game Meats Pty Ltd* (2001) 1 ALR 185. This involves asking what a reasonable person of ordinary sensibilities would feel if found in the claimant's position. While there were doubts about using this test among other judges – such as Lord Nicholls who felt it blurred the differing questions of what is private and what interference is proportionate – their views are compatible in that it is what the claimant objectively thinks which matters – a view shared in *Murray v Big Pictures (UK) Ltd* [2008] EMLR 12.[7] This is therefore more effective in giving claimants protection than the approach of the Court of Appeal in *Campbell* which looked at what the reader felt.

Even if the information is private, the second question to determine is whether this right to keep the information private should, on balance, outweigh the competing right of the defendant to publish the information. Clearly, this balancing act needs to be undertaken to give effect to the freedom of expression, which is essential in a democracy as part of a free press. However, the merits of a free press must be balanced with ensuring responsible behaviour and respecting the rights of people to a private life. This requirement is not surprising as both Articles 8 and 10 state that each right may be restricted where necessary in a democratic society so as to give effect to the other; neither takes precedence.

In *Campbell*, Baroness Hale stated three factors to consider when performing the balancing exercise to ensure that any interference is proportionate and necessary. First, there must be a pressing social need, essentially a similar issue as the first requirement of whether disclosure is in the public interest. This has allowed the tort to be used in relation to photographs (*Murray*).[8] Secondly, any interference must be proportionate to the legitimate aim of meeting that social need. As such, the extent of the interference must be enough to protect the

[7] Naturally, you have to evaluate the differing views in *Campbell*, but this then gives the impression of a law in a state of confusion. By referring to what later cases have said on this point, you can argue that the new tort is coherent and understood. If it wasn't, there would be questions as to how effective it is, which would impact on the quality of the proposition which you are advancing.

[8] You need to discuss how the tort, once established, has been applied as this goes to the heart of how wide-ranging the protection is and, therefore, whether a general tort is needed.

[9] Outline how the balancing exercise works, then give an opinion as to what this means and how the results flowing from the exercise arise. Someone's right will have been interfered with and so you need to decide whether this has been done fairly, as this goes to the heart of whether the tort is good or not.

opposing right and no more. Finally, the reasons advanced for the interference must be logical and sufficient to justify it. The party which satisfies these most effectively will succeed in the aim of preventing or obtaining publication. This will be warranted as they have demonstrated that their interference with the other's right is necessary to give effect to the social need while not being too overbearing.[9]

The new tort offers protection, going further than simply revealing private information, as seen in claims regarding photographs. The sensible development of the tort in line with ECHR jurisprudence means that a general right exists by default, yet this has not been detrimental to free expression nor restricted the press. The balance at the tort's heart provides the flexibility to ensure that the latter is only curtailed where justified.

✓ Make your answer stand out

- As well as the Arden article in the question, read in full McLean, A. and Mackey, C. (2007) Is there a law of privacy in the UK? A consideration of recent legal developments. *European Intellectual Property Review,* 29(9): 389–95, which makes the argument that lies at the heart of the question.

- Make sure you leave plenty of time for discussion as to how the tort works and whether its application means a general tort is not needed, as this is the principal premise of the question, not why we don't have a general tort.

- If you think that a more wide-ranging general tort is needed, give your own views as to what form this may take and the scope of it. This will really show that you have a deep level of knowledge and understanding of the issue.

- Consider the political implications of judges developing the law on this issue and whether Parliament should be left to draw up any law deemed necessary.

! Don't be tempted to . . .

- Feel the need to discuss *all* of the different cases which have taken place recently. Stick to those which have added something new to the development of the tort and assess the merits of that development.

- Describe in narrative form the development, make sure you evaluate it at each stage.

- Get too tied down by a discussion of the other actions which may be brought, as the question is directing you to focus on the misuse of private information.

Question 6

'First, the good name of a company, as that of an individual, is a thing of value. A damaging libel may lower its standing in the eyes of the public and even its own staff, make people less ready to deal with it, less willing or less proud to work for it. If this were not so, corporations would not go to the lengths they do to protect and burnish their corporate images. I find nothing repugnant in the notion that this is a value which the law should protect.' (*Per* Lord Bingham in *Jameel* v *Wall Street Journal Europe Sprl* [2006] UKHL 44 at [26])

Exploring the judicial reasoning in the case, critically assess whether Parliament was right to effectively overturn the decision of the majority with the passing of section 1(2) of the Defamation Act 2013.

Diagram plan

The minority
- Companies can be just as powerful as government institutions
- Reflects the importance of freedom of expression
- The rule helps to protect the soul of an individual which companies do not have
- Injury to commercial assets in other torts requires proof of damage

The majority
- Company reputations are of monetary value
- Their profits flow from the amount of custom, which in turn is dependent on the public's perception
- Impacts on the quality of staff they can attract
- Creates different rules for different corporations or hits non-trading corporations

A printable version of this diagram plan is available from **www.pearsoned.co.uk/lawexpressqa**

Answer plan

→ Set out what defamation is and what it seeks to protect and in doing so, briefly distinguish between libel and slander.

→ Discuss the justifications for not requiring proof of damage in libel and why this is not contested for individuals.

→ Comment briefly on the challenge to the rule in relation to governmental bodies.

→ Consider what the reason was for incorporating the change and making the position different for trading corporations.

→ Evaluate which reasoning best suits the modern trading corporation.

Answer

The issue here is whether corporations should be treated differently from individuals when it comes to libel and have to prove financial damage. This is important as corporations place great value on their reputation and they have always been treated equally by the courts. However, section 1(2) requires them to now show more harm than individuals. It is submitted that it was justifiable to alter the rule for trading corporations in order to protect the public interest.

[1] This is the most important part of this paragraph as it explains why we have the rule. Therefore, focus more on this than what defamation is, as this will provide the foundation upon which the actual arguments take place.

Defamation's purpose is to protect one's reputation from harm where a statement is published which refers to them and would tend to lower their reputation in the minds of right-thinking people. Defamation takes two forms: slander which is a transitory statement, or libel, which is a statement in permanent form. Reflecting the fact that this permanence means the statement is more easily disseminated and any reputational damage is more durable over time, there is no requirement in libel to prove the damage did occur. This is further justified on the basis of the difficulties of an individual establishing that the loss was due to the statement.[1]

[2] While this may seem slightly off tangent, you should briefly cover this case and the principle which it determined as you can use this later in support of Baroness Hale's view when you look at the minority view in *Jameel*.

Traditionally this rule applied to all claimants (***South Hetton Coal Co. Ltd v North-Eastern News Association*** [1894] 1 QB 133). However, the first successful challenge was in ***Derbyshire County Council v Times Newspapers Ltd*** [1993] AC 534. It was held that government institutions could not sue to protect their governing reputations as otherwise it was contrary to the public interest. Defamation claims could be used to censor criticism. In a democracy, governmental bodies should be subject to criticism: otherwise, party political systems could not function[2] as they are based on trying to undermine confidence in your opponent's competence.

[3] Using this wording here gives you the scope to seamlessly proceed to discussing the majority or the minority, depending on your viewpoint. Remember to lay out the view that you ultimately favour second, as this will mean your answer will end on a stronger note and flow into your conclusion.

That a company should be able to bring an action has always been acknowledged; what has long been disputed is whether they should benefit from the same rules as individuals.[3] However, with the passing of section 1(2) of the Defamation Act 2013 companies which trade for profit must show, as individuals must, that the statement complained of has caused, or is likely to cause, serious harm, but for them this now means serious financial loss. In doing so, this has effectively overturned the decision in **Jameel v Wall Street Journal Europe Sprl** [2006] UKHL 44 at [26] which only recently held that both types of claimant should be treated alike.

In **Jameel**, Lord Scott opined that a corporation's reputation is an asset of monetary value; this is why many advertise on TV shows and sponsor events. Companies try to enhance their reputation by association for commercial advantage. However, if their reputation suffers, these opportunities are reduced, leading to lost custom and ultimately profits. Weir (1972) suggests that as this is financial injury it can be proved evidentially, unlike with individuals, and thus should be proved.[4] At first glance this seems a strong point. Lord Scott, though, felt that it was not so simple for companies to prove this loss and attribute it to the statement. Trade variations happen for a variety of reasons and so it is difficult to show that loss resulted from the published statement. Lord Bingham agreed with these sentiments, highlighting that a corporation's reputation also impacts on those wanting to work for it. Therefore, reputations should be protected by a favourable judicial verdict as this carries more weight than a denial by press release. Significantly, Lord Scott also noted that such a change would exclude corporations from obtaining interim injunctions.

Lord Hope's opinion was that the arguments for change could not be soundly based in principle as they singled out trading corporations for differential treatment from non-trading corporations. The distinction was because, as Lord Hope noted, bodies such as charities would find it even harder to put a value on their loss let alone prove it. However, this distinction has now been entrenched by the Act and is arguably unfair in light of the similar evidential difficulties both types of corporation may face and the equal asset value of each's reputation.

Notwithstanding the **Derbyshire CC** case holding that there were distinctions between public authorities and corporations, Baroness Hale felt that, today, the boundary is blurred with multinational corporations wielding enormous power.[5] As such, she felt it may well be of democratic interest to similarly open such corporations to 'uninhibited criticism'. It is important to reiterate that Baroness Hale was

[4] By including this here, you make the arguments in favour of the rule stronger as you are fully testing them at the same time. You will also have a greater degree of cohesion to your answer than if you include this later on with the specific arguments of the minority.

[5] This links your answer to the discussion of *Derbyshire CC* and why you discussed the issue of public authorities.

[6] By highlighting these you show some wider knowledge, and strengthen the assertion that this was a modest development of the law with wider support.

[7] Include some practical examples as to how the majority's arguments can be rebutted, as these will carry more force than a purely jurisprudential argument.

[8] Obviously, as the House was split, it is worth showing your knowledge of each judge and explaining what side they were coming from.

[9] As you have just ended the previous paragraph with why there is no practical reason for the rule, it is beneficial to highlight that you are now addressing the remaining arguments advanced by the majority. As the answer is about supporting the legislation by arguing against the majority, it is important to include Lord Hoffmann's brief views on the issues as this allows you to counter the theoretical reasons of the majority.

[10] This allows you to end on a strong note with high-level judicial endorsement for your concluding argument.

not suggesting removing standing from trading corporations. Indeed, she did not even advocate that loss must be caused: simply that they must prove that the statement was likely to cause them financial loss. Reflecting the view of the Faulks Committee on Defamation, this was a slight modification of the position advanced in **Derbyshire CC**, and is the position adopted by the Act.[6]

This obviously raises the majority's contention that proving such loss may be difficult. However, this is not necessarily the case. Companies, particularly large corporations, will have year-on-year sales figures and so can contrast the period following the publication to previous years'.[7] As companies do now, an assessment of external factors could be made in order to determine whether any loss was caused by those factors such as bad weather or the holding of national events. Furthermore, under section 1(2) concrete evidential proof is not required so causative uncertainties will not be detrimental. The loss must simply be shown to have been 'likely' to be caused by the statement. This is easier to do when looking at the size of the claimed loss and the nature of the statement in light of other external factors. Therefore, on a practical basis there was no need to maintain the rule.

Lord Hoffmann, supporting Baroness Hale,[8] somewhat countered Lord Hope's theoretical issues regarding creating distinctions.[9] He noted and agreed that a company's reputation is a commercial asset, but felt not requiring proof of damage would mean that defamation is at odds with other torts such as malicious falsehood. This could be justifiable in that defamation serves a different purpose. However, Lord Hoffmann felt that the justification for not requiring proof by individuals is that their reputation is part of their 'immortal' self – it is their soul. Therefore, it warrants greater protection. However, as a company has no soul there was no reason to treat it more favourably in defamation than in other torts dealing with harm to commercial assets.

Therefore, while there are strong practical and theoretical difficulties in treating trading corporations differently, they are not insurmountable. Further, reflecting the new landscape identified by Lord Steyn in **Reynolds v Times Newspapers Ltd** [2001] 2 AC 127 that the starting point should be free speech, they *should* be overcome.[10] To favour the protection of a company's reputation without proof of damage is, in Weir's view, a 'grim perversion of values' and therefore it is right that Parliament stepped in and legislated on the basis of the minority decision.

Make your answer stand out

■ Read *Jameel* in full so that you can draw on all of the judicial opinions in support of your arguments, as each judge says something different. You can then show deep and wide-ranging knowledge of the issue.

■ Consider the earlier versions of the Act, including Lord Lester's draft Bill, and the Parliamentary debates over this issue. The provision was not always going to be included in the Government's legislation, and you can get the full range of arguments for and against its inclusion by reading these. You can then build them into your answer.

■ Also read the Report of the Faulks Committee on Defamation (1975), Cmnd 5909 to which their Lordships referred and which made a recommendation on this point. It would also be beneficial to look more closely at the views of Weir, T. (1972) Local authority *v* critical ratepayer: a suit in defamation. *Cambridge Law Journal*, 30: 238, which is his case commentary of *Bognor Regis Urban District Council* v *Campion*.

■ Undertake a comparative evaluation with other jurisdictions which do require a company to prove actual damage.

! Don't be tempted to . . .

■ Spend too long on what defamation is; you can take it almost as a given in the question that it is known. The question is assessing your understanding of what its purpose is and thus why the damage rule is or is not needed.

■ Avoid stating which position from the case you prefer, as this is ultimately what you have been asked to argue.

www.pearsoned.co.uk/lawexpressqa

 Go online to access more revision support including additional essay and problem questions with diagram plans, You be the marker questions, and download all diagrams from the book.

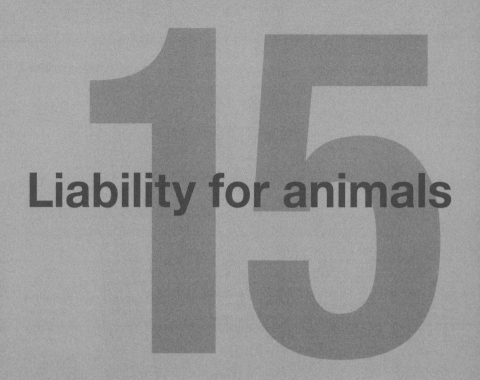

Liability for animals

How this topic may come up in exams

Animals themselves may feature in a number of topics such as negligence, nuisance or trespass to land; however, here we are looking at the specific topic of liability under the Animals Act 1971. Although a small area, it can be quite complicated. You will need to know the wording of the statute and understand how the words have been interpreted by the courts. The Act's complexity means that you should not discount a question on the suitability and effectiveness of the legislation. In terms of problem questions, you should make sure that you have also learnt the more fringe provisions of the Act as well as the main duty provisions.

■ Before you begin

It's a good idea to consider the following key themes of liability for animals before tackling a question on this topic.

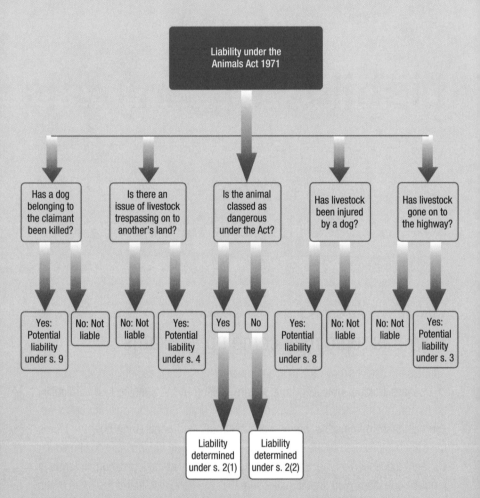

A printable version of this diagram plan is available from **www.pearsoned.co.uk/lawexpressqa**

❓ Question 1

Stoney Grove Farm is owned by Sarah. In furtherance of a sale of her horse, Harold, Sarah had contracted with Reg to transport Harold to the buyer, Mitch. However, just as Reg was at the exit of the farm, a car crashed just up the road. Spooked by the loud bang Harold bolted from the trailer and ran off. Harold ended up in a nearby house, owned by Pete, and had trampled all over his ornamental rose garden. Pete lost a day's pay by not being able to go to work as he had to secure Harold. Furious, Pete beat Harold with a broom handle, injuring his hind leg. Pete then tied Harold up and went off to work all day without leaving any food or water.

Additionally that day, Maddy took her seven-year-old son, Gil to visit the farm. Gil has brought his pet Springer Spaniel, Minky, with him, even though she had just given birth to puppies.

Minky is normally a playful dog and never any trouble. However, since the birth, Minky becomes agitated when away from her litter. Suddenly, the farm's peahen, Grace, appears from around the corner and startles Minky, who starts to bark wildly. Minky then proceeded to chase after Grace who had fled in a frightened state following the barking.

A farm-worker, James, managed to grab Minky, but she turned and bit his leg, allowing her to escape his grasp. Fearing for the safety of Grace, who was backed into a corner by Minky, another employee, Susan, shot Minky dead. James's wound from the bite required multiple stitches, and he was unable to work for a couple of weeks.

Advise all of the parties as to their potential liability for the actions of the various animals.

Diagram plan

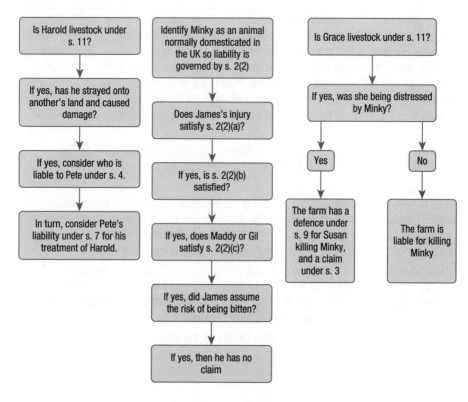

A printable version of this diagram plan is available from **www.pearsoned.co.uk/lawexpressqa**

Answer plan

→ Establish who potentially has a claim and against whom.

→ Deal with the issue of Harold's escape first as it is more isolated from the other events.

→ Take James's injury next and establish the type of animal you are dealing with.

→ Work your way through section 2(2), outlining and applying the requirements for liability.

→ End by considering the issue of Minky's death.

Answer

[1] As you have not been told specifically what aspect of the law that you need to consider their liability under, identify it straight away to show the marker that you have picked up on the main issue of the question.

[2] Save yourself time in the exam by shortening the Act's name so you do not have to repeat the name of the legislation.

[3] As each issue relates to a different provision of the Act separate them out and deal with each in the order that they occur. As this issue is detached from the other events/claims it also makes sense to deal with this one first.

[4] Use the wording of the Act where you can to demonstrate why you are discussing the issue and your knowledge of it.

[5] As matters within the Act are dealt with in whole sections of the Act, your answer will look better if you can be specific as to which part of the section is relevant for the point that you are making.

These incidents raise several issues regarding potential liability under the provisions of the Animals Act 1971[1] (the Act).[2] It will be argued that Maddy will be liable to James as the ultimate keeper of Minky; the farm will not be liable for killing Minky and may, in fact, have a claim for any injury suffered by Grace; and Reg is likely to be found liable to Pete for the damage caused by Harold as Harold was in Reg's possession at the time but, in turn, Pete will be liable to Harold's owner.

The first issue[3] is the potential liability for the damage caused by Harold to Pete's rose garden. Harold falls within the definition of livestock contained in section 11 as horses are expressly listed. As Harold caused damage by trespassing on to Pete's land, a claim arises under section 4 of the Act, and liability rests with the person to whom the livestock belongs. The issue of who Harold belongs to is uncertain as we are told he was being transported in furtherance of a sale, but we do not know whether that sale had been completed. However, this will not matter as section 4(2) provides Harold belongs to Reg for the purposes of liability as Harold was in Reg's possession at the time. Reg should be advised that unless Pete had a duty to fence his garden and thus keep livestock out, which is unlikely on the facts, he will be held strictly liable. With regards the injury to Harold, whilst Pete had the right to detain Harold under section 7(3) he is liable himself to Harold's owner, under section 7(6), as Pete has not exercised reasonable care, nor supplied adequate food and water.

In determining liability for James's injury, Maddy should be advised that although Minky is Gil's pet, he cannot be liable as under the Act only the 'keeper' is liable. The keeper, under section 6, is normally the person who owns, or has possession of, the animal, and where this person is under 16 the keeper will be the head of the minor's household. Whilst not told whether Maddy is 'the head of the household',[4] as Gil's mother she is likely to satisfy the Act's wording for the purposes of liability.

The next issue is whether Minky is classified as dangerous or not as different criteria applies depending on this. Maddy should be advised that section 6(2)[5] provides a two-limb definition, providing first that a dangerous animal is a species not commonly domesticated in the British Isles. A dog is commonly domesticated in Britain and so liability

267

for Minky will be determined by section 2(2) which deals with non-dangerous animals.[6] The subsection provides a three-limb test for liability. First, the damage must be of a kind which Minky was likely to cause unless restrained, or which, if caused, was likely to be severe. This is satisfied as a dog can be said to be likely to cause a bite injury unless restrained. Even if Maddy were to argue that a Springer Spaniel is less likely to bite in comparison to other subspecies of dog, it was held in *Curtis v Betts* [1990] 1 WLR 459 that dogs are dealt with as a general category and not by subspecies. The next requirement is that the likelihood of the damage was either down to permanent, abnormal characteristics for that species, or due to normal characteristics which arise in the species at particular times or in particular circumstances. Since *Mirvahedy v Henley* [2003] UKHL 16, these are deemed alternative reasons for liability. As we are told that Minky has become agitated whenever she is away from her litter, the bite could be said to fall under the latter basis. This is supported by the bite occurring when Minky was being restrained. Therefore, the bite was a result of the particular circumstances of the case. Finally, for liability to be imposed, the keeper needs to have actual knowledge of the characteristics. From the facts, it would appear that Maddy would have known of these characteristics, particularly as we are concerned with dogs biting at particular times – facts which are widely known. Maddy may argue that James assumed the risk of being bitten by trying to restrain Minky. While this may have some merit, James's position is perhaps more akin to that of a rescuer and so the defence will fail. There may be contributory negligence on his part, but more facts would be needed.

The final issue to advise on is the killing of Minky. Maddy should be advised that any potential claim could be brought against Sarah rather than Susan under the doctrine of vicarious liability. This is because we are specifically told that Susan is a farm employee, and it would seem clear that she was acting in the course of her employment as she was seeking to prevent Minky attacking Grace. In the event that this is not the case, a claim could still lie against Susan individually. Normally, a claim would arise under trespass to goods and would seem straightforward on the facts; however, section 9 of the Act provides a defence where the defendant can show that the dog was killed while protecting their livestock, which a peahen is classified as under section 11. Section 9(3) stipulates when a person will be deemed to

[7] You need to mention this first as the defence is only for the protection of livestock. Therefore, if Grace is not livestock, the matter is closed and the farm would be liable for Minky's death.

[8] By analysing the facts of the incident within the actual question, you will strengthen your answer by giving firmer justification to your reasoning.

[9] Although we are not told of this, you should raise it to show your knowledge as it is potentially an issue, indicating what the position is either way.

be protecting livestock. Importantly for the present incident, Paragraph (a)[7] states that this will be where a dog is worrying livestock, and there is no other means of ending the worry. It is clear that Minky was still worrying Grace at the relevant time as she had already chased her into a corner. Maddy should be advised that, while she may argue that the worrying could have been ended by some other means, this is unlikely to succeed as James had already tried to restrain Minky and was bitten. This suggests that, when combined with the fact Grace was cornered, Susan could legitimately claim that there was no other means of protecting Grace.[8] This is particularly likely to be the case under section 9(4) as this requirement is satisfied if Susan reasonably believed this to be the case. Maddy should be advised that Sarah's defence will be lost under section 9(1)(b) if Sarah did not notify the police within 48 hours of the shooting. If this was not done, then she would have a successful claim against Sarah. Further, if Susan was not acting in the course of her employment and, therefore, was the sole defendant, Susan would not have a defence as Grace was not her livestock. However, Maddy should also be advised that if Grace has suffered any injury as a result of being chased by Minky, then Sarah would have an action for this injury under section 3 of the Act.[9]

To conclude, it appears that Maddy would have no redress for Minky's death and, in fact, may well be liable for claims under the Act by James, and by Sarah for any harm suffered by Grace. Reg is meanwhile liable to Pete, but Pete will have some liability himself for Harold's injury.

✓ **Make your answer stand out**

- Illustrate your understanding of the doctrine of vicarious liability by going into more depth if you feel that you will have the time.
- Be precise with the provisions that you refer to by indicating the subsections of the Act. This will show that you have a much stronger level of knowledge of the Act.
- Illustrate your understanding of the wider law by discussing the possibility that if the farm did not inform the police, there is a similar common law defence from the case of *Cresswell* v *Sirl* [1948] 2 KB 311.
- Consider the possibility of liability under any other torts, such as trespass or negligence, even if only to confirm the Animals Act 1971 as the best choice for any claim.

Don't be tempted to . . .

- Spend too much time on the vicarious liability aspect of the question or, alternatively, ignore it altogether in order to save time.
- State as definite certain facts, or presume their non-existence, just because the question is silent on the matter: for example, whether the farm has a claim under section 3 of the Act.

📝 Question 2

'If section 2(1) can be said to be drafted with commendable simplicity, the same cannot be said for section 2(2). The drafting, which has attracted four decades of judicial and academic criticism, is grotesque.' (*Per* Maurice Kay LJ in *Turnbull* v *Warrener* [2012] EWCA Civ 412 at [4])

Critically evaluate how case law has approached the issue of interpreting section 2(2) of the Animals Act 1971 and assess the extent to which the matter has been resolved.

Diagram plan

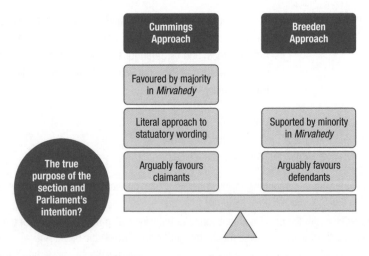

A printable version of this diagram plan is available from **www.pearsoned.co.uk/lawexpressqa**

Answer plan

→ Outline the overall purpose of the legislation and the specific purpose of section 2(2).

→ Analyse the provisions of the subsection and explain what the requirements for liability are.

→ Evaluate the differing approaches to interpreting the section by the Court of Appeal prior to *Mirvahedy*.

→ Discuss the reasoning in *Mirvahedy* and evaluate the consequences of the decision on the application of the subsection.

→ Consider the need for any further reform.

Answer

The issue to consider is how the courts have approached the matter of interpreting the section in light of the issues with how it is drafted and the extent that clarification has been achieved. The case of ***Mirvahedy v Henley* [2003] UKHL 13** is significant as the law was in a state of uncertainty due to contrasting views in previous authorities as to the appropriate interpretation of the subsection. It is argued that the case has resolved the difficulties by clarifying the law, and despite some concerns regarding the decision, the law is now in a settled and satisfactory state.

[1] By quoting passages from specific judges in the case, you will show a deeper level of knowledge of the case.

[2] Although the question is concerned with section 2(2), you still need to discuss what is said by section 6 as this dictates what animals are governed by section 2(2).

Liability for animals under the common law was described by Lord Nicholls[1] in ***Mirvahedy*** as 'notoriously intricate and complicated'. The Animals Act 1971 sought simplification, but the language employed in section 2(2) caused complexity and uncertainty. Section 2(2) deals with liability for injury by all non-dangerous animals. This phrase, owing to section 6,[2] captures all animals which are commonly domesticated in Britain regardless of whether certain subspecies may be more dangerous than others: for example, Rottweilers compared to Labradors. The fact that the subsection is to be applied in such a vast range of scenarios heightens the need for clear wording and a solution to the previous lack of clarity which had caused problems.

[3] As this is the paragraph of the subsection at the root of the problems, this should form the main part of your answer, so you should just briefly outline what Paragraphs (a) and (c) state.

The subsection has three requirements which must be satisfied in order for liability to be imposed. Two requirements, Paragraphs (a) and (c), have been successful in simplifying matters. Paragraph (a) provides that the damage must be of a kind which the animal is likely to cause unless restrained, or which if caused is likely to be severe. Paragraph (c) requires that the characteristics of the animal which cause the injury be known to the keeper, their servant, or a member of their household who is under 16. The key requirement is Paragraph (b).[3]

This links to Paragraph (a) by providing that the likelihood of damage or the likelihood of it being severe must be due to characteristics of the animal. The difficulty regarded what the requirement meant, and the nature of the characteristics in question as the requirement clearly has two limbs. The paragraph states that the cause must be a permanent characteristic of the animal which is abnormal for that species, 'or' the cause was a characteristic which 'is not normally so found except at particular times or in particular circumstances'.[4] The purpose of this paragraph,[5] according to Lord Nicholls in *Mirvahedy*, is to limit the circumstances when liability will be imposed by providing a precondition of liability in addition to (a) and (c). However, it has been held that the wording is 'inept' (per Nourse LJ in *Curtis v Betts* [1990] 1 WLR 459) and has an 'elusive' meaning (per Lloyd LJ in *Breeden v Lampard* (unreported) 21 March 1985).[6] It is the second limb which has caused difficulty, with contrasting judicial opinions over whether it was an alternative head for imposing liability, or merely a clarification of the first limb. Clarity was hindered by the fact that the cases forming both sides of the debate were not before the court in the opposing cases.[7]

The first interpretation comes from *Cummings v Grainger* [1977] QB 397 which concerned a guard dog biting a trespasser. It was held that, while dogs are not normally prone to bite, when they are guarding their territory they may do. Therefore, while this was considered normal behaviour in the circumstances, were it not for a valid defence, liability would have arisen. The merits of such view are that it falls within a literal interpretation of the statute.[8] The use of the word 'or' would indicate that this is an alternative to the first limb. The difficulty with this interpretation is the generality of the meaning it gives. It results in liability always arising, as one would always be able to point to a set of circumstances and say that they are particular to that species. Liability would be imposed even though the behaviour was normal, such as a bitch biting someone who approaches her pups.[9]

Breeden v Lampard provides the second interpretation. A characteristic was said to not warrant being classified as abnormal, and thus subject to strict liability, when it was normal for the animal in those particular circumstances. Therefore, the scenario of a bitch protecting her pups would not bring liability as that is a characteristic which is normal in that scenario. Imposing liability in the view of Lloyd LJ would

[4] As you will highlight in your answer, this phrase is not clear and could be worded better. However, by using the actual statutory wording, you illustrate why there have been difficulties and set up your later discussion.

[5] To fully assess the correct interpretation of the paragraph, you ought to explain what the purpose of it is. Then you can use this purpose as a basis for assessing each interpretation.

[6] As these two judgments form the opposing schools of thought as to how the section operates, by quoting their criticisms you will reinforce the idea that there were widespread difficulties with the section.

[7] Don't just highlight that you *know* the problem, try to show that you *understand* why the problem came about.

[8] As you are assessing and contrasting two opposing interpretations, offer a view as to the merits or otherwise of each interpretation. If you do not, your answer will be lacking in terms of analysis of the section, which is what you have been asked to do.

[9] This is a general example which the cases use to simply illustrate the issue to be determined.

not have any sense as the second limb of the paragraph was merely refining the meaning of abnormality. Oliver LJ agreed that Parliament could not have intended to impose liability for actions which were normal in the animal in the circumstances in question. These views have force as otherwise a non-dangerous animal is being treated the same as a dangerous animal; as the Act makes the distinction, it would seem strange to then treat them alike. Therefore, in contrast to the *Cummings* interpretation, the *Breeden* interpretation would essentially never result in liability. Negligence could perhaps be relied on though instead.

The issue in *Mirvahedy* was whether a keeper is liable for damage caused in circumstances when the animal's behaviour was normal for the animal in question in the particular circumstances of the case. Lord Nicholls felt that neither interpretation 'provides a compelling clear solution', but there was nothing in the section's wording to support the *Breeden* interpretation. Adopting it would depart from the scheme originally advanced by the Law Commission, without any evidence to suggest that Parliament intended such a departure. Lord Walker acknowledged that the distinction made as to the dangerousness of the animal implied that strict liability can never arise for a non-dangerous animal which is behaving entirely normally, as their behaviour would have to be abnormal. However, he also noted that this implication was not clearly spelt out and as such the language of the Act suited the *Cummings* interpretation 'more naturally' as a matter of language.

In conclusion, the fact that two judges dissented in *Mirvahedy* and subsequent cases have favoured them highlight that some problems remain. However, the case does resolve previous problem of conflicting interpretations and so gives clarification to the matter. The literal wording of the section supports the *Cummings* interpretation. The use of 'or' is critical to defeating the reasoning in *Breeden* that the second limb is a refinement of the first. Without anything to support a counter purpose to the section, the adoption of the literal rule for statutory interpretation must be undertaken. Fears that liability would now always result caused a vast increase in animal insurance premiums, leading many riding schools to close. However, these fears have proved unfounded, with subsequent cases not finding liability.[10] However, perhaps the only solution to definitively settle the matter is for new legislation.

[10] If you highlight this, it helps to illustrate whether the case was right or wrong. Depending on your view, put these in the order that you think helps the point you are making.

Make your answer stand out

■ Draw on more of the background to the Act, such as the Law Commission (1967) report, to more fully support what the purpose of the section was.

■ Incorporate the dissenting opinions of Lord Slynn and Lord Scott as to why *Mirvahedy* should have been decided differently.

■ Explore the cases following *Mirvahedy*, particularly *Turnbull* v *Warrener* [2012] EWCA Civ 412 to consider in more depth the merits of the different approaches in *Mirvahedy* and the extent that the law could be said to be settled.

■ Supplement your answer with academic opinion on the discussion arising in *Mirvahedy*, such as Howarth, D. (2003) The House of Lords and the Animals Act: closing the stable door. *Cambridge Law Journal*, 62(3): 548–51.

■ Consider how reform may look if you consider the matter has not been settled.

! Don't be tempted to . . .

■ Give specific detail as to the rules of statutory interpretation.

■ Discuss the other provisions of the Act in order to show that you have knowledge of them, the question is specific to section 2(2) and the particular difficulties that that has caused.

www.pearsoned.co.uk/lawexpressqa

Go online to access more revision support including additional essay and problem questions with diagram plans, You be the marker questions, and download all diagrams from the book.

Bibliography

Arden, M. (2010) Human rights and civil wrongs: tort law under the spotlight. *Public Law,* January: 140–59.

Bailey, S. (2010) What is a Material Contribution? *Legal Studies* 30: 167.
Barker, K. (1993) Unreliable Assumptions in the Modern Law of Negligence. *Law Quarterly Review,* 109: 461–484.
Beever, A. (2009) Transferred malice in tort law?, *Legal Studies,* 29(3): 400–20.
Buckland, W.W. (1935) The duty to take care. *Law Quarterly Review,* 51: 637.
Buckley, R.A. (1984) Liability in tort for breach of statutory duty. *Law Quarterly Review,* 100: 204.

Davies, M. (1982) The road from Morocco: *Polemis* through *Donohue* to no–fault. *Modern Law Review,* 45(5): 535–55.

Faulks Committee (1975) *Report of the Committee on Defamation.* Cmnd 5909.

Geach, N. (2012) The nuisance of the proprietary interest: Lord Cooke's dissent in *Hunter* v *Canary Wharf Ltd* [1997] AC 655, in N. Geach and C. Monaghan (eds) *Dissenting Judgments in the Law.* London: Wildy, Simmonds & Hill Publishing.
Giliker, P. (2006) The ongoing march of vicarious liability, *Cambridge Law Journal,* 489: 492.
Giliker, P. (2010) *Lister* revisited: vicarious liability, distributive justice and the course of employment. *Law Quarterly Review,* 126: 521–4.
Gore, R. (2012) Loss of chance, Lord Hope's dissent in *Gregg* v *Scott* [2005] UKHL 2 in N. Geach and C. Monaghan (eds) *Dissenting Judgments in the Law.* London: Wildy, Simmonds & Hill Publishing.

Hedley, S. (1995) Negligence: pure economic loss: goodbye privity, hello contorts. *Cambridge Law Journal,* 54(1): 27.
Heuston, R.V.F. and Buckley, R.A. (1996) *Salmond and Heuston on the Law of Torts.* London: Sweet & Maxwell.
Hodges, C. (2001) Compensating patients: case comment on *A* v *National Blood Authority* [2001] 2 All ER 289. *Law Quarterly Review,* 117: 528.
Hoffman, L. (2005) Causation. *Law Quarterly Review,* 121: 592–603.
Hope, Lord (2013) Tailoring the Law on Vicarious Liability. *Law Quarterly Review,* 129: 514.

Howarth, D. (2003) The House of Lords and the Animals Act: closing the stable door. *Cambridge Law Journal,* 62(3): 548–51.

Howarth, D. (2006) Many duties of care: or a duty of care? Notes from the underground. *Oxford Journal of Legal Studies,* 26: 449.

Howells, G. and Mildred, M. (2002) Infected blood: defect and discoverability: a first exposition of the EC Product Liability Directive. *Modern Law Review,* 65: 95.

Hunt, M. (1998) The 'horizontal effect' of the Human Rights Act 1998. *Public Law,* Autumn: 423–43.

Jones, M., Dugdale, A. and Simpson, M. (eds) (2014) *Clerk & Lindsell on Torts.* London: Sweet & Maxwell.

Law Commission (1967) Report, *Civil Liability for Animals,* No. 13 www.bailii.org/ew/other/EWLC/1967/13.html.

Law Commission (1969) Report, *The Interpretation of Statutes,* No. 21 www.bailii.org/ew/other/EWLC/1969/21.html.

Law Commission (1973) Report, *Liability for Damage or Injury to Trespassers and Related Questions of Occupiers' Liability,* No. 52. London: HMSO and www.bailii.org/ew/other/EWLC/1973/c52.pdf.

Law Reform Committee (1954) *Third Report: Occupiers' Liability to Invitees, Licensees and Trespassers.* London: HMSO.

Lee, J. (2008) Causation in Negligence: Another Fine Mess. *Professional Negligence,* 24: 194.

Markesinis, B.S. (1989) Negligence, nuisance and affirmative duties of action. *Law Quarterly Review,* 105: 104.

McDonald, B. (2005) Blameless? *Public Interest Law Journal,* 34: 15–17.

McLean, A. and Mackey, C. (2007) Is there a law of privacy in the UK? A consideration of recent legal developments. *European Intellectual Property Review,* 29(9): 389–95.

Ministry of Justice (2014) *Guidance on section 5 of the Defamation Act 2013 and Regulations: Complaints about defamatory material posted on websites.* www.gov.uk/government/uploads/system/uploads/attachment_data/file/269138/defamation-guidance.pdf

Morgan, P. (2013) Vicarious Liability on the Move. *Law Quarterly Review,* 129: 139.

Mullis, A. and Scott, A. (2012) The Swing of the Pendulum: Reputation, Expression and the Re-centring of English Libel Law, in D. Capper (ed.), *Modern Defamation Law: Balancing Reputation and Free Expression.* Belfast: Queens University Belfast Press.

Mullis, A. and Scott, A. (2014), Tilting at Windmills: the Defamation Act 2013. *Modern Law Review,* 77(1): 87–109.

Murphy, J. (1996) Expectation, losses, negligent omissions and the tortuous duty of care. *Cambridge Law Journal,* 55(1): 43–55.

Murphy, J. (2004) The merits of *Rylands* v *Fletcher. Oxford Journal of Legal Studies,* 24: 643.

Murphy, J. (2007) The juridical foundations of common law non-delegable duties in J. Neyers, S. Pitel and E. Chamberlain (eds) *Emerging Issues in Tort Law.* Oxford: Hart Publishing.

Murphy, J. (2010) *The Law of Nuisance.* Oxford: Oxford University Press.
Murphy, J. and Witting, C. (2012) *Street on Torts.* Oxford: Oxford University Press.

Newark, F.H. (1949) The boundaries of nuisance. *Law Quarterly Review,* 65: 480.
Nolan, D. (2005) The distinctiveness of *Rylands* v *Fletcher. Law Quarterly Review,* 121: 421–51.

Ogus, A.I. (1969) Vagaries in liability for the escape of fire. *Cambridge Law Journal,* 27(1): 104.
O'Sullivan, J. (2007) Suing in tort where no contract claim will lie: a bird's eye view. *Professional Negligence,* 23(3): 165–92.

Reece, H. (1996) Losses of chances in the law. *Modern Law Review,* 59: 188.
Rogers, W.V.H. (ed.) (2010) *Winfield and Jolowicz on Tort.* London: Sweet & Maxwell.

Stanton, K. (2006) Professional negligence; duty of care methodology in the twenty first century. *Professional Negligence,* 22(3): 134.
Stapleton, J. (1994a) In restraint of tort, in P. Birks (ed.) *The Frontiers of Liability.* Oxford: Oxford University Press.
Stapleton, J. (1994b) *Product Liability.* London: Butterworths.

Teff, H. (1998) Liability for negligently inflicted psychiatric harm: justifications and boundaries. *Cambridge Law Journal,* 57: 91–122.

Weir, T. (1972) Local authority v critical ratepayer: a suit in defamation. *Cambridge Law Journal,* 30: 238.
Weir, T. (1992) *A Casebook on Tort.* London: Sweet & Maxwell.
Weir, T. (2006) *An Introduction to Tort Law.* Oxford: Oxford University Press.
Williams, G. (1960) The effect of penal legislation in the law of tort. *Modern Law Review,* 23: 233.
Winfield, P.H. (1934) Duty in tortious negligence. *Columbia Law Review,* 34(1): 41–66.

Index

Tried and tested

What law students across the UK are saying about the **Law Express** and **Law Express Question&Answer** series:

'I personally found the series very helpful in my preparation for exams.'
Abba Elgujja, University of Salford

'Law Express are my go-to guides. They are an excellent supplement to my course material.'
Claire Turner, Open University

'This is the best law Q&A series in my opinion. I think it's helpful and I will continue to use it.'
Nneka H, University of London

'These revision guides strike the right balance between enough detail to help shape a really good answer, but sufficiently brief to be used for last-minute revision. The layout is user friendly and the use of tables and flowcharts is helpful.'
Shannon Reynolds, University of Manchester

'I find them easy to read, yet very helpful.'
Rebecca Kincaid, University of Kent

'The information is straight to the point. This is important particularly for exams.'
Dewan Sadia Kuraishy, University of Manchester

'In the modules in which I used these books to revise with, generally the modules I found the most difficult, I got the highest marks in. The books are really easy to use and are extremely helpful.'
Charlotte Evans, Queen Mary University of London